The Anatomy of Loneliness

ETHNOGRAPHIC STUDIES IN SUBJECTIVITY

Tanya Luhrmann, Editor

1. *Forget Colonialism? Sacrifice and the Art of Memory in Madagascar*, by Jennifer Cole
2. *Sensory Biographies: Lives and Deaths among Nepal's Yolmo Buddhists*, by Robert Desjarlais
3. *Culture and the Senses: Bodily Ways of Knowing in an African Community*, by Kathryn Linn Geurts
4. *Becoming Sinners: Christianity and Moral Torment in a Papua New Guinea Society*, by Joel Robbins
5. *Jesus in Our Wombs: Embodying Modernity in a Mexican Convent*, by Rebecca J. Lester
6. *The Too-Good Wife: Alcohol, Codependency, and the Politics of Nurturance in Postwar Japan*, by Amy Borovoy
7. *Subjectivity: Ethnographic Investigations*, edited by João Biehl, Byron Good, and Arthur Kleinman
8. *Postcolonial Disorders*, edited by Mary-Jo DelVecchio Good, Sandra Teresa Hyde, Sarah Pinto, and Byron J. Good
9. *Under a Watchful Eye: Self, Power, and Intimacy in Amazonia*, by Harry Walker
10. *Unsettled: Denial and Belonging among White Kenyans*, by Janet McIntosh
11. *Our Most Troubling Madness: Case Studies in Schizophrenia across Cultures*, by T. M. Luhrmann and Jocelyn Marrow
12. *Us, Relatives: Scaling and Plural Life in a Forager World*, by Nurit Bird-David
13. *The Likeness: Semblance and Self in Slovene Society*, by Gretchen Bakke
14. *The Anatomy of Loneliness: Suicide, Social Connection, and the Search for Relational Meaning in Contemporary Japan*, by Chikako Ozawa-de Silva

The Anatomy of Loneliness

SUICIDE, SOCIAL CONNECTION, AND THE SEARCH FOR RELATIONAL MEANING IN CONTEMPORARY JAPAN

Chikako Ozawa-de Silva

UNIVERSITY OF CALIFORNIA PRESS

University of California Press
Oakland, California

Library of Congress Cataloging-in-Publication Data

Names: Ozawa-de Silva, Chikako, author.
Title: The anatomy of loneliness : suicide, social connection, and the search for relational meaning in contemporary Japan / Chikako Ozawa-de Silva
Other titles: Ethnographic studies in subjectivity ; 14.
Description: Oakland, California : University of California Press, [2021] | Series: Ethnographic studies in subjectivity ; 14 | Includes bibliographical references and index.
Identifiers: LCCN 2021016933 (print) | LCCN 2021016934 (ebook) | ISBN 9780520383487 (hardback) | ISBN 9780520383494 (paperback) | ISBN 9780520383500 (ebook)
Subjects: LCSH: Loneliness—Social aspects—Japan—21st century. | Suicide—Anthropological aspects—Japan—21st century. | Social media—Japan—Influence.
Classification: LCC BF575.L7 O385 2021 (print) | LCC BF575.L7 (ebook) | DDC 155.9/2—dc23
LC record available at https://lccn.loc.gov/2021016933
LC ebook record available at https://lccn.loc.gov/2021016934

25 24 23 22 21
10 9 8 7 6 5 4 3 2 1

for Chan Chan

Contents

Acknowledgments

When I think about this project, I cannot help thinking about "interdependence," a well-known concept in Buddhism, and my personal favorite. This book would not have been possible without so many people's kindness, acceptance, and understanding. There are too many people whom I want to thank to list them all here, and I am aware there are many people who must have assisted me in indirect ways that I don't even know of. Conducting field work is always a humbling experience. I was often touched by the kindness of my interlocutors, people who made this project possible and were so generous with their time. Each person who was involved in the process of this project played a unique and invaluable part.

When I reflect on how this book project started, I have to go back over twenty years to the year 2000. I was a visiting research fellow at Harvard University, where I found the Friday Morning Seminar (FMS) of Harvard's Medical Anthropology program continuously inspiring. That was probably when I began my long-term interests in subjectivity and loneliness. I would like to thank Drs. Mary-Jo Good and Byron Good, who were running the FMS during my visiting year and who have provided long-term support and kindness ever since. Among the many inspiring presenters at FMS, I would like to thank Dr. João Biehl and Dr. Robert

Desjarlais for sharing their work with us. I still remember their talks and discussions to this day and have internal dialogues with their books each time I read or teach them.

I am grateful to Dr. Arthur Kleinman who, knowing about my work on internet group suicide in Japan, encouraged me to develop this into a book project on loneliness at a time when I was wondering about whether to move on to a completely different (and less emotionally taxing) subject. Dr. Junko Kitanaka also played a major role in making my research possible, inviting me to spend my sabbatical year as a visiting professor at her institution, Keio University in Tokyo, where she introduced me to a number of key figures in psychiatry and suicide research. She also read drafts of my articles on suicide and provided much insightful feedback. Dr. Kenji Kawano, then at the Japanese National Center of Neurology and Psychiatry (NCNP), and currently a professor at Ritsumeikan University, invited me to meet his team at NCNP, who were all working on internet group suicide and suicide among youth, and to a number of other meetings, workshops, and conferences. Among the team members at NCNP, I also would like to thank Dr. Yōtaro Katsumata and Dr. Sueki Hajime for generously sharing their research and time.

I am so grateful to Dr. Yukio Saito, the founder of the Inochi no Denwa suicide crisis hotline, who met with me several times to share his vast experience and introduced me to a number of additional experts in suicide and mental health in Japan. His kindness and sincere commitment to suicide prevention touched me deeply. I thank also Dr. Tetsuji Ito at Ibaragi University for including me in his Qualitative Methods Working Group on 3.11 in North Ibaragi. I would also like to thank and acknowledge Dr. Ichiro Yatsuzuka, a member of this working group, who kindly gave me permission to use pictures he took during our visit to North Ibaragi in this book. I am grateful for his kindness and kind words.

I would also like to thank the students who volunteered to do interviews with me, whose narratives make up a chapter of this book. They often spent two hours in an interview, and several agreed to multiple interviews. Their sincere attitude to their lives, their warm feelings toward their family and friends, and their sharing of their hopes and anxieties about their futures moved me and provided insight into several key issues of this book. Although their names have been changed here to protect their identities, I remember them fondly and hope to meet with them again in future.

At Emory University, I am so grateful to the numerous colleagues and graduate students who read draft chapters and provided detailed feedback and discussion. The chapter on North Ibaragi and the 3.11 disasters in Japan was heavily revised after receiving this feedback, and my students in particular encouraged me to not shy away from speaking about my personal experiences as the events unfolded. Dr. Anne Allison, Dr. Claudia Strauss, Dr. Bobby Paul, Dr. Suma Ikeuchi, Elena Lesley, and others all read the entire book manuscript (some of them multiple times), and their comments and suggestions have unquestionably strengthened it. I am so grateful for their interest, time, and insight.

I also would like to thank Dr. Tanya Luhrmann, the series editor at University of California Press, for her valuable feedback and constructive suggestions, and for being such a wonderful friend and colleague over so many years. Dr. Rebecca Lester and Dr. Clark Chilson served as reviewers for the manuscript and provided extensive and invaluable comments that have improved the work greatly. I am grateful for their time, their sharing of their expertise, and their belief in this book.

I would like to express my gratitude also to Kate Marshall and Enrique Ochoa-Kaup at UC Press. Their tireless work really made the process of publishing this book as smooth and stress free as it could be. I would like to thank Audrey (AJ) Jones, who is completing her PhD in anthropology at Emory, and who is an amazing scholar with a meticulous eye for editing. Her ability to edit; provide key comments; and assist with the references, endnotes, and formatting of this work has been supremely valuable, and I am so grateful for her help.

My very special thanks go to my husband, Brendan Ozawa-de Silva. Without him, I would not have been able to complete this book project. Words cannot capture what his support has meant for me. There were days when I thought I wouldn't be able to turn this project into a book. He sat and listened to me and helped me to gain clarity of mind regarding what the main theme of this book ought to be, and he was there when I was emotionally drained to boost my spirits. If there is one person who was most influential in the way this book became what it is, it is Brendan. He suggested much of the scholarship outside of anthropology, especially from psychology and neuroscience, that informs this work and its arguments. He has expanded my scholarly horizons for the past two decades and has been my comrade throughout my life since we first met. I am eternally grateful for his standing by me no matter what.

I would also like to thank the management and staff at the Rafa Nadal Sports Center and Academy, including Rafa himself and his family, as a site where important writing of this book took place. Brendan and I fell in love with the charming island of Mallorca a few years ago and spent several weeks at the Sports Center, writing in the mornings and afternoons, then relaxing at the spa and working out at the gym. Watching Rafa practicing on court for three hours at a time and then later in the gym, even through Christmas, was a daily reminder of the power of persistence and methodical hard work, while the congenial atmosphere was a reminder that work, family, and community need never be at odds.

This book revision was completed during the first year of COVID-19. The pandemic greatly increased interest in loneliness and social isolation, and I was invited to give several talks on these topics. I hope the experience of COVID-19 will teach us the importance of human connection and will result in more research on loneliness and social bonds. Speaking of such bonds, I would like to end by thanking my parents, who have raised me and supported me throughout their lives. Without their support and understanding, I would not have had the chance to study and eventually to become an anthropologist in the United States. Thank you, mom and dad, for allowing your daughter to leave Japan and study abroad, which must have been worrying at times! I value your trust in me.

The research for this book was made possible by a National Endowment for the Humanities Fellowship for Advanced Social Science Research on Japan and internal funding from Emory University, including a seed grant from Emory University's Religion and Public Health Collaborative.

A Note on Language

To avoid confusing general readers who are not familiar with the order of Japanese names, in which the family name comes first, Japanese names in this book are given personal name first, family name last. I sometimes use the Japanese honorific ending "-san" to refer to individuals instead of "Mr." or "Ms."

I use pseudonyms for the college students I interviewed, other interlocutors such as those in North Ibaragi whom I interviewed, as well as the suicide website visitors whose posts I cite. Where I do use real names, such as Dr. Kenji Kawano and Dr. Tetsuji Ito, it is with their permission.

Introduction

DISCONNECTED PEOPLE AND THE LONELY SOCIETY

> Loneliness is a major social, educational, economic, and health issue that will reach epidemic proportions by 2030. . . . At the moment there are no interventions. Where are they? I can't find any.
>
> —Prof. Stephen Houghton, University of Western Australia

Loneliness is everybody's business. We have all at times felt lonely, left behind, left out, or abandoned. This is perfectly normal, because—as this book shows—the roots of our ability to feel lonely lie in the very nature of our brain and biology, our need for social connection, and the nature of what it means to be a person, a self. As human beings, we experience a continuous tug of war between our need to belong and connect socially and the fact that our consciousness, self, and subjectivity are defined by a sense of separation from what is "not me."

Some people, however, experience not just moments of loneliness, but loneliness as an enduring state. They feel excessively lonely. This affliction is not necessarily a mental disorder or mental illness; it is not reducible to a sickness of the body or the mind. However we may categorize it, it is an affliction of subjectivity, meaning that it is true in the experience of a person but not necessarily visible to people on the outside. A person may be surrounded by family and friends yet be feeling terribly lonely. The fact that this is becoming increasingly common in modern societies should be a cause for concern.

A GLOBAL EPIDEMIC OF LONELINESS

If loneliness is neither a physical condition nor a mental disorder, what is it? That is one of the key topics this book aims to shed light on: the anatomy of loneliness. One of the most important messages of this book, however, is that the anatomy of loneliness is not the anatomy of a single individual, but of a type of society.

When we think of loneliness, we probably think of a single, solitary individual. But in contemporary times, loneliness is actually a social issue. This is especially the case in highly industrialized societies, where public officials are calling widespread loneliness an "epidemic." Newspapers like the *New York Times* and the *Guardian* have run features reporting that loneliness is as serious a threat to human health as obesity and smoking, if not worse. In 2018 UK prime minister Theresa May asserted that "loneliness is one of the greatest public health challenges of our time" and appointed the country's first ever minister for loneliness, Tracey Crouch, to lead a cross-government initiative to curb it.[1]

This change occurred in response to studies that found nine million people in the United Kingdom "often" or "always" felt lonely. In the United States, a survey taken in 2010 found that more than a third of American citizens over the age of forty-five felt lonely.[2] In 2017 former US surgeon general Vivek Murthy called loneliness a "growing health epidemic" and mentioned that a study found social isolation to be "associated with a reduction in lifespan similar to that caused by smoking 15 cigarettes a day."[3] Other studies have found that the reduction in lifespan caused by social isolation exceeds that of obesity and substance abuse, increasing risk of mortality by 26 percent.[4] Collaborative research between psychologists and geneticists has found that chronic loneliness changes gene expression in ways that make the body less healthy and more susceptible to illness.[5] Leading researchers in loneliness have argued that long-term loneliness is associated with general negative mental health outcomes, such as depression, anxiety, and suicidal ideation.[6] Contemporary scholarship is therefore focusing on loneliness as not merely an individual matter, but a public health issue that negatively impacts both physical and psychological health, even increasing the risk of mortality.[7]

Until recently, suicide prevention policies, including those by organizations such as the World Health Organization (WHO) and US National Institute of Mental Health (NIMH), have tended to focus largely on treating depression. Suicide researchers, on the other hand, emphasize that there is no simple link between depression and suicide. Instead, they point to additional factors such as having someone who committed suicide in one's family, suicide as a learned option and behavior, and upbringing.[8] Researchers who focus on positive mental health as something beyond the absence of mental illness, such as Corey Keyes, have also argued that "languishing," understood as a deficit in emotional, social, and psychological well-being, is more detrimental and more predictive of future suicide than mental illness. As a result, those who are suffering from depression but have meaning in life, good relationships, and so on may be at lower risk for suicide than those who do not suffer from mental illness but are languishing and lack these other factors.[9] This suggests that studies of mental health and suicide should consider factors such as social support and loneliness. Keyes and others characterize flourishing or positive mental well-being as being not merely the absence of mental illness, but the presence of psychological and social well-being, including meaning in life.[10]

LONELINESS AND SUICIDE

This book did not start off as a project on loneliness, but as a research project on suicide in Japan that gradually led to uncovering loneliness as a critical underlying issue. In 1998 suicide rates jumped suddenly and sharply in Japan—by 50 percent in some age categories—and they remained elevated in the following years. This caused significant alarm in Japan and raised many questions. Initially, the spike in suicides was seen as being caused by two things: Japan's economic stagnation and depression, particularly depression caused by factors such as unemployment. The spike in suicide was seen as being a problem primarily impacting men in their forties to sixties who faced economic uncertainty and unemployment due to the bursting of Japan's bubble economy in the early 1990s.

This picture was imperfect from the beginning, however. For one thing, the spike in suicides happened not only among working-age Japanese men, but also across multiple age categories, including adolescents, who experienced an increase in suicide of 50 percent in a single year. Second, the narrative of economic stagnation leading to depression leading to suicide did not fit the subjective reports of those who were attempting or committing suicide, nor did it easily account for the emergence of entirely new forms of suicide, such as internet group suicide.

The long-term economic stagnation and concurrent increase in irregular employment (part-time and temporary work) affected not just the middle-aged, but also the younger generations who grew up in the post-bubble economy. Two signs of how young Japanese were being significantly impacted were the rise of those categorized as NEETs (not in education, employment, or training) and an increase in the phenomenon of social withdrawal, or *hikikomori*, wherein young people do not leave their rooms or houses for extended periods of time—six months to several years—instead remaining secluded and entirely dependent on their parents or caregivers for their food and other necessities of life.[11]

In 2003 I initiated a study of individuals who frequented Japanese "suicide websites."[12] I wanted to understand why suicide rates had spiked in Japan, as well as why a number of new forms of suicide were emerging, particularly internet group suicide, in which individuals come together online and then agree to meet in person to commit suicide collectively, despite being strangers. It did not take me long to discover that the problems expressed by suicide website visitors were rarely about unemployment or work conditions; neither were they about depression. Rather, the most common themes that emerged were loneliness, a lack of meaning in life, and a lack of feeling needed by others. None of these were common themes in the discourse on suicide taking place in Japanese scholarship or media. Yet when I discovered these common themes among suicide website visitors, I realized that these same themes were emerging across Japan in various ways. They were turning up in books, films, television shows, and the new forms of companionship services that I call "the commodification of intimacy." I realized that my research had to focus not just on suicide, but also on the deeper underlying issues facing young Japanese, especially the issue of loneliness.

A number of social commentators have pointed to these underlying issues as problems affecting modern societies in general, not just Japan. In 2016 the Dalai Lama wrote in an op-ed for the *New York Times*:

> We all need to be needed. . . . The problem [in prosperous countries] is not a lack of material riches. It is the growing number of people who feel they are no longer useful, no longer needed, no longer one with their societies. . . . In America today, compared with 50 years ago, three times as many working-age men are completely outside the work force. This pattern is occurring throughout the developed world—and the consequences are not merely economic. Feeling superfluous is a blow to the human spirit. It leads to social isolation and emotional pain, and creates the conditions for negative emotions to take root.[13]

The Dalai Lama has frequently expressed his opinion that focusing too much on material well-being, while neglecting the more human, emotional, and social dimensions of well-being, is leading to increasing problems of anxiety, loneliness, and loss of meaning. As we will see, political economists of Japan have come to a similar conclusion that a narrow focus on material well-being is leading to a crisis of subjectivity.

THE LONELY SOCIETY

This book deals with not just the loneliness of a single person, or of a few people, but of a society—that is, a type of society that makes people feel uncared for, unseen, and unimportant: the lonely society.[14]

This phrase is intentionally paradoxical. *Society* means people being together and living together, engaging socially. To be in society means to not be alone. But it does not mean that one does not *feel* alone. This book suggests that there are forms of society that make people feel cared for and connected, that instill in people a sense of belonging. At the same time, there are forms of society that do the opposite. Every society falls somewhere along this scale, but as societies continue to develop economically, it is increasingly concerning that they seem to be moving in the direction of the lonely society.

What characterizes the lonely society? Why are societies becoming lonelier? And what, if anything, might be done to change the tide of this steady movement toward loneliness? These are the questions that drive this book. Throughout my research over the past twenty-five years, conducted primarily in Japan and the United States, I have come to the conclusion that a lonely society is not just one in which a very large number of people feel lonely—what some have called a "loneliness epidemic." That is just the first condition. It is also a society whose people do not feel taken care of and cared for by society as a whole, and whose structures promote a sense of loneliness rather than one of belonging and connection. Finally, it can also be a society or community that is lonely as a unit, in that it is not closely connected to other societies and to humankind as a whole or feels abandoned, neglected, marginalized, or disenfranchised. These are the three conditions of what I call "the lonely society," and I explore each aspect in detail in this book.

STRUCTURE OF THE BOOK

The structure of this book parallels the path I took in writing it. After this introductory chapter, chapter 1 outlines my theoretical approach, with a focus on the topics of subjectivity and empathy. Chapters 2 and 3 deal with my initial research on suicide, suicide websites, and internet group suicide in Japan. Chapter 2 provides an overview of suicide in Japan and then describes the phenomenon of internet group suicide. Chapter 3 then focuses on suicide websites and their visitors, examining what their comments and discussions tell us about the subjective experiences of Japanese people considering suicide.

Although my research began with a narrow focus on suicide, I grew increasingly interested in the underlying issues of which suicide, suicide websites, and internet group suicide are manifestations. This led me to a follow-up research project in which I interviewed a few dozen young, college-aged Japanese to investigate their views on suicide and meaning in life and to see whether their comments would differ from or reflect the sentiments I had come across on suicide websites. The results of this study are presented in chapter 4. The interviews were complex and varied, but they reveal many lines of congruity between the college-aged Japanese I interviewed and the thoughts expressed by visitors to suicide websites.

I was disturbed to find that the sentiments expressed by suicide website visitors about lack of meaning in life, loneliness, and the "difficulty of living" (*ikizurasa*) had a strong resonance in Japanese society far beyond the confines of suicide websites.

As my research evolved, I felt the need to identify not only problems and challenges, but also solutions and reasons for hope. I developed an interest not only in suicide and loneliness, but also in resilience, human connection, and other factors conducive to individual and collective well-being. After I had already collected substantial ethnographic data on suicide, isolation, and loneliness, the triple disaster of "3.11" struck Japan. On March 11, 2011, an earthquake, a tsunami, and a nuclear disaster occurred in the Tōhoku region of Japan, involving nuclear reactors in Fukushima. This series of disasters resulted in some twenty thousand casualties and displaced more than two hundred thousand people in Japan.

The 3.11 disaster and its aftermath show that the physical displacement of hundreds of thousands of people and the subsequent experiences of social isolation are only part of the story. The loss of homes, communities, and entire cities led to significant challenges for residents of the affected areas, but the subsequent moral injury caused by the perceived mishandling of the situation by government, media, and corporations led to feelings of isolation, abandonment, and hopelessness. Just as feeling at home is connected to a sense of belonging and wellness, so can displacement and living in exile evoke feelings of loneliness. Belonging and connection can mean feeling connected not just to people, but also to places and environments. 3.11 is a flashpoint in seeing how the political, economic, and social structures of society make people feel disposable—in this case, not just individual people but entire communities. Chapter 5 examines these physical and social disasters related to 3.11.

The challenging circumstances, however, also led survivors to band together to find new ways of surviving and make meaning, including a greater focus on "bonds" (*kizuna*). Just as survivors resisted and expressed resilience against the physical disasters of 3.11, they also resisted and expressed resilience against the way they were being treated by the media, politicians, support services, and corporations. The response of the community that I visited, North Ibaragi, sheds light on the way that individuals and communities can push back against the dehumanizing trends that make people feel disposable. They taught me important lessons about resilience and resistance that I believe can and should be applied more broadly. Chapter 6 focuses on these questions of moral injury, resilience, human connection, and resistance.

Chapter 7 concludes the book by returning to some of the theoretical questions raised in this introduction and by laying out two related theories that have emerged from my research. The first has to do with the importance of cultivating empathy and compassion in societies as an antidote for loneliness, as well as the importance of doing so not just on an individual level, but also on interpersonal and systemic levels. The cultivation and recognition of human connections, I argue, serve as a direct antidote to loneliness, and mutual respect, empathy, and compassion allow those connections to take root and grow.

The second theory is the "relational theory of meaning." This is a theory of meaning in life that is not based on a single driving purpose or a cognitive understanding of what life means, but rather on how people feel they matter to other people: the meaning we have in the eyes of others. Up to now, the various disciplines that tackle the study of meaning in life, including psychology and anthropology, have neglected this important intersubjective dimension. From my research, however, it is relational meaning in life that is most relevant for addressing loneliness.

These two theoretical approaches are closely connected. Rethinking what meaning in life is, or what it can be, should not be just an individual endeavor, but ultimately the endeavor of a society. As I demonstrate throughout the book, the structures of our societies reflect and reinforce our intersubjective assessments of just that meaning, or the lack thereof.

CONNECTING TO BROADER SCHOLARSHIP

This book is written for a general audience, so the reader is not expected to be an expert on Japan, anthropology, psychology, or the study of loneliness and suicide. When engaging in existing scholarship, I attempt to do so in an accessible way and explain the relevance of the literature. For academic readers in particular, it is worth laying out briefly here the three specific areas of scholarly debate that this book engages. The first of these consists of the anthropology of Japan and Japan studies. Within this area, debates center around both the issue of how Japanese people construe their sense of self and how this does or does not resemble Western notions of selfhood and the nature of Japanese modernity (and again, to what extent it does or does not resemble modernity in Western countries). In particular, scholarship on Japan poses the interesting question of whether neoliberal reforms intended to address the country's economic stagnation can be effective if they neglect the characteristics of Japanese selfhood and the subjective dimensions of the precarity being experienced in Japan today. This book offers an ethnographic investigation that sheds light on this question, so I return to it in detail in the final chapter.

The second area this book engages is anthropological literature on suffering, resilience, and the "anthropology of the good." The latter is a call to anthropologists to focus not only on suffering, but also on ethics and people's conceptions of "the good" as something that may motivate them. A key debate in this literature is how important conscious, reflective conceptions of the good actually are when it comes to explaining behavior. The focus in this book on meaning and purpose in life (*ikiru imi* and *ikigai*), as well as on resilience and community care, directly addresses this debate.

The third area the book engages is literatures in psychology, positive psychology (the study of human happiness and flourishing), and contemplative science, namely the interdisciplinary study of meditation and contemplative practices. Although I do not examine contemplative practices directly here as I did in my previous book on the Japanese contemplative practice of Naikan, key themes in both positive psychology and contemplative science include compassion, empathy, and meaning in life—and the role that these play in individual and collective human flourishing.[15] This has led to the coining of phrases such as the "science of happiness" and the "science of compassion." Debates in positive psychology include the role that meaning in life plays in flourishing and well-being, as well as what constitutes meaning in life. I directly engage this debate in several chapters of this book and then present my own theory in the concluding chapter.

MYTHS ABOUT LONELINESS

Although loneliness is a common human experience—indeed, as I argue, a universal one—there are several ways in which it is typically misunderstood.

Following are what I have found to be common myths regarding loneliness that I want to address at the outset.

Myth 1: Loneliness Is a New (Psychological) Problem in Society

Despite the recent spate of media articles touting an "outbreak of loneliness" or a sudden epidemic of loneliness, we should not think that the recognition of loneliness as a serious social and public health issue means that it is somehow a new problem for humanity. Loneliness is as old as recorded history, and since it almost certainly comes from our evolutionary past and the fact that we are social animals who cannot survive independently, one could argue that it even predates humanity itself.

Loneliness is something most people, if not everyone, have experienced at some point in their lives, even if only for brief moments. Separation, the loss of loved ones, being left behind (even temporarily as a child), or simply being in a new and unfamiliar environment can trigger feelings of loneliness. From an evolutionary and psychological perspective, loneliness involves built-in psychological mechanisms not limited to humans but present in other mammalian species and likely bird species as well. This is because all mammalian and bird species require maternal care to survive during and after birth, meaning that being left alone for too long would be equivalent to death. Social death and physical death are intertwined for all mammalian species, including human beings. Given this basic fact, it is no wonder that the immune and stress systems of not only humans, but other mammals as well, become activated when we experience loneliness.

Loneliness is therefore not just an aspect of our social reality, but of our biological and evolutionary reality as well. It is based on our strong wish and need—even on a physiological level—to bond, belong to, and connect with others and places, which results in our establishment of caring support systems that are advantageous for our own well-being, our families, and our societies.[16] Developmental psychologists argue that loneliness begins from the first moments of life, when infants experience moments of losing the attention of their mother or other caregivers.[17]

Thus, although we do seem to be experiencing an increase in loneliness in modern neoliberal societies, it is important that we recognize that loneliness involves something quite ancient in us that is not merely psychological, but truly bio-psychosocial.

Myth 2: Loneliness Is a Form of Depression or a Symptom of Underlying Depression

It is easy to conflate depression and loneliness, but the two must be kept conceptually distinct. Subsuming loneliness as one kind of depression, or viewing loneliness as a symptom and manifestation of depression, is common but misleading. It is certainly the case that loneliness and depression often co-occur.[18] But to completely reduce loneliness to depression would be to fail to address the specific causes of loneliness.

Among loneliness researchers, loneliness and depression are considered two distinctive constructs.[19] Psychologists Letitia Peplau and Daniel Perlman argue that depression is the broader concept, in the sense that depressed people are not always lonely.[20] But it is also the case that people who are lonely are not always depressed. According to the American Psychiatric Association, depression is a medical illness, and its symptoms include a sad or depressed mood, loss of interest or pleasure in activities once enjoyed, feeling worthless or guilty, difficulty thinking, and thoughts of death and suicide.[21] Loneliness, on the other hand, is always relationally oriented and refers to negative and unpleasant emotional feelings people experience coming from a wish to be with someone and not be alone, or from not feeling at home in their surroundings.[22] Loneliness fundamentally reflects how a person feels about their relationships and their place in the world, or lack thereof.[23] Depression, on the other hand, is not necessarily relationally oriented. Psychologist John Cacioppo even argues that depression is self-oriented, while loneliness is relation oriented.[24] While I agree that loneliness is a subjective experience focused on a perceived lack of fulfillment with regard to relationships, I still see it as ultimately self-focused, in that it involves focusing on the deprivation of oneself rather than on the needs or experiences of others.

In sum, even though depression and loneliness can both be debilitating, depression is a general feeling of sadness, hopelessness, or dejection, while loneliness involves feelings of social pain induced from feeling and perceiving a lack of close or meaningful relationships, connections, and belonging. Like depression, social, environmental, physiological, affective, and cognitive factors all play a role in the experience of loneliness, but we would certainly do loneliness a disservice to reduce it to clinical depression in every instance. This would leave out the large populations of people who experience and struggle with loneliness but would not be classified as suffering from depression.

Myth 3: Loneliness Means Being Alone

"Being alone" and "being lonely" sound similar, and often go together, but they are conceptually distinct. Clearly one can be physically alone and not feel lonely, and one can similarly feel lonely while surrounded by others. As human beings, we are strongly conditioned to feel discomforted when left alone or left behind. This is most noticeable when we are small children. Social connection creates safety and protection from potential enemies. Ample research suggests that we are evolutionally wired to desire bonds, connections, affection, and belonging, and to fear social rejection.[25]

Often in the popular press, and even occasionally in some research articles, loneliness and social isolation are considered together as if they were the same thing.[26] A recent article in the *New York Times* states that "rigorous epidemiological studies have linked loneliness and social isolation to heart disease, cancer, depression, diabetes and suicide" and that "loneliness and social isolation are associated with a reduction in life span similar to that caused by smoking 15 cigarettes a day and even greater than that associated with obesity."[27] Yet loneliness and social isolation are not the same thing, as the majority of researchers recognize. Social isolation is a physical and social reality; loneliness is an affective and subjective reality. While there is nothing wrong in studying both social isolation and loneliness, problems arise when we conflate the two. One such problem is that we may fail to find appropriate and effective solutions. We may be addressing social isolation, while the underlying problem of loneliness remains unaddressed. The key here is that loneliness is a subjective experience involving *perceived* and *felt* social isolation.[28] While isolation is *being* alone, loneliness is *feeling* alone.

As we will see in chapter 5, on communities that were displaced by the 3.11 disasters, people can also feel lonely when they are away from the places to which they feel connected and where they feel a sense of belonging, particularly the places where they feel at home (*ibasho*). Displacement, exile, forced migration, and refugee status (even simply moving to a different city or country for work or study) can result in feelings of loneliness. This is because our sense of belonging includes not just people but also environments. The role the physical environment plays in experiences of belonging and loneliness has largely been ignored in the study of loneliness, despite its being a very common experience.

Myth 4: Loneliness Is Mainly a Problem for the Elderly

Loneliness is commonly assumed to be a serious problem only among older people. Reflecting such tendencies, a vast amount of loneliness research focuses on the elderly and their social isolation. There are several journals dedicated to gerontological health, such as *The Journal of Aging and Health*, *Aging and Society*, *The International Journal of Geriatric Psychiatry*, *Reviews in Clinical Gerontology*, and *Gerontology*, and these journals include a considerable amount of research on the health impact of social isolation among the elderly.[29] However, we have seen that social isolation and loneliness are not the same thing. And beyond the elderly, loneliness research remains a very small field.

This is a problem, because despite the well-known fact that social isolation can be a serious issue for older individuals, there is little evidence showing that loneliness is principally a problem only for the elderly.[30] Some research suggests that children in late adolescence experience the most intense forms of loneliness, and that this intensity gradually decreases in middle adulthood, only to then slowly increase again at older ages.[31] Psychologists Jenny de Jong Gierveld and colleagues cite that more than 60 percent of high school students report sometimes experiencing loneliness. The authors connect this to the "development of increasing expectations about social relationships, friendships, support, and intimacy."[32]

At the same time, statistics suggest that the incidence of loneliness among the elderly has remained constant over the last fifty years, with about 10 percent reporting themselves as lonely. One study going back to 1948 shows the ratio of chronic loneliness among older individuals as steady for seventy years, with 6–13 percent of those surveyed saying they feel lonely "all or most of the time."[33]

The recent perceived spike in loneliness in multiple countries therefore cannot be attributed to older individuals alone and suggests that we need more research on loneliness across the lifespan. Manfred Beutel and colleagues note, "In line with previous findings our data suggests that younger age groups are more affected by loneliness. Thus, the investigation of the prevalence of loneliness and its impact on mental health in individuals under 35 years old would be desirable."[34]

DEFINING LONELINESS

We have noted a few things that loneliness is not. How then can we define what loneliness is? I briefly provide a few definitions taken from the research literature on loneliness before presenting my own definition, which I use throughout this book.

In their "Loneliness and Social Isolation" in *The Cambridge Handbook of Personal Relationships*, de Jong Gierveld and colleagues refer to Cacioppo, Fowler, and Christakis's concise and yet insightful definition that loneliness is "perceived social isolation."[35] They also cite Perlman and Peplau's definition: "The unpleasant experience that occurs when a person's network of social relations is deficient in some important way, either quantitatively or qualitatively."[36] In a recent special issue of the *Journal of the American Medical Association* (*JAMA*), loneliness is defined as "a distressing discrepancy between desired and actual levels of social contact."[37] These recent definitions distinguish loneliness from social isolation and emphasize the cognitive appraisal and perception of experiencing loneliness.

In his influential book *Loneliness* that was published in 1961, psychologist Clark Moustakas argues that there are two kinds of loneliness in modern life: existential loneliness and loneliness anxiety, or the loneliness of self-alienation and self-rejection.[38] According to Moustakas, existential loneliness is intrinsic to and unavoidable in human life and is associated with both "pain and triumphant creation."[39] Existential loneliness is a real loneliness of genuine experience (e.g., losing someone who was close to you), and for Moustakas it is a central and unavoidable aspect of human experience.

Loneliness anxiety, on the other hand, results from a person being "unable to experience life in a genuine way, unable to relate authentically to his own nature and to other selves."[40] People feel loneliness anxiety when they desire intimate and authentic relatedness to others in vain, which results in feelings of nothingness or inauthenticity. Moustakas argues this is a form of self-estrangement and that fear of such loneliness is common in modern life. Those who suffer from this form of loneliness are suspicious of others, feel inferior, exhibit helpless rage, and hold a desire for revenge as a result of being left out of life. Moustakas sees this latter form of loneliness as a type of "disturbing anxiety."[41]

In 1974, sociologist Robert Weiss published a seminal book, *Loneliness: The Experience of Emotional and Social Isolation*. Weiss, a leading attachment perspective advocator, classifies loneliness into two types. The first is emotional loneliness, which he describes as an acute feeling of emptiness and abandonment. This happens when a person loses their partner through divorce or death. According to Weiss, this kind of loneliness will only be resolved when a person starts a new intimate relationship. The second type is social loneliness, characterized by a lack of social network support.[42]

Among more recent studies, de Jong Gierveld and colleagues classify loneliness into three types: (1) positive loneliness, (2) negative and positive loneliness, and (3) negative loneliness.[43] Those who exhibit positive loneliness are long-term meditators who voluntarily withdraw themselves from social interactions and contacts. Negative and positive loneliness is akin to what Moustakas describes as "existential loneliness." This kind of loneliness is an unavoidable aspect of human life, leading to both experiences of doubt and uncertainty and the potential for self-growth.[44] The third type is what most people usually consider loneliness and what the study of loneliness deals with. Elsewhere, I have myself coined the term *afflictive loneliness* to capture the negative dimension of loneliness and differentiate it from other forms of loneliness.[45] Afflictive loneliness is chronic loneliness that is experienced as an affliction, something that feels unbearable or very difficult to bear.

In contrast to the deficit approach, Perlman and Peplau argue that there is no direct connection between loneliness and lack of relationships.[46] According to them, cognitive discrepancy is key for approaching loneliness, and subjective evaluations of existing relationships are what determine feelings of loneliness.

In this book I draw from the work just discussed to define loneliness as "feelings of dissatisfaction that arise with regard to relationships to others or to the environment." By using the word *feelings* in the plural, I aim to point out that loneliness, even when it is experienced as a chronic state, comes and goes, ebbs and flows, and is impermanent—meaning that it is always in a state of change—and also that there can be multiple forms and manifestations of loneliness. In using the word *feelings*, it is also important to stress that loneliness is not just a psychological phenomenon, but a biological and social one as well. When subjectivity and affect are discussed in this work, as I explain in detail in the next chapter, they are approached as a bio-psychosocial process. Thus, while I agree with other scholars that loneliness can and often does involve a perceived deprivation of a type of relationship that a person considers important to their happiness—and indeed, this used to be the definition of loneliness I used myself—I now find that this addresses only the cognitive dimension of loneliness. Loneliness can be "felt" in and by the body even when it is not fully cognitively understood by the person who feels lonely and who struggles to put into words what they are feeling and experiencing. As we will see, such feelings can result from loss, displacement, marginalization, not finding a place or niche of one's own, or unmet expectations.

I believe it is extremely important to recognize the evolutionary and biological roots of loneliness and our need for human connection, as these roots help explain why loneliness is so deeply seated in the body. By using the term *dissatisfaction*, I also aim to highlight the importance of society and culture in shaping expectations for relationships and happiness, often in idealized or unrealistic ways, including the idea that one should never feel lonely. Emphasizing the importance of affect and the body, therefore, should not mean we ignore the important role of cognition in subjectivity and the way it is shaped by the structures of society. By using the term *relationships*, I point to relational meaning, bonds, and "sharing a world"—all concepts that are explored at length in this book. Finally, by using the phrase "or to the environment," I point out that loneliness, as we shall see, can involve the absence not only of satisfactory relations with other living beings, but also of social and physical places where one feels one belongs and where one feels "at home." By omitting "an individual's" feelings, I aim to point out that loneliness can and often is experienced collectively—as paradoxical as that may sound—and that it is shaped by processes that are not just individual, but social, cultural, and political as well. Each part of this definition, therefore, points to an important aspect of "the anatomy of loneliness" that is explored in detail in the chapters of this book.

Our foray into the anatomy of loneliness is not without hope. As noted earlier, in recent years, an "anthropology of the good" has encouraged anthropologists to focus not only on the "suffering subject," but also on topics such as value, morality, empathy, and care.[47] This line of inquiry pushes us to follow the process of cultivating the good by investigating the values and insights conducive to liberation, well-being, and flourishing. This is precisely what I attempt to do in this book, examining individuals who may be suicidal, lonely, isolated, and marginalized, yet who are also resilient, resistant, wise, and insightful. Throughout the book, I seek to examine how the groups and individuals I have studied conceive of the good and their "purpose in life" (*ikigai*), and how they create their own spaces and push back against internal and external structures that suggest they are disposable, worthless, and unnecessary. I also investigate how society and culture could be reconfigured to promote empathy, connection, and resilience against loneliness, and I end with a final chapter on what loneliness, and those who have suffered from it, can teach us.

1 Subjectivity and Empathy

> In my work with the defendants (at the Nuremberg Trials 1945–1949) I was searching for the nature of evil and I now think I have come close to defining it. A lack of empathy. It's the one characteristic that connects all the defendants, a genuine incapacity to feel with their fellow men. Evil, I think, is the absence of empathy.
>
> —Capt. Gustave M. Gilbert, US Army psychologist (1950)

As we have seen, loneliness is not *being* alone; it is *feeling* alone. While exploring the experiences of loneliness that are presented in this book, I came to understand more clearly how loneliness is actually fundamentally connected to the nature of subjectivity itself. The purpose of this chapter is to outline some of the major theoretical arguments put forward in this book, particularly regarding the interrelated nature of subjectivity, empathy, and loneliness, and then explain what I understand to be their methodological consequences for the anthropological study of what I call "afflictions of subjectivity" such as loneliness.

Several notable theorists in sociology and anthropology have explored how subjectivity is structured by the interplay of internal and external processes, one of the most notable being Pierre Bourdieu. Bourdieu used the term *habitus* to explain how subjectivity—individually and collectively—comes to be shaped by social structures which it then operates to replicate and perpetuate. Habitus refers to the postures that an individual or group of people in a society come to hold both mentally and physically toward others and their environments—that is, their way of relating to and perceiving the world. He famously and somewhat cryptically defined habitus as "systems of durable, transposable dispositions, structured structures predisposed to function as structuring structures, that is, as principles which generate and organize practices and representations that can be objectively adapted to their outcomes without presupposing a conscious aiming at ends or an express mastery of the operations necessary in order to attain them."[1] Importantly, this quote suggests that these structures of subjectivity need not be consciously accessible.

What do these internal structures of subjectivity consist of? What is their inner architecture? Although subjectivity can and has been defined in a number of ways, for the purposes of my work I define subjectivity as "first-person experience and the internal structures of body and mind that shape experience." Subjectivity is *that* a person experiences, *what* they experience, and *how* they experience it. As this may appear as abstract and vague as Bourdieu's definition to some, I present here with greater specificity what I believe to be a few of the key internal structures of subjectivity and how each relates to affective states such as loneliness.

For clarity of presentation, these theoretical and methodological arguments, as well as the background literature supporting them, are collected in this chapter, and the ethnographic basis for these arguments follows in the subsequent chapters. As a result, these arguments and claims may appear to some to be insufficiently or only loosely substantiated at first. I hope that readers will judge whether the ethnographic data presented in subsequent chapters lend them further support. In the conclusion of the book, I return to these arguments and tie the threads together regarding what they reveal about loneliness and how I think they can support future research.

THE JANUS-FACED NATURE OF SUBJECTIVITY

The first and most fundamental structure of subjectivity is what I call the "Janus-faced nature of subjectivity," referring to Janus, the Roman god of gates and transitions, who has two faces looking in opposite directions.[2] Put simply, subjectivity is a process of differentiation that establishes a divide—albeit a porous one—between what is "self" and what is "not-self," or "other." It establishes two sides that operate at one and the same time: subjectivity looks out and looks in. This liminal process results in the continual establishment of a membrane that stands at the threshold between two interdependent and mutually co-constituting sides. They are co-constituting, because to speak of self implies what is not-self, namely the environment and others, while to speak of something that is "other" implies "self." It is a process, because it is ongoing and not static, and because what is constituted as "self" and "not-self" can shift across contexts and time. This process is itself what we call *subjective experience* or simply *experience*, since it contains and establishes the subject of experience and the objects or content of experience.

To understand this concept, it is helpful to take each side of this membrane on its own first before putting them together. The first side is the aspect of subjectivity that "looks out." As human beings we are social animals who participate in a shared symbolic world with others. This "shared world" aspect of subjectivity means that our meaning making, our language, our concepts, our values and beliefs, our assumptions and attitudes, and the very way we experience our environment and ourselves are all co-created with others. Sharing a world is both essential to our ability to communicate and exist with others and foundational to our felt need for others, acceptance, and belonging, what developmental psychologist Philippe Rochat has called "our basic need to affiliate."[3] The fact that we share a world enables empathy, care, and compassion, but it also means that we experience pain when we are socially isolated, ostracized, bullied, disrespected, neglected, or marginalized. It is from a recognition of this structure of subjectivity that researchers argue that all subjectivity is intersubjectivity; that all experience is intersubjective; and that all meaning, language, and culture are social in nature. Seen from this perspective, to be a self is to be interdependent with others; one is and becomes a self in relation to others.

Yet this "looking out" has a twin side, "looking in." This refers to the fact that we also experience ourselves as a "self" separate from others and from our environment. Phenomenologists since Edmund Husserl have noted that a fundamental structure of experience is that it is always oriented toward an object (the other), which is called *intentionality*, but that at the same time it is always experience "for me" and "to me." This is because to be an experiencing subject presupposes non-self objects to experience as well as a self that experiences.[4] In fact, this very differentiation of self from environment is what it means to have a self and to be an organism that seeks to survive. As neurologist Antonio Damasio points out, if organisms made no differentiation between themselves and their environments, they would not seek to survive, nor would they approach food and safety and flee danger.[5] Viewed from this perspective, to be a self is to be separate from others; it is to be alone.

When an individual feels physical pain, for example by stubbing their toe, they will often signal that experience to others, through a vocalization, facial expression, or gesture. Others seeing that can experience empathy on the basis of the shared nature of experience and meaning making. In fact, they may wince, and neuroimaging studies suggest that they may experience similar, although not identical, neural activation, as if experiencing that pain themselves.[6] This speaks to the shared nature of experience. At the same time, that same individual may be going through emotional pain that is undetectable and invisible to others. Even if they try to communicate that pain, others may fail to understand or empathize. The fact that we have uncommunicable experiences speaks to the private nature of experience.[7]

These two sides that are established in subjectivity appear contradictory, yet they form a basic and fundamental dynamic of subjective experience: that we exist interdependently and individually, that we both share a world and are alone, and that both are fundamental to the nature of experience itself. Indeed, they are two sides of the same membrane—hence the term *Janus-faced.* This two-sided nature also creates the essential conditions for loneliness. Loneliness exists in and as a result of this liminality, which is why it is not ancillary but a fundamental problem and condition of human experience.

SUBJECTIVITY ESTABLISHES THE SELF, SURVIVAL, AND AFFECT

The other structures of subjectivity explored here all derive from, and are implied within, this one basic structure of subjectivity as a process of differentiation, but for purposes of clarity, I elucidate each one in turn here. The second structure of subjectivity is its role in establishing the self. Subjectivity is the process that creates the self. It is interdependent not only because it arises through an interaction of organism and environment, but more fundamentally from the fact that it is this very process of differentiation that establishes the organism as something distinct from its environment. This distinction can be considered one of the most basic characteristics of selfhood.

This perspective can be seen as the opposite of what we might call the naïve perspective on selfhood, which is that it is the self's existence that results in subjectivity and not the other way around. After all, the fact that we exist seems indubitable. But why do we exist—that is to say, why do we exist as beings that experience ourselves as something other than our environments? From what we know about the constitution of our brains and nervous systems, the establishment of ourselves as conscious and sentient beings that take our own existence for granted is the result of neural processes; thus, it is these processes that allow us to feel that give rise to our sense of existence and our sense of self. Instead of Descartes's "I think therefore I am," we might say, "I feel therefore I am" or "I feel therefore I think I am." Experience establishes existence and precedes essence.

SUBJECTIVITY IS PLASTIC

As human beings with higher cognition, for us selfhood is something that can become much more elaborated than the mere capacity for sensation, and numerous anthropologists and cultural psychologists have noted the various ways in which selfhood can be shaped and the different construals of selfhood that may be promoted in different societies and cultures.[8] Notably, for example, psychologists Shinobu Kitayama and Hazel Markus have suggested that Japanese people favor interdependent construals of selfhood as compared to the independent construals favored in North American and European societies.[9] As Kitayama notes, these variations are possible because of the plasticity or malleability of subjectivity and the dynamic manner through which subjectivity constitutes selfhood.[10]

Just as fundamentally, the processes of subjectivity can be altered in fundamental ways by violence and trauma, illnesses such as schizophrenia, and other experiences. Anthropologist Byron Good points out that cultural phenomenological approaches that treat experience as an invariant, neo-Kantian process may provide "a profoundly inadequate basis for a theory of subjectivity," particularly as they tend to leave out such complex psychological experiences as well as the role that social, historical, and political processes play in the shaping of subjectivity.[11] Like the present work, Good sees a role for empathy to play in anthropological research on subjectivity, although he rightly cautions that empathy cannot be limited to attending solely to what is verbally communicated. In his excellent monograph *Vita*, which focuses on a single interlocutor, and in his coedited volume *Subjectivity*, anthropologist João Biehl shows that subjectivity is an ever ongoing and relational process whereby individuals wrestle to make sense out of murky, uncertain, and incommensurable circumstances, and therefore attending to such lived experience may require new approaches to ethnography, even including aesthetics.[12]

Once the self is established at this most basic level, survival becomes a meaningful concept. The establishment of a self as something distinct from an environment also establishes, as a necessary by-product, the idea of survival; namely, if the integrity of this self is not protected, it will merely become part of the environment again, through death and dissolution of its elements. Self implies survival, and survival implies movement toward those things that promote survival and away from those that threaten survival. From this develop the fundamental components of affect, which begin at the most basic level in the form of sensations. To survive, an organism has to be able to sense what promotes its welfare and what threatens it and react accordingly. For emotion researchers like Damasio, this basic constitution of the self as something that must survive drives the development of sensations in the nervous system, and then a fuller elaboration of emotional life in birds, mammals, and human beings. For many researchers on emotion in psychology and neuroscience, emotions are best understood as evolved mechanisms for survival.[13] Thus, we can say that the third structure of subjectivity is its affective nature: subjectivity establishes affect, and affect—the ability to feel in ways that support survival—is fundamental to subjectivity.

INTERSUBJECTIVITY AND SOCIETY

The Janus-faced nature of subjectivity should help to elucidate what is meant by *intersubjectivity*, and this is the fourth structure of subjectivity explored here. Because subjectivity is the differentiation of self from others (other people and the environment), because its membrane is porous and has sides that look in and look out, and because we as human beings are social animals who depend on maternal care and on one another for survival, it is only natural that our subjectivity is not an independent entity but a process that is co-constituted by society and the subjectivities of others. As psychiatrist and anthropologist Laurence Kirmayer notes, "Experience itself is interpersonal and intersubjective in origin."[14]

As human beings, our survival is not merely an individual matter. As with all other mammalian species and like all bird species, human offspring depend entirely on maternal care to be born into the world and to survive, a fact that is increasingly pointed to by primatologists, comparative psychologists, and others as an explanation for why we see commonly prosocial emotions such as empathy and gratitude and prosocial behaviors such as consolation, helping, and cooperation across mammalian and bird species.[15] Offspring are not born to be self-sufficient, and human beings have an especially long development period before reaching maturity. At any point in this period of development, if support from caring others were withdrawn, the offspring would die. Even after reaching maturity, we humans continue to depend on countless others for our food, shelter, and other necessities of life. This means that just as survival depends on feeling and affect (the very condition of being sentient), so does human survival depend on *social affect*: feelings about ourselves and others, belonging, empathy, acceptance, trust, and intimacy, as well as the absence of these—social rejection, exclusion, and so on—which is feared because it is associated with threats to survival and possibly death. It should not be a surprise, therefore, that social rejection and exclusion typically result in extreme stress among human beings as well as other mammalian species.[16]

This evolutionary history elucidates why our need for belonging is built into our physiology and psychology, such as through the way human bodies respond to caring, affective touch.[17] It also seems to explain why people sometimes fear social death (embarrassment, exclusion, being ostracized) more than physical death; it also helps to explain why shame and fear of embarrassment can be such powerful motivators for behavior. In speaking about potential embarrassment, it is common in both the United States and Japan to say things like, "I'd rather die!"

Yet just as we are social beings, the nature of our biology and psychology makes us individuals as well. As noted earlier, the very structures of subjectivity, consciousness, and selfhood establish a sense of separateness of mind, body, and person. Important aspects of this sense of separateness increase over the course of human development. For example, it takes time for very young children to develop increasing sophistication in what psychologists call "theory of mind": the ability to understand others' mental states as different to one's own. Up until around the age of four, children tend to fail the "false belief test," in which they need to recognize that what they know might not be known to others. Over the course of development, sensitivity to the possibility of exclusion increases in parallel to the development of the human brain. Children learn that people can be untruthful and untrustworthy, that people can say things they do not mean. Adolescence in particular is a time when belonging becomes crucially important and exclusion particularly painful, with the brain undergoing significant developments related to social cognition.[18]

SUBJECTIVITY, LONELINESS, AND SOCIETY

We human beings are therefore a paradox. At one and the same time, we are both social beings who depend on connection with others for our survival and individual beings who experience things from a unique perspective not always shared or shareable by others. Both states are grounded in our biology and psychology. Yet together, these two aspects of our humanity result in an inherent tension and potential for loneliness. On the one hand, we have a deep biological and evolutionary need to belong and to share a world, to have intimacy, trust, and safety. On the other, we have an increasing realization that we often do *not* belong, are *not* accepted as we are, and do *not* share a world. It is this tug of war that sets us up for loneliness.

Importantly, the structures of society can ameliorate or exacerbate this inherent condition that we all share: they can help us achieve empathy, genuine intimacy, and human connection, or they can make that connection more difficult. Something so basic and intrinsic to human beings should be of importance to anyone engaged in social science research. Yet as anthropologist Janis Jenkins insightfully notes, "The anthropological tradition of prioritizing mental (values, belief, meaning) over affective (emotions, presentiments, feeling) elements of human culture led to the rise of subfield of cognitive anthropology, but not of affective anthropology."[19] In fact, as we shall see, even approaches to empathy have often become subsumed into a predominantly cognitive approach. In recent decades, however, anthropology has taken a strong interest in subjectivity, and this has led to an interest in internal emotional or affective states.[20] The connection between subjectivity and affect is natural because a key structure of subjectivity is the capacity to feel things: to experience sensations and emotions in a way that is oriented around one's own perceived well-being, or lack of it. Indeed, subjectivity is most commonly defined as the cognitive and affective states of an individual. Anthropologist Sherry Ortner, in an influential article on subjectivity, falls into this category when she defines subjectivity as "the ensemble of modes of perception, affect, thought, desire, fear, and so forth that animate acting subjects."[21] However, after reviewing a number of influential theorists of subjectivity in the social sciences, such as Bourdieu, Anthony Giddens, Marshall Sahlins, and William Sewell, Ortner notes that "there is a particular lack or area of thinness in all their work . . . a tendency to slight the question of subjectivity, that is, the view of the subject as existentially complex, a being who feels and thinks and reflects, who makes and seeks meaning."[22]

CHALLENGES IN STUDYING SUBJECTIVITY

There are a few notable challenges and possible objections to anthropological research on subjectivity. First, subjective states are by definition internal, so they seem to be invisible and impossible to observe. If they cannot be observed, that makes it very difficult to study them rigorously or scientifically. This has even led some anthropologists to conclude that subjectivity and affect are not worth studying, or perhaps are even impossible to study.

Second, subjective states are individual, yet anthropologists tend to be interested in studying the interactions of groups of people within societies and cultures. If one were to study individuals and their internal states, it might seem to detract from the study of communities. Again, this would seem to be a reason to avoid subjectivity in anthropological work. However, as Biehl has shown in his work *Vita*, which focuses on a single person, skillful ethnographers can still explore complex social, political, and cultural dynamics as they manifest within the subjectivity of individuals if they are attentive to innovative methodologies.[23]

Third, perhaps because they are internal and invisible, subjectivity and emotions simply do not seem as real or as important as other things we could be studying. We know that people feel things, but at the end of the day, does it really matter that they do? Surely what is more important is how people actually behave and the way they act. It can appear simpler to focus on behavior and decision-making, which are more accessible to observation, and ignore emotions, feelings, and other subjective states. Moreover, since people are often confused about their own internal states and often report them inaccurately, it might actually be misleading to focus too much on internal states rather than external behavior.

These are all reasonable objections, but they need not prevent us from engaging in research on subjectivity. In this book, I aim to show that it is not only possible to study subjectivity and affect; it is essential. Furthermore, I argue that most anthropologists and other social scientists are already engaged in studying aspects of subjectivity, albeit often indirectly. The study of subjectivity is fundamental to anthropology and always has been.

One of the reasons for this is that what we call society is actually in large part the product of collective subjectivity. As noted, I define subjectivity as first-person experience and the internal structures of body and mind that shape that experience—that is, *that* a person experiences an environment as separate from themselves, *what* that person experiences, and *how* they experience it. This includes a person's experience of themselves (self-concept), their environment, and their "being in the world." This definition is inclusive of the idea of subjectivity as the cognitive and affective states of an individual, but I feel it is somewhat more precise, because states do not arise randomly but are themselves internally structured through the configuration of the body and mind. These primary structures that shape experience are therefore biological, psychological, and physiological, yet they develop interdependently and synchronistically with the organism's interaction with an external environment, including other individuals as well as political and economic structures.

As noted, one of these primary structures—and a particularly important one for the study of loneliness—is the establishment of the self as something separate from the environment, and as something that can survive and can experience well-being and suffering. If we did not have subjectivity—that is, if we did not have emotions, desires, fears, and conceptions about what is better and what is worse—then we would not be sentient beings. To be sentient is to feel. Furthermore, all sentient beings tend to move toward that which they believe will promote their survival, well-being, or happiness, and away from what will lead to pain and death. Sentient beings, to the extent that their nervous systems and cognitive abilities permit them, therefore seek out or create environments that are conducive to their survival and flourishing. What we call society, and all the institutions of our society—political, economic, cultural, and so on—are the manifestations and products of these inner states, reflecting our desire to create conditions that support our flourishing and minimize our distress. When we study these institutions and structures, we are studying the outer manifestations of subjectivity.

Similarly, far from being an impervious interiority, our subjectivity is porous and is shaped by the environments we are born into and live in. Anthropologists and sociologists have long argued this, including Bourdieu through his concept of habitus. Our environments, including the people around us, shape how we think and feel; they often even determine the limits of what we *can* think or feel, and they do so in ways that are largely unnoticed by us and unconscious to us. Thus, our subjectivity is always in dialogue with our environment and with the subjectivity of others; it is social. It even emerges developmentally within a social context: first a fetus and its mother, and then a person surrounded by many others. Indeed, the infant-mother relationship is an archetypal instance of intersubjectivity. As self always develops in relation to that which is not-self, and as subjectivity is inherently social beginning in the womb, all subjectivity is intersubjectivity.

Through development it becomes clear that what we call subjectivity is the product of the interplay of our biology and our environment, including not only our natural/material environment, but also our political, social, and economic environment.[24] On a biological level, we have a need for survival as well as evolved mechanisms for experiencing and navigating the world. Yet as social animals, we are born into an environment that is not just natural and material, but also social. We are born into families and relationships, into social, political, and economic structures, and these all shape the development of our brains and bodies, including our personalities and psychologies. What we call *culture* is the result of this interplay between that material-social environment and our biology. Hence, the most important factors for understanding culture are the natural environment, the social environment, and biology.

SOCIETY AND AFFECT

Society is the collective manifestation not just of people's reason, but also of their affect. Affect is therefore already present in the institutions of a society, its norms, and what we call "culture." It both shapes and is shaped by its environment. This should not surprise us, because what determines happiness and flourishing is not just a matter of reason, but also of feeling. We like certain things and dislike others, yet we can't necessarily explain *why* this is the case. Even when we can come up with reasons, they are often what psychologists call confabulations: stories we tell so that we feel that we understand why we like or do certain things. But ultimately many of our actions are guided by feelings and emotions; what we want and what we fear is not strictly delimited by what is rational. This is why the institutions of our society will always reflect our affective states.

As noted, affect is also social in nature. When we think about emotions, we tend to think of them as individual processes. But emotions are not just individual. For one thing, emotions have both evolutionary and cultural roots; they are the product of an evolutionary past that includes all of humanity (and are therefore not merely individual), and they are shaped by the cultures we live in (and are therefore, again, not merely individual). Furthermore, almost all emotions are social in nature; they have to do with the way we feel about one another and are often accompanied by signals to others.

Indeed, if we look at the etymology of the English word *emotion*, we notice something very interesting. The word's history comes from a public or social stirring or agitation; in other words, it first arose in the sixteenth century to describe not the feelings of individuals but the actions of groups. Later it came to refer to strong feelings, and for several centuries it was only used to refer to strong, negative emotions. Only in the nineteenth century did the word begin to be used to refer to any kind of feeling, including subtler and positive ones.[25]

From this perspective, we can see that the study of subjectivity is neither impossible nor irrelevant. It is actually foundational to our study of culture and society. If we study the norms, practices, beliefs, artifacts, and institutions of a society or culture, we are studying the history and processes of intersubjectivity collectively working itself out. If this is the case, then we must guard against ignoring people's subjective states; we would be looking at one side of the coin, the outward manifestation of intersubjectivity, but ignoring its other side, the intersubjective states of actors. We know from every field of science and social science—and particularly the field of epigenetics—that life is a constant negotiation between environment and organism: the organism's internal state changes in response to changes in its environment, and—in the case of those organisms that can change their environments—the organism changes its environment to promote its own survival and flourishing.

The study of emotions, therefore, should not be limited to psychology or neuroscience; there is an important and critical role for anthropology to play. The work of Damasio and others has done much to dismantle the clear division between cognition and emotion, a division that anthropologist Catherine Lutz, one of the main contributors to the anthropology of emotions, has called "the gendered hierarchy of reason and emotion, a distinction that distorts and divides understandings of human activity."[26] This work attempts to contribute to what Lutz describes as a "mid-range" space: "The unique insights that ethnographic fieldwork provides would advance theory-building in the study of affect by thickening the crucial but neglected mid-range below abstract theories about the nature of the human and the nature of nature and closer to the history of the present."[27] As such, I do draw from generalizing theories of human psychology and behavior, largely taken from psychology and based on empirical (yet often laboratory-based) research, and seek to connect them with ethnographic fieldwork, which is specific, real world, messy, and rich in both detail and ambiguity.

Another important contributor to the anthropological study of subjectivity and affect is Tanya Luhrmann, who notes that "anthropologists used the word 'subjectivity' to refer to the shared inner life of the subject and particularly to the emotional experience of a political subject."[28] Luhrmann argues that a psychological model of emotions can be helpful in the anthropological study of subjectivity: "If subjectivity is the emotional experience of a political subject, then to articulate the psychological structure of the emotion only gives us more evidence to argue that power is inscribed upon our bodies and that moral judgment is a visceral act."[29] The works of Ortner, Lutz, Luhrmann, and other anthropologists are particularly important as we seek to make sense of the ethnographic findings on loneliness and suicide presented in the following chapters.

Anthropologists have played a crucial role in the exploration of emotions as they play out in concrete situations in society, and an interdisciplinary approach that includes anthropology best allows us to see the interplay between individuals and their societies: the constant interplay of the inner dimension of intersubjectivity and the outward dimension of social, political, and economic structures. With some notable exceptions, psychologists and neuroscientists primarily study individuals and occasionally small-scale interactions between a few individuals. Economists, political scientists, and sociologists may study larger scale processes but too often neglect the essential role of intersubjectivity and affect. We know, however, that these processes are being engaged simultaneously and interdependently; therefore, we will benefit from focusing on the interplay and mutual reflection of our inner and outer selves.

Indeed, this interplay is so fundamental that it turns up not just in works of academic scholarship, but frequently also in works of literature. A notable example is the works of Jane Austen. In her novels, Austen expertly investigates the way political economy shapes the subjectivity (perceptions, cognition, and affect) of her characters. Not only that, she chronicles the way transformations in political economy (the shift of power away from the landed gentry that occurred as a result of the Industrial Revolution) result in transformations of subjectivity. At the same time, however, she recognizes the role of biology. Human emotions and feelings are not simply reducible to political economy; they have a long evolutionary history. As a result, despite those political transformations, certain basic aspects of friendship, love, honesty, transparency, trust, and so forth remain constant. Her books can be read as a constant negotiation between these two forces: the shifts in subjectivity caused by transformations of political economy and the constancy of subjectivity that is a result of our slower-changing biology. In fact, the latter sense of constancy is one reason we can still empathetically relate to her characters today, despite the significant differences between the political economy of her time and ours.

WHO COUNTS AS A SUBJECT?

Here I offer a final, but important, note on subjectivity, affect, and emotions. Throughout our intellectual history, our sense of who "counts" as a person has shifted and become more expansive over time, and our theories about human nature have shifted accordingly. There has been a recent revival of interest in Aristotelian virtue ethics across a number of fields, including anthropology, where it has been incorporated into discussions of an "anthropology of the good" to counterbalance a focus on suffering and the anthropology of ethics. I see this as a positive development, but I hope this work can show that an inclusion of other cultural traditions of meaning making and conceptualizing of the "good life" can supplement these efforts. After all, we must remember that for Aristotle, virtue ethics did not apply or extend to everyone; it was a code and a standard designed for a specific type of person—a citizen of a polis (city-state) and typically a man—and indeed it did not even extend to citizens of another polis.[30] Ancient and modern philosophy and theory repeatedly prioritized a certain type of person: male, adult, someone who employs reason and language to make decisions, who is neither intellectually nor physically disabled, and who stands at the center, not the periphery (privileged, civilized, not queer, not enslaved, and so on).[31] It should be clear that that is not a representative picture of humanity; it is a form of epistemological blindness. As part of this picture, cognition and reason have played a central role, and affect has been shunted to the side—at least in part precisely because affect is more universal and is what men of privilege have in common with women, children, enslaved persons, people from other cultures and societies at the periphery, people who are mentally or cognitively disabled, nonhuman animals, and so on. Feminist studies, disability studies, subaltern studies, critical race theory, and other fields have pushed back against this normative and often unquestioned view of what is meant by "a human being." A focus on affect provides us with a way to further that effort; it should provoke a seismic shift in our theory and ethnography. To be a living, sentient being is to be able to feel, and that is what we all have in common; it is not to be able to reason in a sophisticated way or use certain forms of human language. Turning to affect is turning to a dimension of humanity that is more fundamental than "reason," more inclusive, and therefore, in my opinion, more illuminating. It allows us to address, undermine, and correct this prejudiced discrepancy—what I would call a "ratio-normative" orthodoxy—that has thus far unreasonably limited our science, our theories, our research, and hence our conclusions about humanity and human nature.

EMPATHY AND TRIANGULATION AS METHODS IN APPROACHING SUBJECTIVITY

The dynamic between society and subjectivity is especially important if we want to understand subjective states like loneliness and actions like suicide, two of the main topics that I deal with in this book. In Japan, and now increasingly throughout the world, we are witnessing an epidemic of loneliness. We are also witnessing an epidemic of suicide, one of the leading causes of death in virtually every developed nation in the world. This book argues that we can better understand actions like suicide if we attend to the subjective states of those who commit suicide, and this is facilitated by empathy. Suicide is an effect and a symptom, and we need to understand the cause. But unlike traditional approaches to suicide that see it solely as a symptom of individual mental illness, it is becoming increasingly apparent that suicide is at least as much a symptom of a sick society. The working hypothesis of this book—explored in depth in each chapter—is that systems-level processes in society are making people feel worthless, unseen, uncared for, and disposable. These subjective states establish mindsets that make suicide appear a viable, even necessary, option. If we are to address this issue, we must explore the dynamic between society and subjectivity. We must uncover the social, political, and economic practices that are driving us toward lonely societies and driving people to loneliness and even death.

On the one hand, we have individuals and their subjective states; on the other, we have society. The methodological proposal of this book is that we should examine the two together and in relation to each other—both disconnected people and the lonely society—through a sophisticated understanding of subjectivity and methods that explicitly employ critical empathy. *Critical empathy*, as I use the term, involves employing empathy with an awareness of both its potential benefits and its inherent limitations, while recognizing the bidirectional interplay between subjective experience and social, political, and economic structures. Methodologically, it involves placing multiple accounts in dialogue with each other and with the researcher's own perspective with an appreciation of diversity, self-reflexivity and epistemic humility on the part of the researcher, and considerations of the potential for empathy and failures of empathy among all involved parties. I struggled for many years doing research on loneliness and suicide in Japan before arriving at what now seems like a relatively simple and straightforward methodology for balancing multiple accounts with critical empathy. I call this method *triangulation* because it involves three aspects: what I call first-, second-, and third-person approaches. These describe approaches that are more "experience-near" (first-person), are less "experience-near" (third-person), or engage subjective experience dialogically and dialectically (second-person).

First-person is the subjective accounts of individuals. It is clear that if we are to understand subjectivity, we have to pay attention to people's accounts in their own words. First-person accounts are "I" accounts: how a person sees their own experience and relates it to others. A first-person account calls for and depends upon empathy on the part of the reader or listener. This is the most "experience-near" of the three approaches. Disconnection is not just an aspect of objective reality; in fact, if we look at things more objectively, we may conclude that people in modern societies and in the modern world are more connected and interdependent than ever before in human history. But that doesn't mean that people *feel* more connected. Subjectively, as this book shows, people are experiencing disconnection. Why is this the case, particularly in a society such as Japan, which has long been recognized as being highly collectivist and communal?

The second-person approach refers to accounts that are not necessarily coming from a person who is lonely, but that engage the subjectivity of that person dialogically. As we know, the second person is "you"; it refers to someone addressing someone else. This is the way I categorize works of fiction and nonfiction that try to wrestle with the subjective experiences of others, including writers, filmmakers, and so on. Although these people are not necessarily speaking from their own experience, they are interested in the first-person experiences of others. They are interested in subjectivity and want to explore subjective states like loneliness and the mindsets of those who wish to commit suicide. Second-person accounts are important because they engage this subjectivity dialectically and imaginatively, as the reader or viewer is invited to explore situations and experiences as if they were a participant or direct observer within them. These accounts should not be discounted as mere fantasy; they function as social commentary and social critique, especially when they resonate widely within the society they are critiquing. As I show, many films, television programs, and written accounts of loneliness and suicide in Japan can shed significant light on these issues and are worth considering alongside formal scholarship and reporting. Like first-person accounts, what I call second-person accounts depend on empathy to be intelligible and effective.

Third-person accounts include news reports, statistics, much of the scholarly research on suicide and loneliness, and so on. These accounts tend to be far less interested in subjective experience; they are "experience-far." They pay more attention to behaviors and the outer manifestations of subjective states than to the states themselves. They depend least on an appeal to empathy. In some cases, as we shall see, they can exhibit a failure of empathy.

If we are to examine the interplay between society and subjectivity, I believe it is valuable to include all three of these accounts in scholarship, and that is what I have tried to do in this book. This is because including all three types of accounts allows for numerous perspectives and lets us see tensions among accounts and among types of accounts. Statistics regarding suicide and loneliness provide us with important information, but we may decide that the conclusions drawn from them are erroneous if they do not align with first- and second-person accounts. It is possible that prevention efforts are less likely to succeed if they do not connect with first-person accounts. But most important, if we believe that loneliness and suicide are actually symptoms of underlying problems, we are likely to do far better at understanding those problems if we listen to and engage with the subjective accounts of those involved.

DEFINING EMPATHY

If subjectivity is typically understood as the cognitive and affective states of individuals, then empathy can be understood as the capacity to understand and resonate with those states in another. This makes empathy a natural topic of interest for anthropologists and others interested in the study of subjectivity, yet empathy is particularly interesting because it points to both successes and failures in sharing a world. Successful empathy can make individuals feel closer to one another. Failures of empathy can emphasize the distinctiveness, individuality, and private nature of experiences.

Empathy stands at the membrane of self and other. Unsurprisingly, therefore, it perfectly reflects the Janus-faced nature of subjectivity. Much scholarship has tended to emphasize just one side or the other, however, showing how empathy allows for the successful sharing of experiences or revealing that it is prone to failures that emphasize the separate and individual nature of experience. The best way to approach empathy, however, is to recognize that it is inextricable from this dual-natured way that subjectivity is structured, which allows us to account for both its successes and its failures. Standing at the intersection of sharing and separateness, empathy would also appear to be closely related to loneliness. In fact, it prompts the question: To what extent does loneliness involve deficits in giving and receiving empathy?

If it is true that empathy is central to the nature of subjectivity itself, then we would expect it to have a long evolutionary history. That it does is increasingly being recognized. As neuroscientist Jean Decety writes in his introduction to a volume on the social neuroscience of empathy, "The capacity for empathy in humans and their progenitor species developed over millions of years of evolutionary history, in ways that are only now becoming clear. Although it is impossible to travel back in time and observe these developments directly, the evidence for them is available in the neuroanatomical continuities and differences that can be observed across the phylogenetic spectrum."[32]

In the same volume, psychologist Daniel Batson notes that a large number of definitions, many of them contradictory, exist among researchers of empathy. He notes: "Application of the term empathy to so many distinct phenomena is, in part, a result of researchers invoking empathy to provide an answer to two quite different questions: How can one know what another person is thinking and feeling? What leads one person to respond with sensitivity and care to the suffering of another? For some students of empathy, answers to these two questions are related. However, many more seek to answer the first question without concern to answer the second, or vice versa."[33]

Batson notes eight distinct mental states that are at times called "empathy":

1. Knowing about another person's internal state, including his or her thoughts and feelings
2. Adopting the posture or matching the neural responses of an observed other
3. Coming to feel as another person feels
4. Intuiting or projecting oneself into another's situation
5. Imagining how another is thinking and feeling
6. Imagining how one would feel in the other's place
7. Feeling distress at witnessing another person's suffering (empathic distress, personal distress)
8. Feeling for another person who is suffering (sympathy, compassion, empathetic concern)

While each of these eight is distinct, it is possible to condense them into a smaller grouping. In this book, I employ such a reduction. Broadly following the work of Batson, psychologist Nancy Eisenberg, primatologist

Frans de Waal, and others, I understand empathy as a multidimensional construct consisting of affective and cognitive dimensions. I refer to items 1, 4, 5, and 6 in the list as *cognitive empathy*. Items 2 and 3 are referred to as *affective empathy*. When these are both present, I use the term *empathy* in its full sense. Item 7 I refer to as *empathic distress*, and item 8 as *compassion*. While related to empathy, these two states are distinct.

Eisenberg and Richard Fabes define empathy as "an emotional response that stems from another's emotional state or condition, is congruent with the other's emotional state or condition, and involves at least a minimal degree of differentiation between self and other."[34] Researchers disagree about what this "congruence" means. Some empathy researchers, like social neuroscientist Tania Singer, have explored congruence as isomorphic brain activation: if someone witnesses their spouse experiencing pain, their own neural activation of pain networks shows that they are empathizing.[35] For others, congruence does not require the empathizer to have the same emotional experience as the person with whom they are empathizing. Thus, if I see someone experiencing an emotion like fear or anger, I do not need to experience that same emotion (fear or anger) myself to empathize with them.

Eisenberg's concern, and that of many others following her, has been to differentiate between empathy, on the one hand, and the two states it often gives rise to: sympathy (which overlaps with what others, including myself, call compassion) and personal distress. The key difference is that sympathy is "an other-oriented desire for the other person to feel better," whereas personal distress is egoistic.[36] Whereas sympathy leads to altruistic behavior, personal distress (also called empathic distress) leads to helping only in an egoistic way, namely to alleviate the distress one feels when witnessing another's suffering. Recent research on compassion has led to seeing compassion, too, as a multidimensional construct. Clara Strauss and her colleagues identify compassion as consisting of five elements: "1) Recognizing suffering; 2) Understanding the universality of suffering in human experience; 3) Feeling empathy for the person suffering and connecting with the distress (emotional resonance); 4) Tolerating uncomfortable feelings aroused in response to the suffering person (e.g. distress, anger, fear) so remaining open to and accepting of the person suffering; and 5) Motivation to act/acting to alleviate suffering."[37]

An astute observer might notice that all of these definitions of empathy focus on the person who is feeling empathy for another person, not on how the other person receives or responds to the "empathizer." This is perhaps a natural bias of much (but not all, of course) psychological and neuroscientific research. What anthropology brings to the table is a focus on social interactions and culture. In their edited special issue of *Ethos*, psychological anthropologists Jason Throop and Douglas Hollan bring together a number of fascinating anthropological studies on empathy that illustrate the diverse ways empathy can operate and fail, focusing not just on the givers but also on the intended recipients of empathy, as well as on the social and cultural contexts within which processes of empathy operate.[38] The articles by Kirmayer and Hollan in particular focus on the difficulties of empathy and the many possibilities of empathy failing or being misunderstood.[39] Oddly, as Hollan notes, even when the recipient does report experiencing empathy, the timing or nature of that experience may not align with when the empathizer thought they were empathizing.[40]

This ambiguity in the social experience of empathy is one reason I focus theoretically and methodologically on empathy in this work, rather than on compassion. Failures of empathy, as I show, are of direct consequence in understanding the causes and dynamics of loneliness. The other reason is that compassion is specifically oriented toward the suffering of the other and the alleviation of that suffering. Empathy, on the other hand, while supportive of compassion, focuses on understanding and resonating with the experience of the other, which can include but also be broader than experiences of suffering. It seems to me that empathy, therefore, is an appropriate and fruitful area for anthropology as an act of scholarship and inquiry, whereas compassion may be suitable on the level of interventions. Ideally, to avoid misuses of empathy, the two would go hand in hand.

The employment of empathy occurs in multiple ways in this book. First, the methodological triangulation of first-, second-, and third-person approaches would be impossible without empathy. Second, I argue that empathy is intimately connected with loneliness. Third, I argue that lack of empathy in society is a chief characteristic of a lonely society, and that empathy is an important aspect of social and cultural resilience against loneliness and disconnection.

Last, empathy is critical to the work of scholarship itself and to the methodological approach I am suggesting for the anthropology of subjectivity. The presentation of first-person narratives depends on the empathy of both scholar and reader. I am talking about how individuals feel and how they perceive the world. Understanding this requires that to some extent we take their perspectives and *feel into* their feelings. *Feeling into* is the direct translation of the German term *Einfühlung*, which is the etymological origin of the word *empathy*.

Ideally, scholarly engagement with empathy as a methodology involves empathy in the fullest sense of the definitions provided in this chapter: cognitive and affective dimensions supporting compassion and not derailed by empathic distress. This "full" empathy is the way that I use the term here. The cognitive dimension of empathy means being able to take another person's perspective and understand why they see things the way they do and why they might feel a certain way. The affective dimension of empathy is a *feeling with* or an emotional resonance. It means that when we consider another's situation, we are able to use our own feelings to make sense of what we are experiencing and what the other might be experiencing. We resonate on an emotional level; we don't just consider their situation coldly, rationally, and without any of our own affect. The avoidance of empathic distress means that we do not allow our own feelings to overshadow what we are seeking to understand. The process is not about us; it is about the other(s) whom we are trying to understand. Nor do we speak from our own feelings as if we were speaking for the other or pretend that our experience somehow represents that of the other. This ability to not succumb to empathic distress is especially important when dealing with populations who are experiencing distress, suffering, and marginalization, and when dealing with afflictions of subjectivity like severe and chronic loneliness. It is important that empathy be balanced and that scholars engaging in empathy recognize its limits and complications. To forget this would be to fall prey to an illusion, the precise situation that anthropologist Clifford Geertz warned about in his well-known critique of empathy, in which he stressed that anthropologists should not use "extraordinary empathy" as a shortcut or privileged means to speaking for and about others' experiences.[41]

The value of what I am calling first- and second-person accounts is that they allow us to engage our empathy both in the act of scholarship and in the act of reading scholarship. They are what Geertz calls "experience-near." This is an essential component in the study of subjectivity. Since the study of subjectivity is the study of both our rational and affective sides, it should involve both. This does not mean that we set aside reason and merely feel; far from it. It means we recognize that our feelings do matter and count and can actually *aid* our understanding, especially when we are engaging in the study of others' feelings. To wholly forgo empathy would be to fail to recognize the fundamental role emotions and affect play in allowing for and contributing to understanding, and it would mean ignoring a significant amount of recent research on the close links, if not interdependence, between cognition and affect.[42]

NEOLIBERALISM AND MATERIALISM

One of the arguments of this book is that the trend toward lonely societies is related to materialism, specifically an overemphasis on the external, material conditions of well-being while neglecting the social and affective dimensions of well-being—those most closely related to subjectivity. This lopsided approach, when taken to its extreme, reduces human beings to producers and consumers whose value depends on their productivity and consumption, rather than their having intrinsic value, a term to which I return later. If we were robots, with no feelings, no emotions, and no inner life, such an approach would not be a problem. We could increasingly structure our societies, our politics, our economies, and our media in a purely materialistic way that maximized productivity and economic development.

But we are not robots. We do have an inner life. To be human means to have not just behavior and reason, but also affect. Because of this, it matters to us *whether we matter*, and it matters most of all whether we matter to other people. A great deal of our happiness and meaning in life depends on this. In a society where we do not really matter, where we are replaceable, and where we are treated as if we were material objects rather than sentient beings, we are apt to feel unneeded, disconnected, lacking meaning, and lonely. Therefore we need to find a happy medium that balances the importance of external, material conditions for our well-being with the importance of inner, subjective, and intersubjective affective states—which include our feelings toward and about each other.

It has become common in anthropology to offer a criticism of neoliberalism as one of the sources of this push toward materialism and the instrumentalization of human beings. I think there is much to be said for this critique, but I believe it requires two caveats. First, we must recognize that a solution to the problem of people being dehumanized and treated as mere cogs in a system requires addressing both external and internal factors. Earlier I described the dynamic between the intersubjective affect of a society's people and the outer manifestations of that affect in the institutions of society. As I argue in this book, I do believe that the trend toward deregulated markets and the removal of social welfare protections has impacted political, economic, and social institutions in Japan in ways that are readable in the subjectivity of people in Japanese society. It is a common tenet of systems dynamic theories, when applied to societies, that systems shape behavior. That is to say, if people are indeed becoming lonelier and more disconnected, we should see some of the causes for this in society. We may even see a feedback loop from this dynamic between intersubjectivity and the structures of society.

Signs of this feedback loop or vicious cycle do seem evident across Japanese society. In Japanese popular books, magazines, and television shows, and across the internet, there is continual mention of the "precarious" situation that Japan finds itself in. Indeed, anthropologist of Japan Anne Allison's recent book *Precarious Japan* provides an excellent survey and analysis of this situation.[43] Many scholars and commentators on Japan point not just to the suicide rates, but also to shifts in the nature of relationships and intimacy, the meaning and nature of employment and corporate culture, decreasing trust in the government and in large corporations, very low childbearing rates, the decreased willingness of Japanese youth to take risks, and a host of other factors. Japanese society has been aware for some time now that there is a crisis brewing.

Feedback loops can go both ways, of course. In the final two chapters of the book I explore what a virtuous cycle could look like, one in which the people of a society embrace an affect founded on human connection, the relational and irreducible meaning of human life, resilience, and compassion, and in which the external structures of society reflect and support the attitudes, beliefs, and feelings of that subjectivity. Although this area of study—a society's happiness and flourishing—is relatively new for science and the social sciences, there is a growing body of empirical support suggesting that we should look into it further. The World Happiness Report, for example, is an initiative of the United Nations that collects data from over 150 countries to investigate the causes and conditions of a society's happiness and subjective well-being. Moreover, while the symptoms may at times look different, the underlying problems that Japan faces, insofar as they are problems of materialism and excessive neoliberalism, are common in many countries in the world today.

The second caveat has to do with the term *neoliberalism* itself. Although it has come to mean the complete deregulation of markets, a laissez-faire economic philosophy, and the commodification of everything (including human beings), this is quite different from the original intention of the University of Chicago economist Milton Friedman, who is generally credited with having popularized the term as an economic philosophical approach. For Friedman, neoliberalism actually represented a middle ground between unbridled, laissez-faire individualism and collectivism. In his famous essay "Neoliberalism and Its Prospects," Friedman points out the errors of both individualism and collectivism.[44] Of complete laissez-faire individualism, wherein the state has no role other than to maintain order and regulate contracts, he writes that it "underestimated the danger that private individuals could through agreement and combination usurp power and effectively limit the freedom of other individuals; it failed to see that there were some functions the price system could not perform and that unless these other functions were somehow provided for, the price system could not discharge effectively the tasks for which it is admirably fitted."[45]

One such function for which government was necessary, and which could not be left to market forces, was to "relieve acute misery and distress." On this, Friedman wrote, "Finally, the government would have the function of relieving misery and distress. Our humanitarian sentiments demand that some provision should be made for those who 'draw blanks in the lottery of life'. Our world has become too complicated and intertwined, and we have become too sensitive, to leave this function entirely to private charity or local responsibility."[46] Therefore, he argued, "a new faith must avoid both errors. It must give high place to a severe limitation on the power of the state to interfere in the detailed activities of individuals; at the same time, it must explicitly recognize that there are important positive functions that must be performed by the state."[47]

At the time, Friedman was more concerned with the domination of collectivism in economic and governmental policy; hence, he emphasized the need for a movement toward liberalism. But neoliberalism for him was precisely a rejection of both extremes and was importantly qualified by the essential role of government in helping the marginalized in society. More recently, however, the term has come to mean simply the deregulation of markets, a laissez-faire approach, individualism, and the removal of government from all social welfare activities. This appears to be precisely one of the two extremes that Friedman hoped to avoid.

POLITICAL ECONOMY AND SUBJECTIVITY

The question of neoliberalism and the relationship between political economy and subjectivity has a particular dimension when it comes to Japan because Japanese capitalism bears some important differences from capitalism in the United States and western Europe. Capitalism in Japan has been called *collective capitalism* or *corporate capitalism* because it valued the collective as the agent of competition (against foreign companies and foreign nations), not the individual person. For this reason, many early companies in postwar Japan were closely connected to the state, and many still retain close ties that would be seen as highly concerning in countries like the United States. The companies were created with specific policies to establish them as alternative "families" and sites of loyalty for their employees, who were mainly men: hiring students in their last year of university, offering lifetime employment, requiring long work hours so that employees stay at work or at company-organized socializing events late into the evening or night, and enacting policies that made it difficult to fire anyone or replace them with part-time or temporary workers. In 1946, the Japanese political scientist Masao Maruyama presented a highly influential analysis of Japan's political economy and its effects on society. In "The Logic and Psychology of Ultranationalism" (*Chōkokka Shugi no Ronri to Shinri*), he suggested, controversially, that the postwar Japanese state was based on a particular adaptation of liberalism that maintained traditional values of loyalty, hierarchy, and nationalism, which prevented Japan from fully shedding its fascist orientation.[48] Maruyama's thought influenced successive generations of scholarship on Japan's modernization, and many aspects of Japanese society can be seen as the product of a growing nationalist political economy and collective capitalism. Even the role of the Japanese housewife as homemaker and home economist in charge of finances, able to run the family despite the long absences from home of her husband, has been read as the result of an intention to establish a role for women that would support the productivity of their husbands and thereby the productivity of the large companies and the nation itself.

Following Maruyama, scholars of Japan such as Ritu Vij have argued about whether Japan ever passed through a liberalism similar to the trajectory of Western capitalist democracies. If it did not, then neoliberal economic reforms intended to spur Japan's economy out of recession by weakening the structures that have held it stable for so long, including lifetime employment and other policies, could fail precisely because they do not account for the fact that the external forms of political economy are interdependent manifestations of Japanese intersubjectivity. In short, neoliberal restructuring may not resonate with Japanese people on a subjective and affective level. Of this Vij writes, "In the absence of the 'liberal moment' as a feature of social life as a whole . . . efforts to release the normative limits of the culturally coded institutions of Japan's political economy may prove to be self-defeating, signaling a crisis not only of political economy [but also] a crisis of subjectivity."[49] Vij's perspective is very much in line with that of this book when she writes that political economy is the "external structure of subjectivity."[50] For Vij, the success of the "neoliberal turn" is not measured by economic indicators, but rather by "the successful re-shaping of subjectivities that would in turn provide its [neoliberalism's] constitutive conditions of possibility."[51]

Vij concludes her book by asking if there are signs of this crisis of subjectivity. As a scholar of political economy, she does not herself engage in ethnographic research that would directly address her question, although she does refer to the phenomenon of *hikikomori*, Japanese who refuse to leave their homes or bedrooms for anywhere from six months to many years. The research presented in this book can be read as an answer to her and other scholars who have wondered about this question. I think it will show that her intuition was correct: when looking ethnographically at the subjectivities of young Japanese, particularly those who experience and express loneliness, who seek or express a lack of meaning in life, and who contemplate or attempt suicide, we see clear signs of a crisis of subjectivity that appears connected to the political, economic, and social transformations Japan has been undergoing in recent years. This is in line with other works of a similar nature, most notably *Precarious Japan* by Allison, which convincingly chronicles this subjective experience of crisis and precarity across Japanese society.[52] Whereas Allison's book provides a more general overview of Japanese society, this book focuses on loneliness and suicide, particularly through the lens of subjectivity.

2 Too Lonely to Die Alone

INTERNET GROUP SUICIDE

The most terrible poverty is loneliness, and the feeling of being unloved.

—Mother Teresa

SORRY TO CAUSE YOU TROUBLE

MINA: I decided to die today. Sorry to cause you trouble.

NATO DAN: Well, I won't stop you, as I don't think you're serious about it. If you do want to die, then please die quietly without causing trouble for other people. Jumping in front of a train is out of the question. I hear that a body that has died from freezing to death or from carbon monoxide still looks pretty. Well, I have to say, it's too late to regret it after you're dead. Good night. So, does my reaction satisfy you?

The way you are, you're going to be driven into a corner even in the afterlife, too.

MINA: Mizuho-san, have you already died? Would you like to die together? After I've died, I am going to kill myself in the afterlife also. I will certainly not cause anyone any trouble. I ran away from home when I was at elementary school. I don't think there's anyone who remembers me. I'll hide in the woods and take poison, and die by falling into a pre-made hole.

KANTARO: Wait, Mina. Don't die!

MIKA: I really want to commit suicide. I really want to commit suicide because everybody bullies me and I don't want to go to school. God, I want to die. Aaah! I want to die!!!

RURU: It seems no one's around right now. . . . Mika-san, nice to meet you. Mika-san, are you also bullied?

MIKA: Would you like to go to Mt. Fuji's sea of trees? I was about to go. Nice to meet you. I am Mika. Let's be friends, shall we?

RURU: Me too. I tried to kill myself many times and strangled myself. Recently I cut my wrists. . . . But I can't die.

MIKA: When would you like to do it?

RURU: Personally I prefer winter break. The forest will be cold. If we wander around, I think we would die from hunger or cold. . . . Or shall we hang ourselves?

MIKA: Ruru-san, thank you! When shall we do it? I am always free! Please give me a call at home. (xxx) xxx xxxx. Other people, please don't give me nuisance calls! Ruru-san, only you can call me. Are we agreed?

MIKA: Ahhh. . . . Death.

RURU: Got it. I will give you a call tonight. I have to go now as my class is about to end. I wonder when I can come online again. . . .

MARCY [WEBMASTER]: By all means, it's not that I want to prevent you from committing suicide. But I would want you two to understand the responsibility of posting these comments seriously, as it's disgusting. Mika asked for a suicide pal by posting her phone number. In general, such actions tend to give a sense of companionship and the courage to die to people who want to die, but who are half-heartedly suicidal, and who lack the courage to die by themselves. This state of mind comes from our human "herd mentality." Suicidal individuals tend to fall for such techniques, as they tend to have few friends. They can easily come to "depend" on "relationships of mutual trust." Ruru, please check your own head before calling. Mika, be aware that you might end up dragging along someone who might not commit suicide on their own. Anyway, I won't request that this correspondence be deleted, as these two seem to have already written down the contact information. . . . Well, it's your own life, so it's your choice if you want to put an end to it, but please don't ask for company![1]

This dialogue occurred in 2003 and comes from a transcript of an internet suicide website, in this case a chat site, with only the contact information removed. It is not known whether any of the individuals involved ended up committing suicide. Nowadays, a posting that contains personal contact information would be deleted immediately by the webmaster or moderators. This particular website closed in 2018, but many others still exist.

The tone of these communications is illustrative of a great number of posted comments on suicide websites. But why do people wish to die with strangers? This question fueled the beginning of my journey to identify what kind of mental pain and existential suffering these young people are going through.

1998: A TURNING POINT

The year 1998 marked a turning point in Japan with regard to suicide. Prior to that time, and before its sharp increase in suicide rates, Japan had been known as a culture that was tolerant of suicide, seeing it as a matter of personal choice and personal responsibility, rather than of mental or public health.[2] The Japanese national and local governments did not devote attention to suicide prevention. Yet Japan's reputation for being a "suicide nation" (*jisatsu taikoku*) had less to do with overall suicide rates than with the notoriety of highly ritualistic forms of suicide such as *seppuku* (better known as *hara-kiri* in general), *shinjū* (double suicide or family suicide), and the "kamikaze" pilots of World War II.[3]

In the century preceding the spike of 1998, there had already been three earlier waves of high suicide rates. The Meiji government began collecting suicide data around 1899.[4] No reliable data are available for the period before that.[5] The first of the three waves took place from 1913 to 1921, the second during the late 1950s, and the third during the mid-1980s; 1998 marked the beginning of the fourth and most recent wave.[6]

In 1912 General Maresuke Nogi, a Russo-Japanese War hero, committed *shinjū*, a double suicide with his wife, immediately after the Meiji emperor's funeral. There followed a period of elevated rates of suicide, which scholars have called an "indicator of a chronic and debilitating phenomenon caused by modernity and Western individualism."[7] Historian of Japan Francesca Di Marco states that many during this period viewed suicide as a protest against modernity and Westernization and a result of the clash between Western ideas and traditional Japanese notions of family.[8] Eventually, suicide rates decreased with the onset of war with China in 1937, which lasted until the end of World War II in 1945.[9]

The second suicide peak, in the late 1950s, is considered to be a reflection of tensions in Japanese society caused by social, economic, and ideological changes that came in the wake of World War II, including the collapse of the traditional *ie* (family) system in 1947 under the new Civil Law and the altered role of the Japanese religion of Shinto, which had been the state religion.[10] This period is notable for having higher suicide rates among both young and older Japanese. Japan was labeled a "Suicide Heaven for Youth" and a "Suicide Nation for Youth" because the suicide rates of people in their twenties were among the highest in the world.[11] In 1958 the suicide rate in Japan was 25.7 per 100,000 (30.7 for men and 20.8 for women). Di Marco notes, "As soon as the American occupation ended, the Japanese became increasingly convinced that their society had become dysfunctional, and there appeared a growing consciousness that voluntary death might be a reflection of deeper Japanese social maladjustment."[12] Di Marco also cites sociologist Munesuke Mita's understanding of postwar suicide as "the contemporary maladjustment of the Japanese as the outcome of alienation and a feeling of purposelessness in the face of urbanization and machine civilization."[13] Following the peak of 1958, suicide rates started declining, especially among young Japanese, until 1986.[14]

This period of almost three decades of lower suicide rates ended in 1986. That year saw a spike in suicides, to 25,523, the highest number since the end of World War II. The spike was especially notable among youth, who experienced a 30 percent increase.[15] The first of two notable cluster suicides was initiated when a male junior high school student killed himself in January 1986 after suffering from being bullied; the second followed the suicide of a very popular eighteen-year-old female singer, Yukiko Okada, in April.[16] Both cases were widely reported by the mass media, and each triggered a chain of suicides.[17] After this suicide spike in 1986, suicide rates again fell lower, until 1998.

Interestingly, cluster suicides have been a recurring characteristic of each of these suicide waves. In 1903 Misao Fujimura, an eighteen-year-old high school student at the elite Daiichi High School, jumped from the top of Kegon Falls in Nikkō. This location then attracted 40 suicides and 140 attempted suicides between 1903 and 1907.[18] Another similar cluster suicide occurred in 1933 when a twenty-one-year-old female college student, Kiyoko Matsumoto, jumped off the volcanic Mihara Mountain, accompanied and witnessed by her classmate, Masako Tokuda.[19] Following her suicide, more than a thousand people killed themselves by jumping off Mihara Mountain between 1933 and 1936.[20] Both Fujimura's and Matsumoto's suicides appeared to be suicides of resolve. Matsumoto left a note indicating her objection to the traditional marriage system and rejecting women's prescribed role in marriage. Fujimura's suicide was widely regarded as a philosophical expression of free will in a conformist country, due in part to the fact that he carved references to Hamlet and the Latin poet Horace on a tree.[21]

Thus, when Japan's most recent spike in suicide began in 1998, it was not the first time the country had faced such circumstances. This time, however, the reaction was different. Until 1997 the suicide rate had remained steady for some ten years: 18 to 19 suicides per 100,000 people. In 1997 there were 22,410 recorded suicides. In 1998 there were 32,863—an increase of 47 percent in a single year. This wasn't a blip or anomaly. In 1999 the number of suicides was 33,048.[22] The suicide rate remained at that high level for the following decade. In 2003, the number of suicides increased to 34,427.

Deaths due to traffic accidents in Japan number about 10,000 every year. At the new rates, more than three times as many people were losing their lives to suicide as to auto accidents each year.[23] These figures also stand out in a comparative context. In 2003, Japan's elevated suicide rate stood at 27 per 100,000, whereas in the United States the rate was 10.8, and suicide was only the eleventh leading cause of death.[24] In the decade following this sharp rise in 1998, Japan had the second highest suicide rate among the G-8 nations after Russia (34.3 suicides per 100,000 in 2004), and significantly higher than France (17.8 in 2002), Germany (13.0 in 2004), Canada (11.6 in 2002), the United States (11.0 in 2002), Italy (7.1 in 2002), and the United Kingdom (6.9 in 2002).[25]

After 1998, suicide was recognized as a public health issue for the first time in Japan's history, and gradually suicide prevention initiatives began to emerge.[26] The Japanese National Center of Neurology and Psychiatry (NCNP) instituted a suicide prevention working group, and in 2005 the Ministry of Health, Labour and Welfare started a government initiative to lower suicide rates.[27] Part of the reason for this change in response was the very high numbers themselves, but another key reason, as we will see, is that public perception shifted away from seeing these cases as suicides of resolve, choice, or rebellion; rather, it appeared that the subjective states of those committing suicide were different.

SEARCHING FOR REASONS

Why Japan experienced such a dramatic rise in suicide rates in 1998 is a question that has never been fully answered. Such a drastic increase in a single year suggests that some kind of societal strain had reached a tipping point. But what was the nature of that strain, and what were its causes?

In the absence of war or other major historical explanatory events, when compared to earlier suicide waves, the default reaction to the 1998 spike in suicides was to blame it on the economy. Indeed, the Japanese economy had been under strain for some time by then, exerting an increased pressure on society. The media and public experts noted that the rise in suicides had to be the result of financial and psychological insecurity among middle-aged Japanese men in a society that had previously enjoyed extremely low levels of unemployment. The most common explanatory model provided was a three-step process: (1) the long-term economic recession had led to (2) depression among those who were unemployed or concerned about the possibility of losing their financial security, which then caused (3) a rise in suicide rates. Moreover, Japan's economic stagnation had been hit with further blows in 1997, when several well-known Japanese financial institutions failed, including Yamaichi Security, Sanyō Securities, and the Hokkaidō Takushoku Bank.

There are convincing reasons to believe that Japan's economic struggle was an important factor in the sudden increase in suicide. But there are also reasons to think the explanatory model of economic stagnation leading to depression and eventually suicide is too simplistic on its own. For one thing, suicide rates jumped across ages and genders. Japanese middle-aged men did indeed constitute one category that saw a dramatic rise in suicide rates, but so did Japanese youth. Furthermore, the very policies undertaken by the Japanese government to address Japan's stagnation may have had unintended consequences that created additional insecurity and anxiety.

Post–World War II Japan enjoyed steady and rapid economic growth, so much so that it became the world's second largest economy after the United States, until it was displaced from this position by China in 2010. Japan had been viewed as an economic miracle, founded upon a culturally distinctive ethos and value system that included things like "lifetime employment" or *shūshinkoyōsei*, and the "family-corporate system," in which the corporation served as a family for employees.[28] Once someone was employed by a company, the company would look after them for the rest of their lives, with full social welfare and health benefits and a gradually increasing salary every year. The sociologist Chie Nakane has called this a "vertically structured society" or *tate shakai*, with promotion based on seniority.[29]

But since the early 1990s, Japan has experienced long-term economic stagnation. In its search for a solution, successive governments began exploring the introduction of neoliberal economic policies. This included tinkering with the once successful quasi-family corporate model of lifetime employment by making it easier for companies to lay off their full-time employees and replace them with temporary workers. Changes to the Agency Worker Law in 1996 and 1998 increased the number of temporary and dispatch workers who could be hired.

For the first time, large numbers of full-time company employees—called *sarariiman* (salary men or company men)—were being laid off. Most would never have contemplated the possibility of being fired. They were replaced by temporary workers, who lacked the pay, job security, and benefits of a full-time position. Subsequently, under the administration of Prime Minister Junichi Koizumi (2001–2006), more neoliberal policies were introduced, resulting in the privatization of the post office and other institutions. Experienced middle-aged and older employees were laid off at higher rates, and again more temporary workers were hired.

As a result, corporate values and practices shifted. The economic challenge, as often happens, became a social and cultural challenge as well. Unemployment for many Japanese men meant not just losing their financial means, but equally their dignity and self-worth. Murakami Haruki, the internationally acclaimed Japanese author, describes how he received scornful gazes from people whenever he walked around Tokyo city during work hours or, even worse, went shopping. As a writer, he was a rare case of someone who could do this, since he didn't have an office job. But in Japan, men walking around in cities without a suit and tie in the middle of the day can still attract curious or scornful gazes.

GENDER AND AGE

In 2005 the suicide rate for men was 36.1, compared with 12.9 for women, and the number of suicides among middle-aged men between ages 40 and 54 was five times higher than that among women in the same age category. Figures like these were cited as evidence of the link between suicide and the recent economic recession and rise in unemployment, justifying a focus on middle-aged Japanese men.[30] Yet despite the higher suicide rate among men than women in most (but not all) age categories, women in Japan consistently make more suicide attempts per completed suicide than do men. According to the Ministry of Health, Labour and Welfare's report, the gender ratio between men and women for completed suicides is typically about 2.5:1 (24.5:10.4 per 10,0000 in 2017), but the attempted suicide rate among those who eventually committed suicide was twice as high for women as for men (29.3 as opposed to 15.3 in 2017).[31] This suggests a roughly equal number of men and women in Japan attempt suicide. When looking at young women who committed suicide, 46.7 percent of women in their twenties and 45 percent in their thirties had previously attempted suicide, as opposed to 15.5 percent and 17.8 percent for men.[32]

The media's coverage of the sudden suicide spike left out the stories of young people as well.[33] While the suicide rate among men in their forties to sixties jumped to 35 percent in a single year in 1998, the jump for those under age nineteen was 53 percent that year, and 70 percent for girls.[34]

It is estimated that in Japan there are one to two hundred times as many unsuccessful suicide attempts by youths as there are completed suicides; for adults, the ratio of attempts to completed suicides is far lower, at 10 to 1.[35] Thus, while the 720 deaths by suicide in 1998 in the under-nineteen category may seem small, this indicates that there were around 70,000 to 140,000 suicide attempts. Attempted suicide is typically understood as a cry for help and a sign of mental pain. Attempted suicide also places individuals at high risk of completing suicide in the future.[36] It is therefore important to recognize that we cannot rely on completed suicide statistics alone if we are to understand the underlying problems of which completed suicide is merely one symptom. When we take this perspective, we see that the sharp increase in suicide rates in 1998 signals a much larger problem in Japanese society—larger even than the epidemic numbers of suicides by themselves suggest. For some reason, Japan experienced a groundswell of mental pain.

Now, some two decades after the pivotal year of 1998, the question of what led to the sudden increase in suicide rates remains a mystery. Sixteen years later, in 2014, the Ministry of Health, Labour and Welfare acknowledged that while the sudden increase in suicide must have been primarily triggered by the bursting of the bubble economy in the early 1990s, an economic explanation alone is insufficient for understanding why this rise lasted for over a decade.[37]

Around 2010, overall suicide rates started a slow decline again, possibly due to the active implementation of suicide prevention policies. This was celebrated by the Japanese government, perhaps prematurely. The overall decrease in rates did not include Japanese in their twenties and thirties, as reported in the Ministry of Health, Labour and Welfare's annual suicide prevention report of 2015.[38] A further report by the ministry on June 19, 2018, noted that suicide remained the top cause of death among those between ages fifteen and thirty-nine. In fact, Japan is the only country among the G-7 with suicide as the leading cause of death for this age category.[39] In 2020 Japan again saw a slight rise in suicide rates, with women again being a leading category, indicating that this most recent suicide "wave" that began in 1998 may not be over and is proving even more intractable and long-lasting than previous ones.

Due to economic stagnation, the decade from 1991 to 2000 in Japan is referred to as the "Lost Decade." But since the decade from 2001 to 2010 showed little improvement, the phrase has been updated to the "Two Lost Decades" (*ushinawareta 20 nen*). For some scholars, these suicide rates among young Japanese show the impact of the "Two Lost Decades."[40] They argue that pessimism about Japan's precarious future has been the main driving force behind the suicides of young people.[41]

I believe that economic factors have played an undeniable role in the increase in suicide in Japan. But economics is not extricable from social and cultural forces that have proved equally powerful. The economic stagnation led to political changes that altered the laws governing corporations, changing the very nature of work for millions of Japanese. These workplace changes—being laid off; fearing being laid off; having to go on the job market in middle age; working as a temporary employee with no job security, no status, and no benefits—affected people's sense of identity, their relationships, and their family lives. It affected Japanese society in profound ways and changed much of the mood of the country, from relying on a system that had meant security to living under a new system that represented a great deal of uncertainty. But economic factors alone are unlikely to explain the high rates of suicide and attempted suicide among

Japanese youth and Japanese women. Without looking into the experiences of Japanese youth and why they were wishing to kill themselves in record numbers, we are still left with a mystery.

"THE COMPLETE MANUAL OF SUICIDE"

In 1993 an unusual book was published in Japan, and perhaps more unusually, it became a national best seller. The book was *The Complete Manual of Suicide* by Wataru Tsurumi.[42] The book discusses eleven categories of suicide methods, such as hanging, overdosing, and drowning, with instructions on how to use each particular method, the level of pain one will experience, the level of preparation it will require, the level of lethality, and even a description of how one's body will appear after death. The tone is matter of fact. The book is still iconic and considered to be the bible of suicide methods among those contemplating taking their own lives.

Unsurprisingly, the book met with severe criticism. Although it was never censored or banned by the government, some prefectures decided not to allow its sale to minors. Many critics argued that the book would lead to an increase in suicides. This turned out not to be the case, at least not immediately. Others reviewed the book more positively.

In retrospect, Tsurumi anticipated in his manual a theme that was to become very strong over the next two and a half decades: the "difficulty of living" or *ikizurasa*. Nowadays there are numerous books on this topic. Instead of advocating the traditional Japanese cultural values of trying hard, doing one's best, and making the most effort (*gambaru*) to survive life, Tsurumi provided a way out if people found life too tough to keep on living. Knowing that there is a way out, he argued, people might be able to cope with their lives with less pressure. His notion seems to be reflected by the reviews of people who purchased the book.

On the Japanese Amazon website, one person reviewed the book thus:

> It was almost ten years ago when I encountered this book. I was experiencing severe harassment even though I wouldn't quite call it bullying, and I started thinking about suicide. The teachers around me all said, "Don't commit suicide. Let's pull together, because there's a bright future waiting

> for you!" But I couldn't believe such statements. As I was spending my lunch breaks and after school hours at the school library where no one would be around, I confided my circumstances and my feelings in the librarian. Despite my expectation that she would say similar things to the other teachers, the librarian told me "I should probably stop you from committing suicide, but if it's fine with you, then it's fine with me. I'll give you something that will be good for you, so why not come back here tomorrow." She gave me *The Complete Manual of Suicide*. She even said, "With this book, you can choose how to die. You might be unsure now, but you'll find a method that you'll feel 'This is it!' Then you can do it." Since that day, I started reading this book whenever things were tough. I still haven't a suicide method that makes me feel "This is it!" But it is also a fact that I can keep on living thanks to this book. It gives me comfort to think, "I can die anytime. Well, I will die." Thank you, my librarian.[43]

When I accessed this review in 2019, 123 people had found it useful. The sentiment that this suicide manual serves as a safety blanket for people who are having difficulties living seems to resonate with this reviewer's goals. It is also very similar to the posted narratives by suicide website visitors. Another reviewer wrote that they found the book scarier than horror movies and lost any desire to commit suicide after reading it.[44]

Another reviewer, whose review 976 people found helpful, shares her insight as someone who has been suicidal for a long time. She found this book more comforting than people telling her that she should try hard and shouldn't kill herself because doing so would make many people, including her family, sad:

> I've always been thinking about suicide since I was a junior high school student. I kept attempting suicide and failing over and over. Whenever I searched for suicide methods online they all appeared suspicious and I couldn't really trust any of them. But this book provides concrete information, like: you can hang yourself without much height, and you can die from the 10th floor of a building. So I found it very helpful. My heart felt lighter when I read the author's last words: "I don't want to say something tiresome like don't do suicide! My real goal was to provide some way to make life less hard and easier to cope with by sharing my thoughts that people are free to die when they want to and people who wish to live can live." Until I encountered this book, whenever I told people that I wanted to die, they always told me things like "Don't waste your life" or "Try hard and live by making more effort." So I felt a lot of pressure from hearing things like that. But this book

was different. What I'm grateful for in this book is how the author understands suicidal people's feelings and makes us feel it's OK. What I want to say in the end is even though there are some people who say, "Don't commit suicide. Have you thought about how many people you'll hurt and make miserable? Do you want to make your parents cry?" the people who want to commit suicide don't have anyone who cares for them. I myself have been abandoned by my family and I have no friends, no money, and no job. My parents and brothers abuse me saying "Please die soon, you piece of trash." With relations like that, there's no one who will cry for me when I die. When people say things like "Your parents will be sad" to people who are driven into a corner and living in loneliness, those lonely people feel "There are many kinds of people. Don't make light of me." The reality of being lonely is what is most common among people who commit suicide.[45]

LYING DEAD IN THE SHAPE OF A RIVER

On February 11, 2003, a teenage girl opened the door to an unoccupied apartment. When she walked inside, she found three people—a twenty-six-year-old man and two twenty-four-year-old women—lying down side by side, apparently asleep. They lay before her in a configuration that she later described as being like the Japanese character for "river" (川). Beside them were charcoal briquettes in a *shichirin*, a traditional Japanese stove oven. All the windows were tightly sealed with scotch tape. The victims had died of carbon monoxide poisoning.[46]

When asked what she was doing there, the girl confessed to the police that she had actually been aware of the planned suicide. She had met the other individuals online and had initially agreed to participate in the group suicide, but she got cold feet and decided not to go at the appointed time. Later, curious about what had happened, she visited the apartment and found the dead bodies of those she had been chatting with earlier.[47]

This case, with its striking and memorable details, caught the nation's attention and was widely reported. It wasn't the first case of internet group suicide, however. Previously, a thirty-year-old man and thirty-two-year-old woman were found dead in an apartment from the same cause. After the case of the "river" group suicide, the media started reporting on internet group suicides with regularity, providing detailed descriptions of the deaths as well as the existence of numerous suicide websites where individuals could gather to discuss suicide and even plan group suicides.[48]

The next year, in October 2004, seven young men and women were found dead in a minivan in a parking lot on a mountain in Saitama prefecture. There were four *shichirin* ovens in the car, and all the windows had been sealed with Scotch tape. For a few years, this was the largest internet suicide pact. Then in 2006, nine individuals who had met online committed suicide together.[49]

In the course of two years, between February 11, 2003, and December 31, 2004, there were 599 articles on internet group suicide in five of the major newspapers in Japan, and 156 television programs reported on the phenomenon.[50] Suicide researchers warned that the wide media coverage could lead to a chain reaction of more internet suicides.[51]

THE COUNSELING OFFICE OF DR. KIRIKO

When I began my research on internet suicide, I tried to identify the first time the internet was used in Japan as a vehicle to assist and materialize suicide. There is no consensus on what was the very first internet group suicide—defined as meeting via a suicide website and dying together from carbon monoxide poisoning—and it is difficult to determine, because early cases were first treated as ordinary *shinjū* (group suicide, explained in more detail later) before the new category of internet group suicide was established (*intānetto shūdan jisatsu*). Kayoko Ueno notes that the first mention of internet group suicide in *Asahi Shimbun*, a major Japanese newspaper, dates to October 2000, and states that at the time there were 40,000 Japanese websites on suicide, 150 of which were devoted to "how to commit suicide."[52]

Before that date, however, there were already famous cases of the internet being used to facilitate suicide, one of the most infamous of which happened—perhaps unsurprisingly—in the turning point year of 1998. A twenty-seven-year-old man created a website called The Counseling Office of Dr. Kiriko. Using this deceptive name, the young man attracted potential victims, to whom he sent potassium cyanide in order to assist them in their deaths. Six people received potassium cyanide from him, one of whom died from taking it.[53]

FORMS OF INTERNET GROUP SUICIDE

The media reports on the first internet group suicides were sensational and included visual images of the cars used for group suicides, pictures of the charcoal briquettes, and detailed descriptions of the methods used to connect online and commit suicide. This resulted in severe criticism from psychiatrists and suicide prevention experts, who said that such coverage could lead to a copycat effect. Within two years after data on internet group suicide began to be collected, the number of internet group suicides tripled (from 2003 to 2005), with ninety-one deaths (thirty-four cases) in 2005. Eventually the nonstop news reports died down. The national police agency also stopped revealing the annual number of internet group suicides after 2006 in an effort to cut down on copycat suicides. This has made it difficult to get a clear sense of whether internet group suicide has been increasing or decreasing.

However, new forms of group suicide have continued to emerge, indicating that the phenomenon has not stopped. In early 2008, several years after I had begun my research on internet group suicide, a new method became popular: hydrogen sulfide poisoning. The technique for creating this poisonous substance was circulated online. In that year alone, 1,056 individuals committed suicide using this method. Their average age was thirty-one, indicating that internet suicide was mainly attracting young people.

Following the methods of carbon monoxide poisoning and then hydrogen sulfide poisoning, a new trend emerged in the 2010s using social media and social network services (SNS) such as Twitter. Hashtags like #suiciderecruitment!! and #wannadie emerged. Unscrupulous individuals also started to prey upon suicidal people in terrible ways.

THE ZAMA SUICIDE PACT SLAYINGS

The Zama suicide pact slayings were multiple homicides that took place in Zama, Kanagawa prefecture, between August 22 and October 30, 2017, committed by Takahiro Shiraishi, a twenty-seven-year-old man, who murdered his victims in his rented apartment.

Shiraishi was caught after the brother of one of the victims, worried about his sister, who had recently gone missing, started accessing her Twitter account. The brother knew her password because he had helped her set up the account. When she stopped responding to his text messages, he checked her Twitter account and found that she had been using the hashtag #SuicideRecruitment and had tweeted the message "I want to die but I'm afraid to die alone" several weeks before she disappeared. He saw that she had been in contact with one particularly suspicious man. He then started posting from her account to see if anyone knew anything about this man. A woman responded, saying that she thought she knew who it was. Then in collaboration with the police, the woman contacted Shiraishi and asked him to come and meet her at a place the police had staked out. The police then followed Shiraishi from the meeting place back to an apartment. There they found ice coolers and storage boxes that contained 9 severed heads and 240 other body parts and bones.[54] In total Shiraishi had lured and killed nine people before he was caught: a twenty-year-old man and eight girls and women aged fifteen, seventeen (two), nineteen, twenty-one, twenty-three, twenty-five, and twenty-six, three of whom were high school students.

Shiraishi confessed to having used Twitter to find people who were suicidal. One account he used was named *Kubitsuri-shi* or "Mr. Hangman." On this account, he posted statements like "Hanging doesn't hurt" and "Please consult with me if you are seriously in trouble." Referring to the common method of using charcoal briquettes to commit suicide, he posted, "Briquette suicide is indeed quite painful," and recommended hanging instead, noting that he was there to assist anyone who wanted to hang themselves.[55] He also admitted using online searches to find posts and hashtags indicating suicidal ideation and said he would respond to such people. He would tell them that society was full of suffering and he was there to help.[56]

He also had another account called *Shinitai* ("I want to die"). From this account, he used the hashtag *#jisatsuboshū* (recruiting for suicide), pretending he was suicidal to recruit victims. After he was caught, several people who had been in touch with him via Twitter came forward to reveal more about his methods. One woman said she had tweeted, "I am seeking a companion to die together with" with the hashtag #*jisatsuboshū*. Shiraishi responded, and they began corresponding. She recalled that Shiraishi kept insisting that he would like to kill her, because it was so painful to see people who were mentally suffering and he wished very much to alleviate that pain.[57]

Since the Zuma slayings, there have been similar cases involving Twitter. In July 2018, five people were found dead in an apartment. One was the resident of the apartment, a thirty-seven-year-old man. The others included two women in their twenties, a woman in her forties, and another man who remained unidentified. The apartment resident had sent out tweets trying to recruit others to die with.[58] The use of social media has made it harder to stop the recruitment of victims or people with whom to commit suicide. On traditional websites, a moderator can find and delete such posts, but such regulation is uncommon on social media platforms.

TRADITIONAL VIEWS ON SUICIDE

Traditionally, suicide has been considered an expression of an individual's free will in Japan.[59] The rhetoric of a "suicide of resolve," still a very popular notion, suggests that suicide can be the rational decision of a freely choosing individual and therefore is an option to be respected when necessity calls for it.[60] Anthropologist of Japan Junko Kitanaka argues that even though psychiatry has been established in Japan since the late nineteenth century, psychiatrists have had very little impact on the way Japanese have conceptualized suicide. She suggests this may be because Japanese have long normalized suicide, even aestheticizing it and honoring it as an act of individual freedom.[61]

Over the course of my research, especially when talking with and interviewing people in Japan, I realized that this view does have positive aspects. It does not impose an ethical judgment on the family of the deceased that suicide is morally wrong, and by not judging or condemning suicide, it retains respect for the mental pain of those who have committed suicide or are left behind.

At the same time, what is vastly lacking from such a view is the promotion of suicide prevention. There must be recognition that suicide is not always motivated by an individual's rational decision after serious thought and consideration. Rather, people tend to be ambivalent about dying, even at the very moment of suicide.[62] In conversations with me, Yukio Saito, one of the leading figures in suicide prevention and founder of the Inochi no denwa (Lifeline) suicide hotline in Japan, lamented the Japanese government's decades-long lack of interest in suicide prevention.[63]

Any attempt at a cross-cultural understanding of suicide is a complex task that ultimately challenges the standard definition of suicide in the West, which equates suicide with "deliberate self-harm."[64] Although attempts have been made to understand suicide from sociocultural perspectives, suicide in the West has been predominantly understood through the lens of individual pathology. Many statistics indicate that more than 90 percent of individuals who attempt suicide suffer from psychiatric disorders such as depression or psychosis. In Japan, however, one of the dominant features in the rhetoric of suicide has been cultural aestheticization, whereby certain suicides are given a positive cultural valence.[65] In the cases of Yukio Mishima and Jun Eto, two famous writers who took their own lives, the public reaction and mass media reports included praise of their heroism. Overall, Japanese cultural perceptions of suicide are more tolerant than those in the United States, and in numerous cases suicide is viewed morally as a sign of maturity and responsibility.

In his work *Voluntary Death in Japan*, Maurice Pinguet asserts, "The essential point is that in Japan, there was never any objection in principle to the free choice of death—a question on which Western ideology has always found it difficult to pronounce."[66] To this he adds, "If Japanese culture does indeed have an originality worthy of our sustained attention, it must ultimately be sought in an absence of metaphysics and idealism."[67] He traces this absence to the influence of Buddhism, especially the Soto Zen school, with its emphasis on the impermanence of all things. This absence is not a lack, and within it, suicide for Pinguet becomes "a fierce excess . . . an austere necessity . . . which Japan resolved never to surrender on principle, as if she understood how much of the essence of grandeur and serenity vanishes from a civilization when its people let slip their freedom to die."[68] Although Pinguet's choice of language seems to carry with it traces of Orientalism, there is a Japanese tradition, *nihonjin-ron* (theories of Japanese uniqueness propagated by Japanese thinkers), and

Pinguet points out that the term "suicide nation" was coined first by Japanese themselves in the 1950s.[69]

When suicide is not aestheticized and is instead seen as pathology in Japan, it is typically considered a "social pathology." Japan's economic downturn has frequently been cited as contributing to this social pathology and to depression and suicide. There has been a strong tendency in Japanese thought to blame society and to look for causes beyond the individuals themselves.[70] Removing the individual entirely, however, can also have problematic consequences. In her critical examination of the medicalization of *hikikomori* (socially withdrawn children), anthropologist Margaret Lock cautions about the socially oriented medical discourse in Japan. She argues that it is not always liberating, but potentially moralizing and hegemonizing. In short, socially oriented medical discourse has a danger of overdetermining the meaning of people's distress.[71] Thus, directing attention solely to deterministic structural forces can serve to undermine the validity and specificity of individual subjectivity and can erase agency. In her research on end-of-life issues in Japan, anthropologist Susan Long argues that "choice" is not the same as "autonomy," as choices (such as making a decision how to die) are limited within a given context and environment.[72] Since an individual's choice is not separable from social limitations, this calls into question what we consider "individual" and "social."

These two distinguishing factors of suicide in Japan—its cultural aesthetic dimension and the fact that it is seen as resulting from a social pathology—are, in my opinion, also the two factors that complicate the Japanese approach to suicide prevention. Both the strong tendency to want to see suicide as a responsible act in given situations, on the one hand, and seeing the causal efficacy of factors resulting in suicide as residing in society rather than in the individual, on the other hand, inhibit Japan from formulating a clear policy with regard to suicide prevention. The former view has resulted in arguments that preventing suicide cruelly deprives individuals of one of the few free, important actions they can take in an extremely conformist society. The latter view places the entire blame on society by arguing that until the entire Japanese society is restructured, high rates of suicide will be the inevitable result to an immobilizing effect. They therefore represent two extremes that arise from not recognizing sufficiently the interdependence of individual and social factors.

SHINJŪ: DYING TOGETHER

As mentioned, the first cases of internet group suicide were labeled *shinjū*. This can roughly be translated as "group suicide" or "suicide pact," but as I show here, there are some nuances that can make these translations misleading. It's worth exploring the terms related to suicide in Japan because they point to a shift in the way Japan started to view suicides: away from a tolerant view of suicide as a choice and an act of personal responsibility and toward a more Western view, in which suicide is a mental health or public health issue and therefore something to prevent.

In the study of suicide, the term *suicide pact* is used to refer to an arrangement between two or more individuals to die together or at the same time. Unlike mass suicides, in which a large group of people may choose to die together for religious, ideological, or military reasons, suicide pacts are typically made between individuals with a close personal relationship, such as close friends or lovers, and the reasons are diverse and usually highly personal in nature.

In Japan there are multiple terms for suicides involving more than one person. The term *jōshi* describes the traditional idea of lovers choosing to die together because their relationship cannot be accepted in this world and they hope to be reunited in the afterlife. The term *shinjū* (心中) describes a small group of people dying together. However, there is no exact translation for this term, and it has particular historical and cultural connotations that differentiate it from what we may at first consider to be a "suicide pact."

For one thing, the consent of all those involved is not a prerequisite for the deaths to be considered a result of *shinjū*. For example, the terms *ikka shinjū* (single-family suicide), *kazoku shinjū* (family suicide), and *oyako shinjū* (parent-child suicide) describe family members all dying together, but they usually do not involve deciding to commit suicide together. Rather, they typically involve a parent or both parents deciding that the whole family must die. They kill the other members of the family, such as their spouse and children, and then commit suicide themselves.

Outside Japan, such as in the West, these would not be considered group suicides at all, but rather homicide-suicides. In Japan, such cases have typically been seen as involving a parent who is concerned that the rest of the family would not be able to continue in this world upon his or her death. Joseph and Magda Goebbels are an infamous case; when it was clear that the Third Reich was at an end, they poisoned and killed their sleeping children before then committing suicide together. The tendency in Japan is to see *shinjū* as tragic suicide. This is not typically the case in the West, however, where the killing of one's family members without their consent is seen as murder. It should be clear then that the term *shinjū* is not easily translated as "suicide pact," but rather something closer to "dying together."

Obviously, suicide is a troubling phenomenon. In addition, there are several unique and troubling aspects of these internet group suicides: the fact that people were meeting online and discussing their suicide plans openly with others, the fact that they wanted to meet up with strangers and commit suicide with them, and the growing popularity of the method. Suicide is typically thought of as something solitary. If it is shared, one expects or at least hopes that those with whom it is shared would dissuade the person from attempting suicide, not that they would confirm the wish and explain methods to conduct suicide together. Internet group suicide showed that suicide could be social and, moreover, that one could commit suicide with strangers, which might be better, at least to some people, than doing it alone. The existence of a range of terms for dying together, including *shinjū*, suggests that suicide has long had a social nature in Japan. There is a long cultural history of "dying together."

IRRESPONSIBLE SUICIDES

Following 1998 and the rise of internet group suicides, Japanese society's attitude toward suicide started to change, from acceptance to increasing concern. Mafumi Usui, a professor of psychology at Niigata Seiryo University, hosts a popular website dedicated to the topic of suicide in Japan. In an article published by the Associated Press, he is quoted as saying, "Depressed, young people and the Internet—it's a very dangerous mix. . . . When Japan was poor, families did more things together out of necessity, like sharing a bath or eating together, and the community was much more important, especially in rural communities. But now it's increasingly all about the individual. This leaves people more isolated and likely to contemplate suicide."[73]

Usui's comments echo a widely shared sense about the collapse of family in late capitalist Japan: extended families are less common, and many families have only one child, who is left alone at home by two working parents or a single parent. Importantly, though, it also ties suicide to social isolation. Suicide is not a rational choice made because it is the best option in a difficult situation; it is a product of loneliness.

I came across a similar comment after the internet group suicide of nine young Japanese in October 2004. At that time, a Japanese man wrote on the *BBC News* website, "In 70s we were not rich but we had dreams. If we studied and worked hard, we could buy TV sets, cars and so on. We've never imagined that our companies go bankrupt or we get fired for a recession. We are pessimistic and vulnerable. Once we lost a life model, we have a difficulty finding new one [*sic*]. Now adults in Japan are struggling to find new dreams or purposes to live. We have to change or we can't show a brighter future where young people will want to live."[74]

There were other, more critical views. Internet group suicides were viewed as "frivolous" or "non-serious" suicides. Those who committed them, it was claimed, had not sufficiently thought through their reasons to die.

The journal *AERA* released a special issue on suicide in 2003 entitled *Shi ni Itaru Wake* (Reasons for death). The issue included data based on interviews with a hundred Japanese teenagers aged fifteen to nineteen.[75] In response to one question in the survey, "What are the reasons or occasions for you to think about dying?," a number of respondents replied with statements such as, "Just sort of (*nan to naku*) feeling bored," "I am tired of living," and "When I feel unsure about who I am." Such statements parallel closely the statements made by individuals who visit suicide websites. One individual in the study, who had attempted suicide, said, "When I think about it, it's not that I especially wanted to die. I just wanted a break from living. To have died or not to have died—either would have been all right."[76]

Responding to such statements, the psychologist and popular social commentator Rika Kayama wrote, "There is a sense that dying or not dying is a kind of lottery. One sees neither a suicide of resolve to cross over (i.e., to die) nor anything that can be pointed to as a reason. I cannot help but feeling that it is a matter of mood and timing. There is not even any sense of the desperation of really wanting to die."[77]

It has also been argued that such individuals are incapable of understanding life, its depth, and its weight, seeing it instead as something light and virtual; they view death in the same virtual way.[78] Computer games, television shows, films, and so on have been invoked and blamed for this.[79] In 2003, Haruhiko Ikeda, a well-known biologist and social commentator, said, "I feel like telling them 'Don't be so spoiled.' What else can one say to someone who doesn't have the ability to go on living another forty years?"[80] Comments like these suggest that suicide might be more understandable for people at the end of their lives, but not for young people.

As I read various commentaries on internet group suicide by social critics and psychologists, it appeared that the underlying cause of these suicides was neither apparent nor clear and as a result garnered little empathy. Instead, these suicides were seen as irresponsible, thoughtless acts, and those who engaged in them were labeled copycats who were too weak willed to die alone.

THE DANGER OF INTERNET AND INTERNET GROUP SUICIDE AMONG ADOLESCENTS

Several scholars and social commentators have drawn a connection between the increase in suicides and the negative influence of the internet on Japanese youth.[81] Part of the reason for negative attitudes toward internet group suicide seems to be the fear of contagion. In the Edo period an increase in *shinjū* or lover's double suicides resulted from a famous kabuki play by Monzaemon Chikamatsu. The Edo *bakufu* subsequently prohibited funerary services for individuals who died through *shinjū*, a measure to curb the rising number of "copy-cat" suicides.[82] In both the Edo case and the current case of internet group suicide, there is a sense that the "form" of the suicide spreads like an infectious disease and therefore must be contained.

Although the exact relationship between the rise of the internet and the increase in suicide remains unclear, internet access does seem to have contributed to an increase in *hikikomori* (withdrawal syndrome), which refers to the more than one million Japanese who have stopped going to school or work for more than six months (and in many cases for several years, even more than ten), and who instead remain at home, never leaving their houses, and sometimes never leaving their own rooms.[83] In the 1980s, most of these people were diagnosed with schizophrenia and depression. Nowadays, according to one Japanese psychiatrist, Shizuo Machizawa, many of these people do not have either clinical condition, yet still have great difficulty interacting with other people and therefore choose to remain at home.[84] Machizawa points out that the convenience of the internet seems to make them self-sufficient: despite their lack of social skills, they can still develop emotional closeness with others through online means.[85] There is a clear resemblance between *hikikomori* and internet group suicide, as the main communication tool is the internet, and these individuals have reduced social interaction and social support. However, neither internet group suicide nor *hikikomori* is easily explained by primarily citing the economic recession.

Finally, when it comes to adolescents, both the mass media and researchers have tended to attribute suicide to two main causes: *ijime* (bullying) and the competitive school examination system called *juken jigoku* (examination hell). They point out that many adolescent suicide notes say things like, "I am a failure, because I did not make it into such-and-such university," or "I was afraid that I would fail the examination, and I lost hope in life," or "I have been bullied by such-and-such a person. They did this and that to me, and therefore, I am going to die." These letters sometimes seem to indicate that the act of suicide is revenge against the bullies and may include the names of the students who bullied them. Interestingly, however, this aspect of suicide as revenge seems to be missing from most cases of internet suicide pacts. It is clear therefore that one cannot simplify all cases of suicide into one or two reasons such as "examination hell" and "peer abuse," as important as these factors may be in many incidents of suicide.

THE RISE OF SUICIDE PREVENTION FOR INTERNET SUICIDE

Internet group suicide has been viewed as a new type of suicide and has been met with varying responses within Japanese society. Once the police established internet group suicide as a new category in their records, the government quickly took action. The Ministry of Health, Labour and Welfare requested and funded research on suicide prevention for internet-related suicides, and in 2006 the Center for Suicide Prevention was established within the NCNP.[86] Within the NCNP, nine internal and ten external researchers have conducted studies on internet suicide and methods for its prevention. One of the NCNP reports expresses concern about the difficulty of preventing internet-related suicide and the possibility of an increase in such forms of suicide.[87] The report's summary concludes that the victims of internet suicide are primarily young Japanese who are frequent internet users and participate in simultaneous suicides among strangers.[88]

EMPATHY AND SUBJECTIVITY

In my view, the initial accounts of suicide in Japan show a concrete lack of empathy toward those who were killing themselves, both stemming from and contributing to a lack of understanding of the phenomenon itself. The new spate of suicides was initially met with bafflement and sometimes outright derision and disgust. Once I realized that the Japanese government and media were starting to take suicide seriously as an issue, but also that these efforts were being hampered by a lack of understanding of the subjectivity of those contemplating, attempting, and committing suicide, I felt it would be important to study the subjectivity of such individuals in a way that tried to bridge this gap of empathy.

How were these individuals appraising their situation such that suicide appeared to be the best or only way forward? And more deeply, what structures and processes of subjectivity would lead individuals to evaluate their situation in such a way that it seemed the correct or only appraisal? Once I asked this question, I felt it opened up a whole new avenue for exploration, both methodologically and thematically, into understandings of self, other, relationships, and the meaning and value of life.

One concrete result of taking this direction was to pay much more attention to first- and second-person accounts that are experience-near, and to give these narratives the space (*ma* in Japanese) to speak and to be heard by listeners and readers. Deficits in empathy often stem from not taking the time to listen and instead rushing to judgment, analysis, and action based on one's own preformed perspectives and opinions, not recognizing that another person's experience might be quite different from one's own yet equally valid. In the next chapter, I focus on the first-person accounts of individuals who frequented suicide websites. In later chapters, I focus on second-person accounts in films and television shows that explore the themes of loneliness and suicide in the form of social commentary.

3 Connecting the Disconnected

SUICIDE WEBSITES

He distrusted her affection; and what loneliness is more lonely than distrust?

—George Eliot, *Middlemarch*

SUICIDE WEBSITES

I started my research on suicide websites in 2003, the year they began to emerge online. Throughout my research, I have witnessed these sites evolve. In 2003 there was an "anything goes" mentality toward these sites. Sites were not well regulated, and people often shared personal contact information and details of methods for committing suicide. People occasionally asked for encouragement to kill themselves, and others occasionally obliged. Some sites, though a minority, actively encouraged people to kill themselves. Few at the beginning provided information on how to deal with suicidal ideation or seek help.

By 2006 most suicide sites stated that any message containing personal information such as a telephone number, an address, or a time and place to organize the suicide would be immediately deleted by the moderator. In addition, webmasters were highly encouraged to report any posts indicating a planned suicide. The websites started changing their character to instead reflect the nature of self-help groups.

For practical and ethical reasons, it is difficult to conduct ethnographic studies on suicide because it is not easy to identify and interview people who are suicidal. I decided to closely follow suicide websites, paying attention to what people posted about themselves in order to understand why they visited such sites. I wanted to understand why young people who were not directly impacted by the economic recession and unemployment were also at higher risk for suicide.

My initial interest was to understand mental pain and suicidal ideation among young people who were regular suicide website visitors. I was struck by coming across statements like "I am too lonely to die alone," a post I read on a suicide website, and "The person I died with could have been anyone," a note left behind by a woman who committed internet group suicide with a stranger. These made a big impact on me. I started seeing connections between suicidal ideation, intense loneliness, and the wish to connect with someone. However, my main focus was to collect posted narratives from online threads and unpack what kinds of social suffering, existential suffering, and mental pain regular suicide website visitors experienced in order to understand the underlying causes of suicide among young Japanese.

At the end of 2006, entering the word *suicide* into the Japanese-language site of Google yielded 3,140,000 websites, and the phrase "suicide methods" (*jisatsu no hōhō*) returned 22,600 results. The suicide-related website Ghetto reports having had just under a million hits within the first three years after it launched in October 2003.[1] Another site, Suicide Site: A Relaxing Place for Suicidal People, reported over three million hits between its inception and the end of 2006.[2] Both sites reported having one thousand or more visits per day.

In 2018, a search for the phrase "suicide methods" returned sixty-seven million results, but with many more results related to suicide prevention than in the early to mid-2000s. Searching for "suicide websites" doesn't reveal the same number of online suicide discussion websites. Even some of the longest surviving sites, such as Ghetto, no longer appear at the top of the search results, having been replaced by prevention sites. However, as noted in the previous chapter, some of this activity has moved to social media platforms.

Since September 2003, I have regularly visited more than forty of these Japanese suicide websites. Although participant observation is a standard model for ethnography, I found that following the statements of numerous suicidal individuals on more than forty internet suicide sites provided a means of gaining insight into their suffering and their motivations for seeking out communication with others. Among the more than forty thousand available sites on suicide, I narrowed down the list by searching the internet for phrases such as *jisatsu saito* (suicide sites), *shūdan jisatsu* (group suicide), or *jisatsu kurabu* (suicide club) in order to identify suicide websites that were organized and run by a regular moderator with features such as bulletin board services (BBSs) (now more commonly called discussion forums) and chat rooms.[3] I also relied on a website that ranked the most popularly visited suicide sites.[4]

ELEMENTS OF SUICIDE WEBSITES

The majority of the suicide-related websites I visited were composed of the following standard elements: (1) a site guide, (2) a BBS, (3) a chat area, (4) links to other websites, and (5) an area about the webmaster or moderator who ran the site.

Most suicide sites present themselves as functioning for the purpose of suicide prevention, that is, as spaces where suicidal individuals can openly share and discuss their troubles and suffering.[5] However, the sites have been blamed for having a negative influence on children. One site that is opposed to standard suicide sites, for example, is titled Lured into Group Suicide by Recruiters: The Danger of Suicide Websites! This website warns, "Suicide sites function as places for exchanging ideas about suicide. Many have introductions to suicide methods and people can find suicide partners through these sites. There are sometimes vivid, persuasive words on these sites, and there may also be persuasive recruiters who lure individuals to commit suicide. Sometimes there are cases of individuals who initially tried to prevent someone from committing suicide, but who ended up being convinced by that person, and ended up involved in a case of attempted suicide."[6]

In some cases, the moderator is completely invisible, but in others, the moderator has a visible role and regularly responds to visitors' comments like a counselor. On one site, some visitors' comments made it clear that they were visiting the site because they felt the moderator was supportive and understanding.

I decided to concentrate on the BBS discussion forums, as I found these most useful in getting a sense of how individuals contemplating suicide might express their thoughts online. I preferred this method to visiting chat rooms because I did not want to influence the visitors of these websites. Unlike chat rooms, BBSs allow individuals to post their comments on the website with the knowledge that they will be public for the foreseeable future and can be read by anyone. The BBS forums varied from collections of poems to sustained discussions about a theme or topic (such as "afterlife") and a random assortment of monologues that often attracted few comments.[7]

A word should be said about the demographics of suicide website visitors. While it is difficult to know exactly who visits suicide websites, judging from their posts, we can infer that most are students or young adults who are not regularly employed and not in education (NEETs). Many self-identify as being in their twenties or as junior and high school students, who would be fourteen to eighteen years old. In 2004, around the same time that suicide websites were becoming popular, Japanese society started expressing concern about the growing number of NEETs. Like millennials in the West, there was a distinctive characterization of these young people: they were seen as lazy, self-centered, uninterested in seeking gainful employment, and dependent on parents to support them.

ANATOMY OF A SUICIDE WEBSITE

The webmaster is generally the person who creates the suicide website, maintains it, and serves as moderator, deciding whether or not to delete certain posts and intervening when someone appears to be highly suicidal. Sometimes when a site visitor posts that they are in despair or wish to "disappear," "vanish," or die, the webmaster will ask for more information about the person. They may also post, "I'm here to listen to you," or give advice like, "Such feelings will pass eventually, if you can just hang in there for a few days." In other instances, the webmaster may take a stern attitude, admonishing the visitor, especially if they are seeking out other people to die with.

Webmasters of such sites are often people who have attempted suicide in the past or have suffered from severe suicidal ideation. They often mention this in a personal history section on their websites. As a result, some of them end up serving as quasi-counselors. Unlike most professional counselors, the webmasters identify with the visitors as "one of them."

One webmaster, who calls himself Boiled Egg (*Yudetamago*), has been running Ghetto, a popular suicide website, since 2003. Ghetto was one of the first suicide sites to appear with the now standard components of a discussion forum or BBS and live chat rooms. The site is composed of several discussion forums with titles like "Grassland for Suicidal Individuals," a links section called "Suicide Station," and two chat rooms—one open to all visitors and one restricted to members. In a description of the site, Boiled Egg states, "This site's main purpose is to discuss suicide and mental illness. We welcome those who may not particularly want to discuss only sensitive issues such as suicide, but who would like to be connected with others who may have similar problems. For those who are facing a serious situation but still want to live, we recommend that you call the national hotline [*inochi no denwa*]."[8]

Boiled Egg further explains that certain activities are prohibited on the site, including "posting private information such as addresses and telephone numbers," "spurring others on to actually commit suicide or other illegal acts," and "suicide announcements with precise information such as place, date and time."[9] Also prohibited are posting detailed instructions on suicide methods, stalking, and severely criticizing other posters.

On his "site guide," Boiled Egg writes:

> Hey You!
>
> Welcome to *Ghetto*! I am Boiled Egg, the webmaster. This site includes information related to suicide and is called suicide website. The main purpose of this website is to provide mutual aid exchanges for people who have suicidal ideation and mental illness, and to discuss life and death. But it is OK if some people want to monologue.
>
> This website welcomes people who are kind-hearted even if they are deviants, such as those with suicidal ideation, mental illness, or *hikikomori* [social withdrawal], artists, geeks, suits, bookworms, people from dysfunctional families, foreigners, pacifists, victims of harassment and stalkers.
>
> I'm a person in my thirties and I live in a small city on the Sea of Japan coast. I guess I'm just an ordinary person who can't take care of themselves when I'm at home and not at work. When I'm outside, I tend to appear tidier as I make more of an effort to adjust.

Now here's something I would like to especially tell young people under thirty. If possible, try to make it to your mid-thirties. Try to live until then, even if life feels boring or lame. The reason I say this, is we tend to mature mentally and become more stable year by year, and by that age life becomes a lot easier.

You may wonder, "Is that really true?" But I think you'll understand what I mean later, once you get to your mid-thirties. If what I'm saying sticks in the back of your mind, and if you later feel what I said was true, then please tell other young people about this.

If you find yourself trapped by emotional discussions and you get narrowed vision, then you should take some distance from the issue, take a deep breath, and regain objectivity.

If you're about to lose your temper, you can try to maintain being magnanimous by looking over the matter calmly. If you still find yourself flipping out, then calm your mind by imagining a calm sight like the waterside.

If you find yourself frequently flipping out, you may want to search for simple purposes in life [*ikigai*] or explore ways of self-realization that are not imposed on you by others. Incidentally, just like the ingredients in food, simple and natural purposes in life [*ikigai*] or methods of self-realization tend to be safer, and they don't come with side-effects.

People who one-sidedly disrespect the individual dignity of others tend to have their own power taken away too. In the case of societies like Japan that are based on a high degree of trust, those people who are accustomed to investing in acquiring wisdom and knowledge, who are rational and humble, and who are able to respect the precious rights of others tend to gain the most, even if they are slightly different because of things like disabilities. This is true in the case of communities, too, even though the time period and social circumstances also play a role. May the benefits of rationality be with those of you who like this site.[10]

Boiled Egg also has a blog, Spiritual Nomad (*Seishin teki Yūbokumin*), in which he actively writes about books he has read, comments on recent news and social issues, and occasionally shares information about his activities and past:

Incidentally, the old site name of *Ghetto* was *Suicide Circle* and it was reopened as *Ghetto*. In my twenties, I was engrossed in using suicide websites and creating one. When I created *Ghetto*, I was looking forward to the arrival of spring because it was the middle of winter and snowed where I live. Incidentally, I took a leave of absence from college and I was doing various odd jobs. Even though I didn't have any certifications, I worked in computer engineering and programming and also managed computer servers. These experiences and my interest in subcultures turned out to be useful when I created this website.

Incidentally, I've attempted suicide myself in the past. But I didn't choose highly lethal methods, and my attempts were temporary and low-level, closer to self-harming acts. My suicidal ideation wasn't that severe and I feel it's become milder than before. I didn't have much chance to talk about my suicidal ideation with others for a long time, but I used to get carried away and say out of control things. But it's a good thing to write about my past like this, as it enables me to contemplate on myself and my past. That's why it was meaningful for me to use suicide websites and express the issues and problems I've had.[11]

THEMES

As my research continued, I began to see distinctive recurring topics on suicide website forums. The following subsections contain representative suicide website posts grouped by theme. I present narratives and quotations from the sites with minimal commentary so that the reader can get a direct sense of the expressions of suicide website visitors, only including context when I feel it is necessary for better appreciation of the posts.

Loneliness

I become like a dead presence at school.
I am just like a shadow . . .
Am I always going to live alone like a shadow and die like a shadow?
Someone, please love me . . .
I am lonely . . .
—Shadow[12]

My dependency got worse as I started to participate in chat rooms. I feel anxious when I'm alone. I can't leave the computer even for a second. I feel anxious that I'm not needed by anyone. Just being told that I'm necessary would be enough—I would have some peace of mind. I'd do anything asked of me so as not to be disliked. . . . I'm lonely. I can't live alone. I want to be strong. . . . To be honest, I'm becoming unsure of what I'm living for. . . . Since I can't believe in true love, I seek just the words. . . . I want to be loved and needed.
—Saya[13]

I cannot stand loneliness! But I can't trust anyone. I cannot trust anything except myself and my pet.

—Kiki[14]

I feel lonely whenever I'm by myself. . . . I feel like I would like to die, but then I'm too afraid to commit suicide.

—Den Den[15]

I've been alone since junior high school and I'm desperately lonely.
I'm alone at college too, of course, so I eat lunch alone.
Doing physical ed and after-school activities is so painful because I have no friends.
I didn't think I'd be in such a situation even in college.
I wish to retire from everything.

—Melancholy[16]

I'm so lonely! Even at school, I'm so lonely I want to die.

—Shu Shu[17]

Friends, friends, friends, friends.

What are friends? The people around me are all happy people. The people I thought were my friends have all disappeared. A friend I considered my best friend only returns unfriendly responses to me when I contact her now that she has a boyfriend. Even when I say, "Let's hang out again!" she only gives me vague answers. What happened? Did I change? Aren't you the one who changed? How nice, you look happy. How nice, I figure you have many other friends besides me. How nice, I'm jealous, I'm envious, I'm envious about everything in this world. How come you guys can do things I can't do, things that never happen no matter how much I wish for them to? That's enough, that's enough, I don't know you guys. I don't know anyone who used to be my friend. You guys, disappear! I don't need emotions. I hate everything, hate, hate, hate, hate, hate—I hate everything.

—Friends[18]

I want to be alone, but I wish someone were there by me.

—Boa[19]

I don't want to be alone. Even though I'm a failure, I still want someone to love me.

—Kurosuke[20]

Recently I'm not sure why I'm alive. I go to school, do some part-time job, and it's a nothing special, everyday life. But I can't make friends, perhaps because I don't trust people. I always suppress myself and show a fake self. . . . The only thing I think about is life and death. I really wonder why I'm living.

—Jingi[21]

I want to be normal. I'm pretending to be normal. If people find out that I'm not normal, then they will all leave me. Then I'll be all alone.

—Totoro[22]

No Meaning in Life

Why was I born? Who am I anyway? Where am I going to go? I think there is no meaning to life as I do not even know that.

—Aya[23]

It's not that I want to die but rather I don't want to keep on living.
There are happy moments but there's more hardship and pain than happiness.
It's not that I'm bullied, but it's a struggle to keep on living.
I can't have a bright outlook to go out into the world and find a purpose in life [*ikigai*] for my future.
It's tough to be told to have future dreams or goals at school because I don't have any talent or ability to make my dream come true.
I have nothing to have passion or interest in in the first place.

—Poison[24]

I want to die. I want to die. There's no meaning to keep on living. Everyone will have an easy time and be happy once I die. I'm a hindrance.

—Love Heart[25]

I don't understand the meaning in life
I want to depend on someone . . .
I don't have the courage to die
I want to vanish somewhere
I don't know why I go to school.

—Cocoa[26]

I also often think I should disappear! I should vanish from this world. I know that my parents would be quite sad and it would be pretty unfilial behavior towards them. That's why I can't die . . . but I'm living constantly questioning whether there is any meaning for me living in this world. I think it would feel meaningful for me to be alive if I could feel that my being alive was connected to other people feeling grateful to me, or making other people happy, but unfortunately, I haven't felt that way in my life. I feel as if my life has finished already in some way. I would like to recognize positive aspects about myself but it's difficult to because I question whether I'm a normal person. That's why I can't have confidence in myself and can't be proud of myself. I suppose I will keep on living in this way.

—Puffy[27]

It's not that there was something bad.
What a difficulty of privilege—I don't feel anything even if I'm told to be thankful for being able to live today.
I don't have anything I like and I don't have any difficulties, but I simply have no motivation to do anything. What can I do?
I have no motivation to work, no motivation to meet anyone, and I just go on eating and sleeping.
How can I have any motivation? What do I need to do to feel happy?
I can't take it anymore. Why was I born?
I wanted to feel glad to be alive, and I wanted to meet people who make me feel that way
I wanted to say thank you to my mom and dad.
I wanted to be loved, I wanted to be pampered.
It's hard just to exist in this world, and it would have been just fine if I never existed. Has anything good come from my existence? Mom might not have been separated from Dad if I didn't exist.
I'm just a piece of garbage who can't even die.

—Nameless[28]

Feeling Uncared For

What were my newborn hands grabbing?
Why am I never forgiven no matter what I do or where I am? I don't recall doing anything wrong
It's as if I have been chased since I was a newborn baby
Someone please look at me and acknowledge me
Please acknowledge the fact that I am here
Though I shouted and shouted
It didn't reach anyone's ears
It's not that I asked for a lot
I just want my own place, even if it's small

I get laughed at whatever I do
I cannot complain no matter what is done to me
Even when I lose something precious, no one comforts me
The cold world keeps on turning as if nothing had happened
Where can I go to be at peace?
With whom can I be to be at peace?
I've had the feeling of being alone since I was little
Nothing I do mends this feeling
I am always just looking at the crowd
Someone please look at me and acknowledge me
Please acknowledge the fact that I am here
Though I shouted and shouted
It didn't reach anyone's ears.

—No Name[29]

Even if I care for others, no one really cares for me seriously. I can't trust the very few friends I have. All I have is my aging mother. I can't find a job. I'm always lonely. If my mother leaves. . . . I'm so afraid of my future. I want to vanish. Is there any reason for me to exist in this world?

—Chun Chun[30]

I have nothing
I have been asleep through life without making any effort while other people have been living life to the fullest.
As I have nothing there is no reason that other people will pay attention to me but I want to be needed by someone and I want to be a special person for someone.
I want to be praised, recognized and desired.

—Frog[31]

There is no meaning in living for people who are not needed by anyone, right?
It's about myself.

—Trash[32]

Belonging (Ibasho)

I don't have any place I belong to.

—Zoo[33]

Beyond the topics that I have just covered, a number of other themes recur in the posts presented here: finding it difficult to trust others, feelings of abandonment and betrayal, and feeling unneeded or unwanted as if one were trash or garbage (*gomi* in Japanese, that which is to be discarded or thrown out). Another frequently recurring theme is a desire to feel that one belongs, to have a place where one feels at home in one's being or role. The Japanese term for this is *ibasho*, which can also loosely be translated as "niche." Lacking *ibasho* and wanting to find a place where one belongs is a recurring sentiment expressed by suicide website visitors.

Although some come to suicide websites to find others with whom to die, to seek encouragement to die, or to uncover information on how to commit suicide, others come to find comfort or the courage to live. While the internet has been blamed for exerting a negative influence on young Japanese people by providing information on various suicide methods, it has also created new forms of communication and new spaces where people can find at least a modicum of community and a kind of *ibasho*.

Following is an excerpt from a lengthy exchange between two website visitors on the topic of *ibasho*:

> I didn't get into the college. There's no place for me [*ibasho*] in my house now. I couldn't live up to my parents' expectations. I don't know what to do. I can't take it anymore. I want to die.
> Want to die want to die want to die want to die want to die want to die
> Want to die want to die want to die want to die want to die want to die
> Want to die want to die want to die want to die want to die want to die
> Someone!
> I want to die.
> I want to die I want to die.
> I want to vanish.
> I wasn't chosen to do ballet.
> I want to die I want to die.
> I want to die Aaaaaaaaa . . .
> —Ballet Girl[34]

> Dear Ballet Girl,
> Were you rejected by a college entrance exam that was based on admission by recommendation for ballet? Judging by the timing, I'm guessing that is your situation. I searched around for options for people in your situation. It appears that people who want to pursue ballet tend to find a way to move to Tokyo to go to college and attend well-known ballet studios. Getting into an education college in the Tokyo area to try to become a ballet teacher seems another option. Other people go abroad and attend highly regarded ballet

studios while studying English. Of course, consulting with people who are experts is the best, but that is perhaps not easy as your parents are ballet teachers. I wonder whether there is some way to discuss your situation with someone who is an expert in ballet.

In regard to your parents and their students' expectations, there is no need to meet their expectations, really. It is your future. Can you make a living from meeting your parents' expectations or other people's expectations? Can you make money that way? Who knows about your parents' wishes? They could be thinking, "I hope our daughter chooses to go to medical school or become a public servant rather than ballet, which is so competitive and hard to survive in." You should simply ignore any thoughts about your parents' students' expectations. They are strangers to you after all so there is no relevance to your future. Your relationship to their students will end when you leave your parents' house. . . .

Once your feeling of grief is over, you should think about what ballet means to you without worrying about your parents and their students' expectations. Then you might start gaining some insight into your future.

—Kanata[35]

There's no such a thing as ballet for myself. I was doing ballet because that created a way for me to belong [*ibasho*] in my house. It must have been like self-hypnosis where I convinced myself that I was passionate about ballet. The best proof of that is the fact I have no motivation at all to do ballet now.

I feel the air around me gets heavy each time I say I'm going to skip a ballet lesson. I don't know what to do anymore.

—Ballet Girl[36]

I don't think you need to do ballet if you don't want to. You can find *ibasho* anytime you want to. In reality, haven't you created your *ibasho* at school by yourself? Isn't it true that your friends are not people your parents provided for you? That means that it's about time for you to become independent of your parents and create your own *ibasho*. That's the reason people start working.

Why not try going to school earlier, dropping by at some cafe on the way back from school, or going out on your own on the weekend and people watching while having coffee at McDonald's or Mr. Donut? You can just observe people inside the store. There are businessmen, office ladies, housewives, college students, shop assistants, people who work at the train stations, and drivers who all have their *ibasho* that has nothing to do with ballet.

Observe what would work for your *ibasho* as if you were going window shopping or to the zoo. If you still feel like continuing ballet even as a hobby, then find a job where you can afford attending ballet lessons. Once you get a job or go to college, then you will have your *ibasho*.

I highly recommend having coffee alone in the middle of the city where no one knows you when you don't want to meet anyone. You won't end up feeling depressed being alone and withdrawn [*hikikomori*].

—Kanata[37]

The following is another exchange about *ibasho*:

I'm a high school student. I suffer from severe loneliness and alienation at school, so I want to die. It's tough when I return to school after skipping a day, and people look at me with a look of, "Why did you come to school?" No one calls me by name at school. People ignore me.

I was actually very popular during sophomore year and at the beginning of senior year. One day I was left out of my group of five other friends, and I've been treated as someone who doesn't exist at all for an entire month.

I really want to die. Should I hang myself? Once I tried to hang myself, but I couldn't go all the way because the suffocating was painful.

When I went to a high-rise building thinking about jumping from the top, I couldn't bring up that last bit of courage to jump. So I just shuffled about there for a while. Then the police came and saved me after someone reported it.

"Your parents will be so sad if you die. Isn't it so stupid to die? Things will turn out to be better. School is not everything. You can quit school." Many people have tried to encourage me like that.

But I'm in pain. I'm truly in severe pain. It's hard to get rid of my wish to die. I have a question to those of you who have attempted suicide: How can I die for real? Please give me that last bit of courage to die.

—Suicidal Student[38]

I'm in the same situation. It's been less than half a year since I started high school.
I wonder where my own place [*ibasho*] is. No one will be sad if I disappear, right? In that case, I can disappear, right?
I will disappear for real . . . ?
I've had enough.

—Alex[39]

It is possible to read exchanges like these and picture adolescents and teenagers who are dramatizing their situations and in no real danger of committing suicide. That may be true for some, and it was a common reaction in Japan in the late 1990s and early 2000s, when such individuals elicited little sympathy because of the apparent lack of seriousness of their difficulties. That being said, it is important to remember that Japanese suicide rates among adolescents and teenagers rose sharply during this period. Whether these difficulties seem significant from an outside perspective, they resulted in people seeking out suicide websites—not ordinary discussion forums—to post their suicidal ideation. These actions resulted in actual attempted and completed suicides. In chapter 2 I discussed documented cases of actual suicides traced to online discussions and connections. In some cases, the documentation is even on the suicide website itself, such as in the following exchange:

> There is nothing in this life.
> There is no meaning to live.
> What can I do in order to die soon?
> I really am fed up with this world.
> I want to die. I want to die right now.
> —Oh No[40]

> Anyway, I wrote my farewell note.
> Anyway, I went to a psychiatric hospital.
> I was told I'm suffering from severe clinical depression.
> Anyway, I started receiving treatment with medication.
> —Oh No[41]

> That's right. It really is painful. People who have had a similar experience understand that. Everyday life is so painful and there is no safe place. It would be nice if you could find your *ibasho*. Oh No, did you have some hardship at your work? If you're still alive, please respond to me.
> —Wing[42]

> Dear Everyone,
> We are family members of the person who used the handle name Oh No. We are terribly sorry for causing you trouble.
>
> Oh No died yesterday, and we noticed Oh No wrote about this site in their diary. That is why we are writing this.
>
> Despite all your support, this is how things turned out. There are no words.
>
> Thank you so much for your support for Oh No. You helped Oh No so much and we are sincerely sorry for causing you any trouble. Thank you so much.

SUICIDE WEBSITES AS TEMPORARY *IBASHO*

Some Japanese researchers have come to view the internet as an important tool for suicide prevention. Japan's major suicide prevention hotline, Lifeline (Inochi no denwa), introduced internet counseling alongside telephone counseling in 2006, recognizing that some young people with suicidal thoughts prefer interaction via the internet. According to Lifeline's founder, more than 70 percent of those who choose online counseling are under the age of thirty. For the youth of the "internet generation," reliance on the internet has been a part of everyday life, and its role in both suicide and social relationships is multifaceted and complex.

It is quite common for suicide site webmasters and moderators to respond to some posted comments to encourage those who posted them to hang in there, or to contact them so that the moderator can hear detailed information about their mental pain in an effort to comfort them. As illustrated by the excerpts below, the webmaster Demon God (Onigami) is particularly attentive to the visitors' postings when they appear suicidal. Like Boiled Egg, Demon God's popular site has been active since around 2003.

Sometimes visitors revisit a site after an absence of several years. It appears they visit these sites when they are going through a difficult time or when they are suffering from intense suicidal thoughts, and that they stop visiting when they are feeling better. A college student with the handle Defect writes that they have visited the website Site for Suicidal People to Communicate with Each Other for five years, since they were fifteen or sixteen. Defect says that even though they are suicidal, the site keeps them alive. Defect especially likes to read the site right before going to sleep:

> I am posting on this site after a long time. I used to post on this site when I was a freshman at high school wanting to die. I've managed to survive and I'm now a sophomore at college. I hated school but I ended up majoring in education for various reasons. Recently, I've been thinking about how I want to commit suicide by next year. However, checking the posted comments on this site occasionally before going to sleep gives me the courage to persevere [*gambaru*] and makes me want to hold out. I hope the people who visit this site can find life easier to live as a result.
>
> —Defect[43]

The following posts come from the suicide website Demon God's Bulletin Board, run by the webmaster Demon God, who is an active participant in the discussion forums. One visitor called Yoshie writes:

> I found this site many years ago. It has been many years since I've wanted to die but have been unable to kill myself, and I was surprised to find that this website was still active when I was organizing my bookmarks. I'm very happy to see your website is still active as most of the old mental health-related websites have closed down. I'm spending every day unable to die, even though I really want to. My days just go by merely breathing. My life is absolutely worthless and meaningless and I am quite sick of it but I intend to live for another year or so. I'd like to visit this website to post my request to find someone who would die with me, but I know my post would be deleted or this website might even be shut down due to such a post. I no longer want to make another failed suicide attempt.
>
> —Yoshie[44]

Following is a post by a young woman and a few people who replied to her, including the webmaster Demon God:

> I never imagined I'd end up posting on this site when I found it a year ago. It's taken a lot of effort for me to live, trying not to be full of regret, even if I may have to reflect on what I've done with a critical lens. But this year was nothing but regret—everything. My life was completely changed in this one year. Even if I try to return to how I used to be by going out, my anxiety and fear over what I might encounter stop me from going out. Every day I think about how easy it would be if I could just "reset" everything, even if that means death. It's better to end my life now than constantly being beset by endless fear with no exit. This is my choice even if people tell me that it's just running away. It seems utterly pointless trying to become a strong person.
>
> —Reiko[45]

> Dear Reiko,
>
> Greetings. It's all right, because no one who visits this site is strong. When people work hard towards one thing, regret tends to follow. There is a dark side even to the appearance of someone who works hard. Death can't "reset" your life. Only emptiness and nothingness remain after death. Time will eventually open an exit door for you if you allow yourself to remain still without pushing yourself. Please don't push yourself.
>
> —Demon God[46]

> Dear Reiko,
> Death won't serve as your emergency exit. It might create further pain if you try to reach out for it. It will either end up being a completed suicide or a failed attempt, but I think the result is the same. You don't need to try hard. You don't need to take any action if you can't move forward. Please treasure right now and the present moment.
> —ZaZa[47]

This is another post by a visitor, with a response from Demon God:

> Just like the title of my thread says, what is the meaning of life? I have no hobby, I can't even go out. Every day I'm so scared of my dad, and I can't play games. The only way to release my stress is to cut my wrists and take it out on some inanimate objects. Should I die after being told I can't do these things?
> —Girl A[48]

> There is no point in trying to seek meaning in life. Once we die, we can't even think about such things.
> —Demon God[49]

The coming and going of suicide website visitors in some cases attests to the changing and impermanent nature of feelings of loneliness, something Boiled Egg alluded to when he encouraged visitors to his site to try to live until their mid-thirties. In some cases, website visitors explicitly share that a change in circumstances resulted in their being accepted in society, which ended their suicidal ideation:

> By the way, my environment has changed and I am now surrounded by people who accept me so I stopped thinking about death at all. At one time I really wanted to die.
> —Kuru[50]

WANTING TO DIE "FOR NO PARTICULAR REASON"

> For some reason, I am lonely . . . all alone. . . . I wish I had not been born. . . . Life is long. . . . I will serve out my life! Please come and take it if there's anyone who wants it.
> —Alice[51]

> For no good reason, I am living. For no good reason, I want to die . . . but I'm afraid of pain and I'm afraid of meeting Yama [the Lord of Death in Buddhism] in hell, and it doesn't matter much about living. I don't know what I want to do. . . . I just want to die. I wonder why.
>
> —Nantonaku [No good reason][52]

> There's nothing wrong with my life. It's not that I am facing any economic hardships or anything like that, but I just don't have a reason to keep on living.[53]
>
> It's not that I want to die, but I also don't want to live.[54]
>
> I'm so tired. What's the point of living any longer? But I don't want to die in pain. I want to vanish in a second.
>
> —Bum[55]

There are many posts that do not explicitly connect a wish to die with an absence of meaning. However, many posts express uncertainty with regard to what to do in life, which seems to be a milder awareness of an absence of meaning. Such individuals seem to be situated on a borderline, as they do not wish to experience any pain that might be involved in dying, yet they express the sentiment that neither living nor dying would make much difference to them. Committing suicide often has a connotation of action and intention, but these individuals express a great deal of passivity. They seek a painless death, and dying with others seems to be one way of eliminating some of the pain of death.

In Japanese, the term *nantonaku* means "somehow," "for some reason," or "for no particular reason." *Nantonaku* is used when a person cannot think of a good reason or can't identify a reason, such as, "For some reason I want to eat a hamburger right now," or "I don't know why but for some reason I don't like him." Contrary to the idea of a "suicide of resolve," a large number of suicidal people in Japan want to die but can't identify any particular reason why they feel this way. This is a distinctive aspect of recent trends of suicide in Japan and is one reason such cases failed to elicit empathy from some Japanese commentators.

WANTING TO DIE WITH OTHERS

> I can't die even though I want to die.
>
> I can't die because I'm scared to do it, even though I want to die. I feel I could die with someone.

I will wait for my comrade who wants to vanish [with me].

—Chibi[56]

Hello, is there anyone who wishes to fly in the sky like me?
Hey, suicide is not scary if it's done with two people!
So I'm seeking company. Is there anyone?

—Ken[57]

I've been wanting to die and have been thinking about suicide methods. Please let me die with you.

—Issho[58]

If it is all right with you, would you like to die with me?

—Cookie[59]

I no longer wish to suffer. But I'm too afraid to die alone. Is there anyone who wishes to die with me?

—Ellie[60]

Are you suicidal and would you like to die with me? I don't have the guts to die alone. I'm asking for people who would like to die with me.

—Together[61]

Is there anyone who wants to die but who can't die alone? Please, let's die together.

—Maru[62]

Sleeping pills won't kill you. . . . Is there anyone who would like to die using another method?

—Nightmare[63]

Would you die together with me? By the way, I live in Gunma prefecture.

—Gunma[64]

I have been wanting to die and have been thinking about suicide methods. Please let me die with you.

—Misery[65]

If it is all right with you, would you like to die with me?

—Run Run[66]

This selection of quotes recalls the earlier discussion on internet group suicide and is another recurring theme I discovered: the wish to die, but not alone. The tone of suggestions to commit suicide together is often alarmingly casual, sometimes even pleading or supplicatory. The actual nature of these relationships is difficult to define. On the one hand, the individuals are strangers who likely mean very little to each other. On the other hand, the fact that they are thinking of doing something together—even if it is suicide—creates a bond and requires a relationship of trust. This is evident in comments like, "Will you be my friend? Will you die with me?" This is a strange kind of friendship, and for the many Japanese who believe in the continuation of life after death, a strange kind of companionship on the journey from this life to the next—a journey that they may not have the courage to undertake alone. As I quoted earlier, one woman who died with a man she had just met over the internet stated in her will, "It's sad to die alone. It could have been anyone."[67]

Taken on their own, strong feelings of isolation, loneliness, and alienation may not be so distinctive or unique when considering suicide, but the choice to die with others, especially strangers, is less usual. In Japanese society, dying alone is stigmatized; it is a cultural imperative for family members to be present when a person dies. Long writes, "The potential for loneliness of the dying seems to be a particular concern, expressed not only in words (for example, *kodoku na shi*, 'lonely death'), but also in the vast importance placed on *shini me ni au* (being there at the moment of death)."[68] In most cases of individual suicide, one might not actively wish for others with whom to die. In cases of group suicide, however, the wish to avoid a "lonely death" seems to remain. Even the choice of the *shichirin* stove itself is significant, for it is a nostalgic symbol of comfort, togetherness, and communal action, like gathering around for a barbeque.

THE AFTERLIFE

> Akihiro Miwa [a TV personality] said that even if you commit suicide and die and are reborn, it's just like running away. Since you haven't overcome your problems, you'll just repeat the same thing again and again in future lives. So it's meaningless to commit suicide.
>
> —Mimi[69]

> The mainstream view is that life is one time, but I think life repeats many times. That way, I think people can lead an easy life, be kind to other people, not become desperate, and be unselfish. I think looting occurs during disasters because people think you only have one life. Regarding suicide, I don't think it's a solution to end this life, so I won't do it. I think I would just have to go through the same thing again in my next life.
>
> —Knight[70]

Discussion of the afterlife is not uncommon in the chat rooms and message boards of Japanese suicide websites. However, there is no standard view of the afterlife in Japan. Christianity represents less than 1 percent of the Japanese population, so the idea of an eternal heaven or hell is not very popular among Japanese. Japan has been more strongly influenced by Buddhism, which holds that people are reborn countless times in a cycle of rebirth.

While the vast majority of Japanese families do have some connection to one of many Buddhist traditions, these ties are often more traditional, only playing a role when someone in the family dies and a funeral needs to be arranged. Statistics on the number of practicing Buddhists are therefore hard to find. Even fewer Japanese would self-identify as Shintoists, although many visit Shinto shrines on certain ceremonial days like New Year's.

While ideas from these religious traditions have permeated Japanese society and culture, leading many to participate in ceremonies on particular days of the year, regular participation in organized religion, such as attending a church, mosque, or synagogue every weekend, is relatively uncommon in Japan. Furthermore, unlike exclusive affiliation with a large monotheistic religion, religious affiliation with Buddhism and Shintoism is generally considered nonexclusive in Japan.

Japanese who do attend a service regularly are usually affiliated with the "new religions" and "new new religions." These are sects that combine elements of Buddhism, Christianity, and other traditions, and are often organized around a particular charismatic religious leader. However, many Japanese regard these movements as suspect, particularly after the 1995 Aum Shinrikyō sarin gas attack in Tokyo, which was carried out by a "new religious sect."

Thus, the religious makeup of Japan bespeaks significant openness and variety in how individuals may envision the afterlife. One such envisioning takes place in the 1998 film *Afterlife* (*Wandafuru raifu* or "Wonderful Life" in Japanese) by Hirokazu Kore-eda, a film that was influenced by and partially based on the narratives of hundreds of "real-life" Japanese.[71] In the film, the afterlife is portrayed neither as heaven nor as hell, but as a place of transition, one where individuals get to choose the single memory that they will keep from the life they have just completed. This idea of death as a transition from one state of being to another, whereby the next state is not an eternal, fixed state of bliss or pain, is important in understanding views toward suicide in Japan, and I return to it later when considering the views of Japanese college students toward suicide and death.

ANALYSIS OF THEMES

Loneliness and an absence of meaning in life seem to be closely connected and highlighted as reasons for suicide in the comments left by individuals on suicide sites. There is often a sense of inner conflict. On the one hand, they experience intense loneliness when alone, but on the other hand, they feel mistrustful of others and do not like social settings. In certain cases, these feelings seem to combine in the wish to die with others. In other words, they want to escape the pain of loneliness and absence of meaning in this life while remaining in connection with another person or persons, because to die alone would be too painful.

As noted, many visitors to suicide websites speak of lacking a place of their own, a niche or place where they belong (*ibasho*). This seems to parallel expressions of lacking meaning and purpose in life (*ikigai*) and wishing to have such purpose and meaning. Many people also feel that no one cares about them, no one accepts them, and no one is their friend. When these posts are taken together, it seems that there is a collective lack of belonging (*ibasho*), meaning (*ikigai*), acceptance, and care from others. At the same time, there is a strong urge to be accepted and cared for by others, which would result in finding belonging and meaning.

This suggests that at the heart of the website visitors' feelings of loneliness is a lack of a sense of being cared for by others and a lack of feeling meaningful to others. Not feeling that one is meaningful to others leads to feeling that one has no place of belonging and that one's life has no meaning. Social connection (*kizuna*) appears central, as does feeling that others have empathy and compassion.

This may also help to explain the strong wish to die with others. Since one cause of the pain expressed by suicide website visitors is loneliness and a lack of social connection, there is a wish not only to escape the pain of this life, but also to escape the pain of loneliness and disconnection. Dying with another person serves both purposes—or at least it seems to.

SUICIDE AS AN ESCAPE FROM PAIN

I noted earlier that a large number of visitors to suicide websites (most likely the majority) are young individuals in their teens or twenties, and that many of them fall into the category of NEETs. Unlike US society, Japanese society does not emphasize the link between adolescence and puberty as a period of biological turmoil.[72] Rather, it is seen as a period in which one engages in highly competitive examination preparations (for junior high school, high school, and college) while training to become a responsible adult.[73] However, as psychologist Katherine Pike and anthropologist Amy Borovoy note, adolescence in Japan is not emphasized "as a time of emerging autonomy and independence" but rather "as a time of social integration, great energy, and potential, rather than as a turbulent time of transition and antisociality."[74] Anthropologist Merry White also notes that adolescence in Japan is the period to prepare and discipline individuals for social relations in adulthood.[75]

Adolescence, of course, takes on varied significance in different cultures and lasts for different periods of time according to diverse cultural logics. In Japan, the period of *seinen-ki*, often translated as adolescence, is very prolonged and can last from ages fifteen to twenty-four (as defined by the Ministry of Health, Labour and Welfare, for example), because many young Japanese remain living in their parents' houses and continue to lead financially dependent lifestyles after high school or college graduation. While it is common to consider people who are in high school and college (fifteen to twenty-two years old) as being in *seinen-ki*, in some cases this period can be conceived of as extending to as late as age thirty-four.[76]

This period of youth or adolescence precedes becoming an adult, which in Japan comes with a strong emphasis on being a responsible member of society. Japanese use the term *shakai jin* as an equivalent of "worker," but it literally means "a person of society," emphasizing a sense of belonging but also of social responsibility and a social role. For women, being a mature adult is intimately connected with motherhood, and Pike and Borovoy even describe the prevalent view of "motherhood as the only route to maturity."[77] Higher education is still seen as a period for women to train to be good wives and mothers, especially at two-year junior colleges.[78] For men, being a mature adult is strongly associated with being employed at a company and being financially responsible for one's dependent family.

Adolescent suicides have often been characterized by the intention of punishing others, for example, with the thought, "If I die now, I will make all those bullies feel bad about themselves." But the latest group suicides show no sign of wishing to punish others, and the method of carbon monoxide poisoning seems to lack dramatic appeal. Rather, it seems to be popular because it is perceived as the most painless and comfortable method. In addition, suicide in Japan has often been characterized as a way to "take responsibility." Through one's strong connection and affiliation with a larger entity—the nation, the company, one's code of honor—one commits suicide as a form of corporate atonement. Yet recent adolescent suicides and group suicides, such as internet suicide pacts, seem to be quite the opposite of this. Rather than arising from a sense of connectedness and self-sacrifice, they seem to indicate a fundamental disconnectedness or *anomie*, as discussed by sociologist Émile Durkheim.

These suicides are also, however, clearly characterized by pain and expressions about the unbearability of that pain. Strong emotionality and a strong aversion to pain and suffering, with a corresponding lack of awareness of impermanence—the realization that all things will pass and that nothing is forever, including one's current feelings of pain and isolation—also appear to be characteristics of adolescence and young adulthood. This seems to be echoed in the recommendation by website host and moderator Boiled Egg that visitors to suicide websites make an effort to live until their thirties, with the idea that their resilience to pain will increase over time.

SUICIDE CLUBS AND AGENTS OF DELUSION: POPULAR CULTURE REPRESENTATIONS OF INTERNET GROUP SUICIDE

If suicide is not being used as a way to punish others or make a dramatic statement, and if it is not arising as a form of sacrifice or corporate atonement, is it possible to think that these suicides are an attempt to seek something better, a relief from the pain of loneliness and separation? To what extent are the thoughts and feelings expressed in the postings of suicide website visitors reflective of Japanese society and youth more broadly?

To answer these questions, we can turn to Japanese popular culture and media. When we do so, we see that the crisis of subjectivity evident in the narratives of individual Japanese suicide website visitors is widespread enough to appear as a central topic in multiple films, television shows, magazines, and books. A number of social commentaries, from television series and feature films to books and online publications, have taken stock of the condition of contemporary Japan and presented a bleak picture of its health. In contrast to "official" explanations of the rise of suicide in Japan, which center around Japan's economic stagnation and individual cases of pathology and depression, these sources suggest that Japanese who visit suicide websites are not isolated pathological cases, but rather victims and signifiers of a deep malaise that is afflicting Japanese society. The individual psychology of such victims is seen as inseparable from a social psychology that is in need of change and healing.

As mentioned earlier, these sources can provide a "second-person" perspective and serve as complementary investigations of intersubjectivity that stand between third-person analysis and first-person reports. This is particularly true for filmmakers like Kore-eda, as we will see, who draw on extensive interviews and research in the creation of their works. Numerous Japanese films made in the twenty-first century have provided social commentaries that reflect and meditate upon the social ills afflicting the country: suicide, unemployment, family breakdown, and isolation.[79] In recent years a large number of films have been produced that deal specifically with the problem of suicide, such as *Suicide Club*, *Suicide Bus (Ikinai)*, *Suicide Manual*, and *Tokyo Sonata*, often exhibiting a level of empathy and insight lacking in many government and media accounts.[80] The film *Suicide Club* and the animated television series *Paranoia Agent* are especially interesting, as they draw attention to Japanese perceptions of the cultural and social-psychological processes that may be involved in internet group suicide.[81] I focus on these two not only because they deal directly with suicide among youth, but also because they provide powerful social commentaries on the rise of group and internet suicide in Japan and the interrelated themes of loneliness, connection with others, and the afterlife.[82]

Japanese studies scholar Sandra Buckley devotes a significant portion of her preface in the *Encyclopedia of Contemporary Japanese Culture* to examining the reflections of loneliness, isolation, and precarity shown in recent Japanese films. As she notes, "Whether the forum is film, the evening news, manga (comics), cell phone messaging, new fiction or reality TV, the contemporary platforms of cultural production and the circulations of the information economy mediate engagement with reality as they continue to impact and shape it."[83] Thus, while these two cases of popular culture are in fact highly dramatized and are not to be taken as factual representations of internet group suicide itself, they do illustrate particular aspects of internet group suicide that have captured the imagination of Japanese social commentators. These aspects have largely been neglected in the approaches taken by the media and the government despite their central importance to an understanding of internet group suicide in Japan.

In 2002, writer-director Shion Sono released the film *Suicide Club*. Inspired by a group suicide in which Japanese teens jumped off the platform of the Yamanote subway station to their deaths, and possibly also by the Aum Shinrikyō sarin gas attack, the film is a scathing and highly disturbing social commentary on the issue of mass suicide and social malaise in post-bubble-economy Japan.

The film begins with fifty-four schoolgirls holding hands on the platform of the Shinjuku subway station. When the train approaches, they say "one, two, three" and jump off the platform onto the tracks, killing themselves. When news comes in that other inexplicable suicides are occurring across the country on the same day, a team of detectives is assigned to investigate the matter. Two days later, a group of high school students are discussing the recent "teen group suicides" while eating lunch on the roof of their school building. As a joke, they stand at the edge of the roof and imitate the schoolgirls who committed suicide at the train station, but after holding hands and saying "one, two, three," a number of them actually jump off to their deaths. The remaining girls standing on the edge of the building look down in shock. Then they too jump off and commit suicide, to the horror of the other students watching nearby.

As the detectives encounter an increasing number of suicides, their investigation gradually exposes the hollowness of their own lives. When a family suicide claims the wife and children of one of the leading detectives, he receives a mysterious phone call from a young boy who asks if he is "connected with himself" (*tsunagatte imasuka*). Upon hearing this, the detective shoots himself in the head.

A television series that similarly addresses group suicide is *Paranoia Agent*, an animated production (anime) created by Satoshi Kon. The series aired from February to May 2004. In it, Kon (known for his full-length animated films *Perfect Blue*, *Millennium Actress*, and *Tokyo Godfathers*) examines a cast of characters who are undergoing problems that reflect a number of Japan's contemporary social ills.

This series seems to suggest that Japanese society is oblivious to the disastrous state it finds itself in. The opening sequence of each episode depicts the main characters of *Paranoia Agent*—a cross section of Japanese society—smiling and laughing in various highly disturbing settings. A woman on the top of a tall city building holds her shoes in her hands (a symbol in Japan of an impending jump to one's death); two boys stand in the wreckage of an ongoing flood; a girl stands upright underwater and smiles, presumably in the process of drowning herself, as a school of fish swims comically by; a man laughs as he plummets head-first through the sky to the earth; a man chatters into his cellphone amid the wreckage of demolished buildings after a disaster or bombing; two women stand in the middle of a garbage dump; a man stands atop a power generator with a large mushroom cloud in the background; and an old man stands on the moon as large-scale explosions register across the surface of Earth. Meanwhile, the lyrics of the opening share the ironic tone of black comedy: "The lost children are a spectacular mushroom cloud in the sky / The lost children are comrades to the little birds that have infiltrated these lands / Touching the sun-kissed lawn with their hands / They are trying to speak with you / Dreams bloom atop benches in the apartment complex / Hold fate inside your heart / Quell your depression / Stretch your legs out towards tomorrow / Don't worry about things like tidal waves."[84] The message seems to be that society is telling us not to worry about natural and human-made disasters; meanwhile, we are dying.

The eighth episode of the series focuses on an internet suicide pact. Three individuals who have met on an internet chat site meet in a public area with the intention of committing suicide together. However, the two men, Zebra (a young gay man) and Fuyubachi (an elderly man on medication), are shocked to see that their third member, Kamome, is not an adult, but a young girl of elementary school age. She is excited to see them and addresses them in a bubbly manner, but they run away. They manage to evade her, despite her protestations, horrified of the idea of committing suicide with a child. The men find an abandoned building, where they burn charcoal in a *shichirin* stove with the intention of dying by carbon monoxide poisoning. They also take a number of sleeping pills and lie down on the floor. However, they are awakened by Kamome's arrival and the demolition of the building.

Upset at having failed to commit suicide, the three then go to a subway station with the intention of hurling themselves before an oncoming train. However, before they can jump off, another young man jumps onto the tracks and is killed. As further attempts to kill themselves fail, the three begin to lament their inability to die. Finally, when Fuyubachi decides to take a pill, he notices that there is just one left. This strikes him (and the viewer) as strange, as earlier in the episode he had already been shown taking his last pill. At that moment, the trio hears the loud sound of black crows flying by them, and the old man is shocked by a sudden realization. The viewer may realize at this moment, as Fuyubachi does, that the three of them are in fact already dead, and have been wandering as spirits or ghosts. A closer look at the scenes following the demolition reveals that their bodies cease to cast shadows on the ground. Presumably, they all died in the building by carbon monoxide poisoning. The episode ends with the three of them happily parading along together and scaring some tourists taking a photograph. The tourists take no notice of them while taking the photo but are shocked when they look at the image in their digital camera, another clue to the viewer that the three main characters are now ghosts.

Irony operates on many levels in the episode: a group of dead people who keep trying to kill themselves become frustrated at their failure to do so and are finally happy when they realize they are in fact dead. None of the characters is depicted as having severe depression or psychosis; rather, they are depicted as ordinary people engaging in out-of-the-ordinary activities. Even their attempt at group suicide is depicted as if they were just going for a picnic, with the young girl not wanting to be left behind. Although no character explicitly gives a reason for wanting to die, some hints indicate that they are all suffering from severe loneliness. Kamome is constantly terrified that the other two will leave her behind and insists on following them everywhere, clearly deriving great comfort from their company. Zebra wears a heart-shaped locket containing a picture of himself with another man, presumably an ex-lover. Fuyubachi is depicted as a lonely old man with a medical condition. Their ordinariness is colored by the fact that they seem to have nothing to live for and hence see death as a blissful release—but a release into what? Their joyous frolicking at the end of the episode is also extremely ironic, since nothing has changed in their condition except that once they realize they have died, they finally feel free. As ghosts they cannot be seen, suggesting that their liberation may be a freedom from society, social roles and expectations, and the burdensome gaze and judgment of others.

EPICUREAN SUICIDE

The people who engage in group suicide in *Paranoia Agent* and *Suicide Club* are all portrayed as "ordinary people," rather than depressed, highly stressed, or tormented individuals who are pathological, out of their minds, or in otherwise extreme and unusual circumstances that drive them to kill themselves. This depiction is concordant with the presentation here of both suicide website visitors and Japanese college students. Although it is difficult to determine whether suicide website visitors have or lack severe psychiatric conditions, they commonly make comments to the effect that "there is nothing wrong with my life. It is not that I am facing any economic hardships or anything like that, but I just do not know the reason to keep living."[85] Sentiments such as, "It is not that I want to die, but I also do not want to live," indicate an ordinariness to their situation that defies common accounts of suicidal individuals, which tend to portray suicide as a dramatic act of last resort or a plea for help. Neither are they typically "suicides of resolve," which are morally motivated suicides that result from immediate, tangible, and pressing circumstances. There is no doubt, however, that they are experiencing existential suffering and that this generalized dysphoric state, which may not be reducible to mental illness or depression, seems to be connected in the minds of many Japanese with the state of Japanese society itself.

A second distinguishing mark of subjectivity in these representations is the need of the presence of others in order to die. *Paranoia Agent* depicts the three suicidal individuals as meeting over the internet and then traveling from place to place together, deriving a sense of comfort from each other's company. When the little girl is left behind by the two men, she is clearly distressed.

This naturally leads to the third point: the wish to die in comfort. In line with the "ordinariness" of the suicides, there is a wish to die as painlessly and easily as possible. One ideal, as noted, is to merely "vanish." This seems weaker than the idea of suicide as a desperate "plea for help," which is a common way of understanding suicide in the United States, and suggests that a different mentality may be underlying this particular form of suicide.

David Samuels, in a piece for the *Atlantic* on internet group suicide, writes of the similarities between this type of suicide and seeking the rest of sleep, a theme that emerges in *Paranoia Agent*: "'Where did they get the idea of using charcoal?' I asked. 'There were rumors on the Internet that to die from briquettes was to die in your sleep,' the young reporter, handsome and open-faced, with a touch of adolescent acne, explained. 'It was a very painless way to go.'"[86]

A last point concerns the very notion of the individual's choice or decision to die. This is highly significant. In contrast to the popular Japanese discourse that suicide is one way that individuals can assert their autonomy in a collectivist Japanese society, suicide pacts seem to involve individuals giving up, or subordinating, their autonomy to a collective decision, a group choice.

Long points out that in Japan, death with a "peaceful face" is considered a good death, while *kodoku na shi* (lonely death) is of great concern.[87] The three aspects of internet group suicides that I have drawn out here—ordinariness, the wish to die with others, and the wish to die in comfort—are consistent with traditional views on what constitutes a good death in Japan. As medical anthropologist Arthur Kleinman notes, "Suicide is a medical issue; but it is also an economic, social relational, moral, and as September 11's tragic global spectacle of suicide terrorist attack made clear, a political issue as well. Suicide prevention, in turn, holds mental, social, psychological, economic, moral and political significance."[88] The moral dimension of suicide that Kleinman highlights relates to the congruence between the characteristics of internet group suicide and Long's description of what constitutes a "good death" in Japan. In contrast to common perceptions of suicide in the United States, the condemnatory negative moral valence associated with suicide is barely present on suicide forums. Thus, there is a split in the moral judgment of internet group suicides between the critical stance adopted by the media and social critics and the stance of popular culture social commentaries such as *Suicide Club*, *Paranoia Agent*, and many others, in which the moral blame for the suicides is targeted more at society itself rather than at the individuals who are the victims of suicide. Of the two, the depictions of the popular culture social commentaries are much closer to the experiences and feelings expressed by the individuals who frequent internet suicide forums. In the study of subjectivity, these second-person accounts are valuable resources.

Given these characteristics of internet group suicide, we might ask how new this phenomenon really is. Group suicide is not itself new in Japan, although the use of the internet to communicate with others and plan a group suicide with others is, as is the use of carbon monoxide poisoning from the *shichirin* stoves. Apart from these aspects, however, many of the characteristics of internet group suicide in Japan resonate strongly with Durkheim's notion of "egoistic suicide," which results from an insufficient integration of the individual into society, and specifically with his subcategory of "Epicurean suicide."

Durkheim's work on suicide has been highly influential in Japan, and numerous researchers refer to Durkheim's categorization of suicide in discussing internet group suicide in Japan.[89] Durkheim's insight into the correlation between changes in society and suicide rates appeals strongly to the sense within Japan that a change in Japanese society is the cause of the elevated rates of suicide and the sine qua non of achieving a solution to the problem. In addition to approaching suicide from the perspective of social factors, Durkheim's work remains influential because his notion that individuals are inseparable from society fits with Japanese conceptions.[90]

Within egoistic suicide, Durkheim notes two subvariants. One is the egoistic suicide of the intellectual. Durkheim gives the example of the protagonist of Lamartine's *Raphäel*, who enters a "spiritual isolation," but we might equally place here the existentialists who, through increasing introspection, conclude that life is meaningless and end it in a dramatic and often violent signaling of the absurdity of existence.[91] The other type of egoistic suicide, which Durkheim calls Epicurean after the Greek philosopher, is "more commonplace": "Instead of reflecting sadly on his condition, the person makes his decision cheerfully."[92] The Epicurean suicide is prepared "to terminate a thenceforth meaningless existence."[93] At the time of death, Durkheim writes, "the sufferer deals himself the blow without hate or anger, but equally with none of the morbid satisfaction with which the intellectual relishes his suicide. He is even more passionless than the latter. He is not surprised at the end to which he has come . . . he only tries to minimize the pain."[94] Rather than seeking out a dramatic, violent, and painful death, or engaging in tortured intellectual contemplation, such individuals, Durkheim writes, "kill themselves with ironic tranquility and a matter-of-course mood."[95] Durkheim's category of Epicurean suicide is interesting because several of the explanations advanced to account for internet group suicide, such as bullying at school, anger at one's parents, and so forth, do not address the many cases that exhibit a matter-of-factness, passivity, and apparent lack of anger at the time of death.

Kirmayer notes that Japanese culture positively values sadness and grief as the appropriate response to the recognition of impermanence and loss.[96] He writes, "Sadness and depression may be given positive social meanings as yielding enhanced awareness of the transient nature of the world."[97] However, it is clear at the same time that these suicides, while characterized by ordinary sadness and loss, are not examples of the development of moral personhood or spiritual awareness, nor are they viewed that way in Japanese society. On the contrary, as noted, internet group suicides have been viewed by the public and in the media as incomprehensible, shocking, and deplorable. They have been partially responsible for the increasing push within Japan to develop effective means of suicide prevention. Thus, Kirmayer's observations may help us to understand the background of why Japan has been so slow to develop policies to address suicide and depression. Japanese culture may have been more tolerant of the mental states associated with intellectual egoistic suicide, namely an investigation of one's existential state, but is now becoming aware that internet group suicide reflects a very different mental state more closely aligned with Epicurean suicide. In the case of internet group suicide, Kirmayer's observations help us understand how suicide can be the result of mental, emotional, and social states that are distinctive and not reducible to the individual pathology of clinical depression.

While helpful, Durkheim's theory does not fully address the questions of "the wish to die with others," which is the most perplexing characteristic of internet group suicide, and the strong wish for a place of belonging (*ibasho*). Furthermore, the prevalence of suicide and loneliness in Japanese popular culture suggests that these themes might turn up even in the lives of young Japanese who do not frequent suicide websites. The following chapter explores these questions by drawing from interviews with college-aged Japanese students on the topics of suicide, loneliness, and meaning in life.

4 Meaning in Life

EXPLORING THE NEED TO BE NEEDED AMONG YOUNG JAPANESE

> "People where you live," the little prince said, "grow five thousand roses in one garden . . . yet they don't find what they're looking for . . ."
>
> "They don't find it," I answered.
>
> "And yet what they're looking for could be found in a single rose, or a little water . . ."
>
> "Of course," I answered.
>
> And the little prince added, "But eyes are blind. You have to look with the heart."
>
> —Antoine de Saint-Exupéry, *The Little Prince*

After realizing the distinctive kinds of mental pain and existential angst among suicide website visitors, I was left with more questions: What kind of loneliness and perceived social isolation do these young people suffer from? What kind of meaning did they want in life, or feel that they lacked? They said very little that would answer these questions. Was there a connection between feeling there is no meaning in life and not feeling needed by others, or were these two independent factors?

I opened this book by noting an interdependent relationship between the structures of society, including its political economy, and the intersubjectivity of its inhabitants. The sudden increase in suicide in 1998 and the high rates over the following years, together with the emergence of new forms such as internet group suicide, could simply have been a result of the availability of new technologies—namely the internet—that facilitated the suicides of those who already wished to die. It also, as I have suggested, could have been the result of shifts in those structures, as anticipated by the work of scholars of Japan in anthropology and political economy. If the latter were the case, we would expect to see a resonance in the subjectivity of younger Japanese more broadly, not just those found on suicide websites. If that resonance were widespread, as would be expected from the significant political, economic, and social tensions that scholars of Japan have extensively analyzed, one would not have to conduct an exhaustive study of younger Japanese to see the effects.

The study on internet group suicide therefore propelled me to conduct further research to identify whether the types of mental pain and existential angst shared online were distinctive only among suicide website visitors or were more prevalent and widely shared among young Japanese. According to the available reported data, the large majority who ended their lives via internet group suicide were in their twenties (52.6%) and early thirties (22.1%).[1] This corresponded to my own ethnographic research on suicide websites. I therefore sought to explore the subjectivity of young Japanese related to the very topics raised by the suicide website visitors: How did they see meaning in life? Did they also find being needed by others important? Did they feel needed by anyone? Did they experience loneliness? To what extent, and in what manner?

Not only were college students in Japan of comparable age to suicide website visitors and those who completed internet group suicides, but they also did not yet hold regular jobs, nor were they married. Furthermore, as observed by Gordon Mathews, who has extensively studied *ikigai* ("purpose in life") in Japan, young adults at college are still in the process of meaning making for their future before settling down to start their own families or take regular jobs.[2] Therefore, I sensed that the search for meaning often found among suicide website visitors' posts might have some resonance with the students.

I recruited students while giving guest lectures at three colleges in the Tokyo area. In total I interviewed twenty-four college students: nineteen females and five males from three different institutions (one national university and two private universities in the Tokyo area). The students' majors varied, including sociology, anthropology, psychology, religion, and economics. There were more female students in all classes I visited, resulting in more women interviewees. These students should not be considered a representative sample of Japanese college students, as they were all recruited in Tokyo, an urban area, and the students who chose to be interviewed by me were naturally self-selected.

The interviews took place from 2009 to 2010 while I was in Tokyo on sabbatical. Most of the students were aged twenty to twenty-four, but a few were in their late twenties and early thirties. Anthropologist Nancy Rosenberger notes in her work on the identity of single women in Japan that young Japanese at this age are often characterized by "postadolescent identity exploration, instability, self-focus, and feelings of 'in-betweenness' and possibilities."[3] I conducted semistructured interviews based on a list of preset questions that addressed their views on suicide, meaning in life, loneliness, the importance of being needed, and what the term *good death* might mean to them.[4] In doing so, I followed the open interview methods practiced by anthropologists of Japan, namely Mathews, Allison, Rosenberger, and others who gather life narratives about subjective experience, values, and beliefs.[5] The interviews took place one on one at a café near the three colleges and lasted from forty minutes to two hours. Overall, male students took less time than female students.

The semistructured interviews I conducted consisted of fourteen questions (see the table). Some questions required only a "Yes," "No," or other one-word response. Others were intended to allow for lengthier answers, including narratives of life stories and episodes from their lives. Some questions, such as, "Have you ever felt that you are needed?," were intentionally placed later in the interview, after interviewees had had some time to reflect on their lives and get into the rhythm of the interview. I also placed this question right before inquiring about *ikigai* or "purpose in life." These were the two themes that had emerged as most important among suicide website visitors.

In order to provide as rich a sense of their views, experiences, and personalities as possible, I first present the statements of several students in narrative form directly and without my analysis. For fluidity of reading, these narratives do not include my interview questions, but it is generally clear to which questions or topics they are responding.

The interviews contain a few Japanese terms that are important to unpack, so I intersperse the narratives with some analysis of these key

Interview Questions

1. If you were to describe death as a color, which color would you choose?
2. What do the terms *good death* and *bad death* mean to you? Can you provide some concrete examples?
3. If you were to describe the afterlife as a color, which color would you choose?
4. Please choose the item(s) which fit the best for you:
    a. After death, everything vanishes and nothing remains.
    b. One goes to heaven or hell.
    c. One goes somewhere.
    d. One returns to nature (earth, dirt, becoming one with the cosmos).
    e. One is reborn or reincarnated.
5. Please tell me your views on suicide.
6. Are there instances where suicide could be a good death? If so, when?
7. What are your thoughts on internet group suicide?
8. Have you ever felt, "I'm not independent, I just go along with the crowd" (*jibun ga nai*)? If so, in what situations?
9. When and in which situations do you feel that you are "being yourself" the most?
10. Have you ever felt that you were needed? Is that feeling important for you in your life?
11. Is purpose in life (*ikigai*) or meaning in life (*ikiru imi*) important for you? Do you have purpose in life? What do you think is your parents' purpose in life?
12. Have you ever felt you have no place to belong to (*ibasho*)? If so, under what circumstances?
13. What are your strengths and weaknesses, publicly (work related) and more personally?
14. Do you think there's a connection between your self-image and other people's assessment of you? Which of the two do you value more?

terms, how they have been treated in scholarship on Japan, and how I chose to translate them. These include *ikigai* ("purpose in life"), *ikiru imi* ("meaning in life"), *jibun ga nai* ("not having a strong sense of independence"), *ibasho* ("belonging" or "a place one feels comfortable"), and *ikizurasa* ("finding it hard to live"), each of which I address in turn.

Although I had not anticipated it, several of the students had direct personal experience with suicide, and one had attempted suicide multiple times. They often became animated while narrating their life stories and several shared that it was helpful for them to talk about things that mattered to them. Some said it felt good to "spit it out" (*sukkiri shita*), and a few even said it was healing (*iyasareru*).

KAORI

I met Kaori, a twenty-eight-year-old female student, in a café in Tokyo. When I asked her whether she had a purpose in life (*ikigai*), she said:

> No, having a purpose in life isn't important for me. To be honest, I don't need it. I don't have much hope and optimism in life. I'd rather die if I could. I'm envious of those who live their lives with purpose (*ikigai*).
>
> I'm not going to kill myself, but the reason I go on living is that a sense of justice and obligation are important for me. My parents have been spending a great deal of money and time on my education. They made that commitment based on the premise of me being alive. So I can't die, because if I did, I would end up negating all the effort they've made. . . . But if it were just me, then although I might not actually commit suicide, I wouldn't have any real reason to keep on living either.

When asked if she ever felt she didn't have a place where she belonged, she said:

> No. I always feel that I belong to my family, so I've never felt like I didn't belong to any place.

My next question asked about her opinions on suicide, to which she responded:

> There are different types of suicide. If someone dies for a good cause, such as to save someone like the Buddha did, or for peace, then that's all right. But otherwise it's not good. I don't think there are praiseworthy suicides nowadays. . . My picture of suicide is that it's not good. But at the same time, I can understand how hard it is to keep on living, since it's hard to live.

Kaori was a very articulate, logical thinker. She was generous with her time, responding to my questions thoughtfully and never in a hasty manner. She appeared to be plainly describing her worldview and how life appeared to her, and she did so in a calm, unemotional tone. She did become emotional and happy when she spoke about her family and how she always felt at home and like herself when she was with them. So where did the thought come from that she would rather die if she could, that it was so hard to live?

KOJI

While Kaori spoke of having no purpose in life and of the difficulty of living, she also clearly stated she would not attempt suicide, and she did not have any direct experience with suicide. Some of the students I interviewed did, however. Koji was a thirty-year-old male graduate student at Tokyo University. The following is an abridged transcript of his responses to my interview questions:

> I studied philosophy as an undergraduate, and then started studying psychology at graduate school here. I told a professor that I wanted to study psychology from the perspective of religion. He told me to visit a distinguished professor of psychology at another university, then that professor recommended me to visit a professor who was also a Jesuit priest. This Jesuit priest was also holding Zen meditation sessions, and when I met him, I said, "Please teach me Zen meditation!" So that's how I started meditating eight years ago. What a peculiar encounter. It's like some kind of karmic connection.
>
> I was a failure already by the time I was in high school. My older brother and older sister were both academically brilliant, but I was attending a high school that was near the bottom of all the schools in Tokyo. My parents were very invested in education. But I was the youngest and was attending this bottom-ranked school. So my dad gave up on me. That was a very good experience for me. Then I kept failing to get into college. It took me three years to pass the entrance exams. So I have experienced failure several times.
>
> As I'm studying psychology now, listening to people is my job. I'm hopeful that my previous experiences of failure come in handy in understanding them. I'm thirty years old now and live on my own.
>
> Well, would it be okay for me to start telling you a rather heavy story? It's the main theme of my research and it's a question I pose to myself: it's that I have witnessed attempted suicide several times. I witnessed someone who was very close to being so powerfully dragged into death. Holding a knife and bleeding . . .

I'm sorry. It was dawn. Under the electric lights, he was being pulled in by death. I tried to stop it but I couldn't do anything. The sense of despair . . . a spectacular sight in a way, his upper body naked. . . . It was my older brother.

He'd been suffering from depression for a long time. He attempted suicide three times. What I'm describing was the first time—no, sorry, the second attempt.

It was dawn. I was writing my dissertation so I was awake. Then I heard my mom screaming, so I went upstairs. I saw my brother in a hazy state of mind already taking sleeping pills. While in this state, he was repeatedly slashing his neck with a knife.

To be honest, all I felt at that moment was, "Why stop him if he wants to die so badly?"

He'd been suffering terribly for ten years. He was in his late twenties at that time. He'd been suffering from depression continuously and it was so bad that sometimes he became unable to speak at all.

He'd wanted to go to medical school. But because of the university entrance exam results, he ended up going to a college that wasn't his top choice. He didn't last there. So he came back home and tried to study again for the next year's college entrance exam. So I witnessed how miserable he was. I was studying philosophy and doing various things like meditation, but none of it was useful in dealing with his misery. I couldn't do anything for him when he made his suicide attempts. My body reacted as if it was on autopilot; my mind wondered, why should I stop him?

That's the reason I ended up studying psychology. I kept wondering: why do we live? At the beginning, I used to wonder, "Why should we stop him from killing himself?" But I came to the conclusion that just thinking about this in my head wasn't enough, so I started working at hospice as a volunteer. I hadn't been able to grasp what death was like on my own, so there I was finally able to experience what death is by witnessing elderly people dying at the hospice.

So I asked, what can I do? And my answer was: I'm alive, and I can keep on living. So I began to think about why I'm alive, and what it means to live. So this is the main theme I'm studying in clinical psychology. I hope to be able to explain these things. I hope to conduct research on these questions.

My brother panicked when the time came for the university entrance exam. My dad was never able to become a doctor himself. So he told me that I had to become a doctor, and my life would be nothing unless I did that. That's the kind of extreme upbringing I got from him. So when I said I'm a failure, what I meant is that I couldn't stay on that track to become a doctor. So the other day when I saw myself in the mirror in a white lab coat, when I was at the hospital for my psychology class, I was surprised and thought, "Wow, that guy in the white hospital coat is me!"

Right after his attempted suicide, I asked my brother how he had been feeling. He said it was like he was opening a sliding door to go into the next world. “The next world”—that’s what he said. He said this world was too painful, so even though it might be a bit painful to kill himself, he had to believe that the world beyond the sliding door was better than this one, even if it was in fact hell. He wanted to leap into the next world.

So it wasn’t to end his life, and it wasn’t a death of convenience. It was his desire to live in that next world. Living in this world was full of suffering for him, so he wanted to live elsewhere. So listening to him, I realized that rather than dying, he was living—trying to live in a different world. It wasn’t about ending his life, but about going somewhere else. Rather than an afterlife, it’s a world we move on to, after this world. And it’s a wonderful place.

But it’s almost funny that the next day, he hated being brought to the hospital, saying it would be so painful to be treated there. I was like, “You just tried to die, didn’t you!” But my mom said it seemed that when he had cut himself, he had carefully avoided critical parts of his body.

His first attempted suicide was by overdosing on sleeping pills that had been prescribed by his psychiatric hospital. Fortunately, he took the pills with alcohol, which caused his stomach to reject them, and he threw them up. If he’d taken them with Gatorade or something then it would’ve been deadly.

Strangely, each time he attempted suicide, my mother found him. Always. It would be around dawn. She’d sense something had happened, and she’d open up his door to find out. There are so many times he wouldn’t have made it if my mom hadn’t woken up and found him. She knows when and which time of year is most dangerous. Like right before the university entrance exam—December. And also New Year’s Eve.

My brother said he knew conceptually that suicide wasn’t good. But he said what was most scary was being possessed by something unknown, some kind of impulse. Then when he comes to his senses, he’s covered in blood. Even to me, when I see him in the middle of trying to kill himself, he looks like someone possessed.

So from these experiences, I started thinking about what it means to live. And I think failure is fine.

Sometimes I wonder if my desire to stop my brother from killing himself was nothing but egocentrism. Shouldn’t I respect his wish to die, his wish to move on to another world? He’s my brother and I love him, so I don’t want him to die, but maybe it’s just me being selfish feeling that way. I believe in suicide prevention, but I’m conflicted, because I also feel I should respect and honor another person’s feeling if they want to commit suicide. Perhaps I should accept it if someone wants to kill themselves. If my brother had died, my thoughts might be different on this—but he’s alive.

> Is having a purpose in life (*ikigai*) important to me? Well, I find having a goal is a burden. Right now, I'm doing this interview, and that's what's important to me. My motto is do your best with regard to what's given to you right now. Right now, to put all my effort into telling you my story is my purpose in life. If my friend asked me to create a wedding film for him, then I would certainly give that my full effort—one hundred percent. That's how I get burnt out, and I do wonder whether I'm where I want to be. Even still, if there's someone who needs me right in front of me, then I'd like to deal with them fully and sincerely.
>
> As for my parents, my brother is my mother's *ikigai*. And my father—he's a dentist who failed to become a full professor. He only became an associate professor, and that was traumatic for him.

IKIRU IMI (MEANING IN LIFE) AND *IKIGAI* (PURPOSE IN LIFE)

Once when relating my research interest to a fellow anthropologist who studies South America, I was met with astonishment about the interest that Japanese take in thinking about meaning in life. "Gosh!" he said, "Meaning and purpose in life? Who thinks about such things? Do Japanese really talk about that regularly?" He did not feel that the topic regularly came up in South America, and indeed, I have not heard it come up much in my time in the United Kingdom or the United States, either.

The conversation sparked a small "a-ha" moment for me. To outsiders, it might appear that Japanese are obsessed with questions of purpose and meaning in life. The topic comes up regularly in the media, in popular magazines, and on television. I often find entire displays in Japanese bookstores featuring works whose titles all contain the phrases "purpose in life" (*ikigai*) and "meaning in life" (*ikiru imi*), as well as the related phrase "finding it hard to live" (*ikizurasa*). Interest in this topic is so great in Japan that it has recently spilled over into English-language self-help books aimed at the international market. These works use the Japanese term *ikigai* untranslated in their titles.[6]

To better understand the narratives of the Japanese students included here, it is important to take a moment to explore these terms and concepts as they take on meaning in the context of Japan, especially as they have been explored extensively in the scholarly literature. *Ikiru imi* consists of two words: to live (*ikiru*) and meaning (*imi*). It therefore literally translates to "meaning in life" in English. It is a commonly known and used phrase. In general, just like the English phrases "meaning in life" or "meaning of life," *ikiru imi* has the connotation of being a grand question, addressing what might be most important in life in a somewhat abstract manner. It evokes philosophical, ideological, and ontological questions. The majority of regular suicide website visitors used this term, *ikiru imi*, and expressed that they did not have any.

The other commonly used Japanese term is *ikigai*. My preferred translation of *ikigai* is "purpose" or "purpose in life," as I think these are the English terms that come closest to the meaning of *ikigai* in Japanese usage, although sometimes it is necessary to translate it as a person's "goal in life." *Iki* means life or living, and *gai* means value or worth, so a more literal translation, preferred by some scholars, is "the worth of living" or "what makes life worthwhile."

Ikigai is considered a unique Japanese term by many scholars, without any exact English equivalent.[7] Mathews translates it as "that which most makes one's life seem worth living."[8] He concludes that it is most often expressed as "family, work, or personal dream[s]" and stresses that the concept is of central importance for Japanese, going so far as to claim that "Japanese selves' key motivation in their shaping is to be found in *ikigai*."[9] Anthropologist Iza Kavedžija translates *ikigai* as "a purpose in life" in her book on *ikigai* and meaning making among aging communities in Osaka, Japan.[10] Referring to Wada, Kavedžija explains that *ikigai* used to be closely connected to the social value of an individual's life in the past, but since the nineteenth century the meaning has become more akin to happiness in one's life.[11]

Noriko Yamamoto-Mitani and Margaret Wallhagen, scholars of *ikigai*, claim that the term "describes a certain state of psychological well-being."[12] They describe a tripartite sequence for *ikigai* that includes "1) a specific experience that creates a sense of worth and happiness, 2) the resultant cognitive evaluation that finds one's life meaningful because of the experience, and 3) the sense of fulfillment and joy that is derived from the cognitive evaluation."[13]

A Japanese psychiatrist and highly influential thinker on *ikigai* in Japan, Mieko Kamiya, and Japanese writer Kazunari Taguchi both argue that *ikigai* is a Japanese indigenous term with a wider connotation than the English concepts of "meaning in life" and "worth of living."[14] Kamiya argues that *ikigai* is both the source of *ikigai* and the feeling *ikigai* itself.[15] For example, a child could be the *ikigai* of a mother, but her mental state of having meaning and purpose is also *ikigai*. This resembles Yamamoto-Mitani and Wallhagen's classification and is similar to English-language usage, in which one can say that one has a purpose in life (a mental state), and that one's purpose is one's children (who are clearly not a mental state).[16] She also argues that *ikigai* is highly personal by nature and provides a value system for an individual.[17] Taguchi also emphasizes the highly subjective and individualistic aspect of this term: for some it is their job, and for others, it may be family, when they go on vacation, or when they have a special dinner. To Taguchi, what is distinctive about *ikigai* is that it is highly "feeling-oriented," whereby people feel that their lives are worthwhile when they are engaging in certain activities. This tangible feeling of *ikigai* is more concrete and down-to-earth than "meaning in life" in English, which strikes him as more abstract and conceptual.[18] Furthermore, this component of "feeling" closely connects *ikigai* to the feeling of happiness. This points to *ikigai* being not just a cognitive understanding of what is important in one's life, but an affective state of subjectivity. Thus, while I prefer and use the translation "purpose in life" for *ikigai*, it is important to stress that this is a felt sense of purpose intimately connected to one's sense of happiness, not merely an intellectual idea.

Yamamoto-Mitani and Wallhagen's study among Japanese women caring for their elderly in-laws reveals a range of responses about *ikigai*: from an acceptance of traditional social roles and finding one's *ikigai* in them ("Caregiving and *ikigai*, after all, for me . . . they are inseparable"), to a more ambivalent intermediate position ("I have to believe that taking care of mother is my *ikigai*. I have to believe that, otherwise I feel empty"), to a feeling that one's social role is a suppression of the self and should not be one's *ikigai* ("It is really sad if caregiving is my *ikigai*").[19] They write that "[the] moral imperatives that underpin the lives of Japanese women are undergoing significant modification. . . . The introduction of more Western institutions has also encouraged more individualistic views of self, family, and well-being."[20]

Yamamoto-Mitani and Wallhagen's study points to the fact that the meanings of words and concepts are dynamic and must be understood in cultural and historical context. Traditionally, *ikigai* was closely associated with gendered social roles, such as one's job for men and caring for one's family and in-laws for women. *Ikigai* has now become more of an open question for many Japanese, who must struggle to find a meaning for their existence without traditional social roles to fall back on.

Mathews notes that a strong sense of *ikigai* is linked with a feeling that one is needed and essential, not merely a nameless cog in the machine that could be replaced without anyone noticing. Again, this points to *ikigai* as an affective subjective state, and it explains why his interviews revealed that "family as *ikigai* tended to breed less ambivalence than work."[21] The comments of suicidal individuals on suicide websites illustrate an absence of feeling needed, a yearning to feel needed, and a corresponding lack of being able to find a reason to live. Company men who realize that they are not essential to their company's survival still need to convince themselves that they are essential in order to make their work their *ikigai* and thereby have a reason to live.[22] Yet the comments of suicidal individuals on suicide websites seem to indicate that they are not integrated into any kind of framework—neither work nor family—that makes them feel essential and needed.

A younger person does not have a clearly defined role or position of responsibility within a company or as a caregiver in their own family. Mathews has noted that for younger persons, *ikigai* comes not from the self's embeddedness in these networks, but from anticipation of future selves and, one would assume, future relational networks.[23] It would therefore seem that the *anticipation* of *ikigai* serves as a kind of *ikigai* when networks of social embeddedness, mutual obligation, and feelings of being needed have not yet been established. What is therefore missing among suicide website visitors is this sense of anticipation: that there is something in the future worth living for that can be clearly envisioned.

As much as *ikigai* is personal, down to earth, feeling oriented, and variable, it is also strongly related to one's stage of life.[24] *Ikigai* is something that one may be searching for when young, similar to *ikiru imi*, but it tends to become strongly tied to social roles once individuals become adults with jobs and a family. The strong connection between *ikigai* and social roles among adults or *shakai-jin* (members of society) has been widely observed by anthropologists of Japan. When Mathews conducted in-depth interviews on *ikigai,* he interviewed fifty-two people between the ages of twenty-one and seventy-eight in northern Japan from 1989 to 1990.[25] Based on his findings, he noted that the majority of people in their twenties responded that their *ikigai* was dreams of what they might become in the future, with a few exceptions of pursuing present pleasures like travel and fine dining experiences. On the contrary, *ikigai* for those in their thirties, forties, and fifties tended to "fit this standard mold of company and family."[26]

This excursus into the context of purpose and meaning in life in Japan will help illuminate aspects of the students' narratives I collected, as well as my choice of interview questions and topics. Mathews's findings on how *ikigai* is affected by age and social roles, for example, was one factor contributing to my decision to interview college students before their *ikigai* conformed to more traditional Japanese adult norms. Like the majority of visitors to suicide websites, college students would still be largely dependent on their parents, unmarried, and without regular employment. Therefore, *ikigai* for them would likely be more akin to *ikiru imi* rather than a prescribed social role related to work or family.

MIE

Kaori had no direct experience with suicide, yet felt that living was hard and her life had no purpose. Koji had the direct experience of his brother attempting to kill himself multiple times. In contrast to both Kaori and Koji, Mie shared that she had herself attempted suicide multiple times. The following is a condensed transcript of my interview with Mie, a twenty-year-old student:

> I lived in Hawaii for six years, from six to twelve. Apart from that I've been living in Japan. Although I lived abroad, it was when I was small, so I'm not considered an "overseas returnee" (*kikokushijo*).
>
> When I was a baby, my mom joined the Buddhist religious organization Sōka Gakkai. She brought me to Sōka Gakkai, but I don't believe in religion or God.

I live with my parents and commute to college from home. I'd love to live on my own—I think it would be a good experience.

What is a good death or bad death? That depends on the situation. I don't care about how I die, but I do care about whether other people are around me when I die, or whether I'm alone. Even if I died in a hospital, if I died alone then that would be a bad death. But if I died surrounded by family and friends, then that would be good. Some people might feel it's not nice to make other people sad by dying in their presence. But then I wonder what it would be like to die alone. So it's difficult. A different thing is whether one wishes to die or not. For example, suicide—I don't think it's stupid to commit suicide. Rather, I think suicide happens when someone is stuck and can't get out of such a situation. So it can't be helped. But of course it would be nice if we could avoid choosing suicide. No one is born wanting to die.

Regarding "bad death," I'd say that it is sad rather than bad. An unfortunate death is being stabbed to death by someone or being murdered. Unless you asked someone to kill you, being killed by someone else is being forced to die. Dying while still regretting something is also unfortunate, and so is death due to an accident.

Something happens and you're under so much pressure, and that's when you commit suicide. It's not stupid to commit suicide. Instead, it's important to figure out what brought that person under so much pressure. I don't think people want to die unless they are in extreme circumstances. Maybe it means that person is weak, but I'd want to know what made them weak.

Of course, it's not great when we think about the people we'll leave behind. But to be honest, when I think about someone who is suicidal, I focus on how much pain that person must have been in.

In fact, I've attempted suicide in the past myself. It must have been around the time when I was in my last year of junior high school and my first year of high school. Yes, it was when I was 15 to 16. In the US, people often say, "Well, just another teen suicide." I was quite aware of that. I hated the fact that I'd be seen as just another teen suicide. But since I myself experienced it, it would be hypocritical for me to criticize suicide. Well, how can I say it—I remember being under pressure. I did think about my parents and close friends, but I was in so much pain.

I can't remember my own actions when I attempted suicide, but I do remember the very last thing I did right before my suicide attempt. I suppressed the circumstances and the feeling of being under pressure from my mind. I was intentionally trying to suppress things, so that I wouldn't be able to remember much. Later, each time I experienced flashbacks, I tried to get rid of those memories from my head. After spending several days intentionally not thinking about those memories, I stopped being able to remember much about my suicide attempts. So nowadays I can't remember much about them. Sometimes the memories do come back, but it's not so frequent anymore. And now I'm okay, even when I do remember things. In the past, I used to feel strange or get depressed whenever I remembered those incidents.

But, how can I say this? It feels like the period when I felt that incredible pain lasted for one or two years. It feels that long, but when I think about it properly, it was only a few months.

I do think it's possible for suicide to be a good death. If someone can save a person who is suicidal then that's good, of course, but otherwise it's much worse—in fact it's cruel—for someone to have to carry the burden of pain for the rest of their life. Regarding my own case, I did it because I was suffering. But mine wouldn't have been a good death, because my suicide attempt was about revenge.

I wanted to take revenge on my parents. I felt really bad about how my friends would feel, but towards my parents my suicide attempts were a pure act of revenge aimed at them. I wanted them to suffer for the rest of their lives.

How can I say it, it's like my surroundings just changed drastically. I didn't do anything—I was such a good kid. So I felt, "I don't deserve this!" When I reflect on it now, I see that it wasn't my parents' fault at all. But I had this strong desire to blame someone, and my parents happened to be the ones nearest to me. But at the same time, I hated blaming my parents, and that made me hate myself so much. My parents were strongly against suicide, so I knew that no matter what, my parents would never commit suicide. So I made my suicide attempts with a strong determination to make them suffer for the rest of their lives after I died.

Still, I intentionally didn't choose a method like cutting my wrists. I thought that cutting my wrists might be effective, but if I failed to die, then I would have to live with the physical evidence of my attempt. For some reason I really thought through these kinds of things strategically.

So I didn't go for cutting my wrists. There's no point attempting suicide unless you have a strong sense of resolve. Also, I thought my parents would scold me badly if I tried and failed. So I felt I needed to make sure that I would die. So it wouldn't have been a good death, since it was an act of revenge.

Even back then, I knew it wasn't my parents' fault. I knew that at the bottom of my heart. But I felt strongly that I needed to blame someone, attack someone. How can I put it? There was no object I could attack. Honestly, I wanted to just destroy everything in my room, I wanted to throw it all away, but I couldn't. It was like I was suppressing myself. I couldn't handle the feeling of "Why do I need to suffer like this?" So my suicide attempts came from these feelings exploding inside of me.

So what I did was I took pills. I didn't have anything like sleeping pills, so I literally just collected all the medicine in my house and swallowed it all at once. That was quite something. I did this three times, each time increasing the number of pills.

Those pills really messed up my taste buds and made me quite nauseated, but I still swallowed them. I was determined, taking more pills, thinking "Who cares?" But I ended up surviving, so I was quite traumatized for a while from the taste of all those pills on my tongue. Since then, even when I have a cold or headache, it's hard for me to take any medicine. I just can't tolerate that taste. If I take a pill, I feel like throwing up. My body developed an allergic reaction to them.

As for internet group suicides, I don't feel sympathy toward them. They're people I don't know. It would be a different story if it were one of my friends doing it. I think it can't be helped if people are in pain. I do think people would feel less lonely and less anxious doing it together in a group. And I think if you can sympathize with others then you might feel it's okay, no matter what may happen later. It might be a feeling of having comrades rather than friends, sharing a sense that you're not alone at the moment of death. So I think it is okay if someone wants to die.

I do understand the experience of just going along with other people (*jibun ga nai*) and feeling empty inside. I started going to a Japanese high school. I don't have many memories of high school. It was quite a meaningless period in my life. It really felt like a clique, and you stuck out easily if you were slightly different from the others. That was super annoying.

Talk about not having a sense of independence (*jibun ga nai*)—I really abandoned any sense of independence when I was at high school.

The reason why I suffered so much back then was because I had to switch from an American school to a Japanese school. One day after I started high school it suddenly occurred to me that the reason why I was suffering so much was because I cared—about everything. So I became indifferent to everything and only showed interest in what was fun for me. I love painting so I painted a lot, but I stopped caring about the future. I thought everything would be fine as long as I enjoyed the present moment. So I should have been thinking about college, but that was a bore. That's how I ended up coming here for college. I thought it's probably better to go to some college, but at the same time, I thought, who cares? So I abandoned myself, I lost myself. Now, though, I feel I'd like to get myself back. I used to think things would turn out just fine, but now I'm twenty and I can't keep having that kind of attitude. So I feel, "I've gotta take back my life."

I found the people around me were so boring and shallow in high school. I became indifferent in order not to lose myself. I intentionally created a wall and drew a line in the sand. I was trying to not lose sight of who I really was by not doing things that I didn't want to do. It's like I was protecting my core. And I stopped expecting much from others.

But I felt so empty. I became extremely materialistic. I was like, "Yes, I love clothing, and I love shopping!" It was fine for a while. It was enjoyable, good. But after a while it made me feel empty. There are so many dresses I haven't worn even once. It was a way of coping with stress. That's how I spent all of high school. Three years.

Then at the beginning of my second year at high school, I thought I should just be indifferent. So then I started college, and I still didn't expect anything from others, and I was afraid of making connections with others. That's also because my best friend moved away. I'm scared of making connections with people and so I avoid it. But I started seeing problems in that attitude.

I feel most myself and comfortable around friends. I had two best friends who supported me when I was going through the period when I was suffering so much. Even when I thought about suicide, I felt so much pain thinking about how it would affect them. Especially this one girl who really supported me. She was a big sister to me though she was younger than me. She understood me and my feelings so well. Because of what I was going though, we only met a few times over several months. But when I did see her, I'd go to her house and she was really there for me. I'm indebted to her. Around other people I'd act stupidly and loud, but at her house I could expose myself and I cried a lot. I must have looked like I was broken. She literally just accepted who I was completely. She never denied me, she never criticized me, and she just wrapped me in her support. Even now, I still feel that, and I'd protect her if anything were to happen to her. Also, when I think of her, I feel, "I won't do that again."

I do think it's important to be needed. People who say, "Oh I'm fine on my own" aren't saying that because they're strong but because it's easy for them. They're only thinking about themselves. But no matter what I say to my mother, she flips it around the other way. The reason I tried to kill myself was because I knew how much she needed me and how valuable I was to her. But on the other hand I knew my best friends needed me too. That's why it wasn't easy to attempt suicide. So which is it? Both my friends and my mother needed me.

But rather than just being with my friends, I specifically feel I am most needed when someone cries in front of me. Crying is different depending on people. Some people can cry fine in front of others, but my friend isn't like that. She really hates crying in front of others and I'm the same way. So when she cried in front of me, I really felt I was needed by her a lot. I also hate crying in public. I don't like the act of crying itself, and I hate it when I cry, but I can really reveal myself in front of this friend. In some way, I want her to understand how much I need her. At the same time, I'm afraid of becoming a source of pressure for her, a burden. I was so indebted to her when I was in high school, but I couldn't do much for her at the time. I owe her so much. If I can meet her again sometime, or if I can live near her, I'd like to do something in return for her kindness to me.

In the past, shopping was my purpose in life (*ikigai*). Shopping and money. Even now I think eighty percent of life is money. But my current purpose in life is to take back my life. Now it's good since I have a goal, but in the past, I was living by abandoning myself and my sense of purpose. It's easier not having a sense of purpose or losing one's purpose, since then you're just roaming around. It's easy having no goal and no purpose, because nothing matters and money is enough. Even if you abandon your sense of purpose, you can eat delicious food if you have money and you can wear pretty clothing with money.

I would also like to find my best friends who moved, especially my friend who really took care of me when I was suicidal without abandoning me or giving up on me. If I can meet the friends who helped me, I would like to do something for them. But that is my side goal and I'm currently interested in doing something with my life.

As for my parents' sense of purpose in life, to be honest, for my dad, it's to take care of my family—so protecting my family by taking care of it. I think it's probably similar for my mom. My mom's relatives and my grandmother live nearby, so she does a lot of things for my grandmother. I know I'm a very important part of my mother's purpose in life and to be honest, that is heavy, if I may say it in a negative way. Right now, my parents are still paying my college fees, so it can't be helped, but I'd love it if they could live for themselves more. Once I graduate from college I'll be twenty-two, and it's weird to still be taken care of by one's parents at that age. That's why I don't want to have children to be honest. I don't want to make my children my purpose in life. I want to live for myself. So even though it may be a good thing to see one's children as one's purpose in life, that's not for me. I'm an only child, by the way.

I have surely felt at times that I had no place to belong to (*ibasho*). My source of belonging was my best friend, the one who took care of me so much during the tough period I was going through. But she didn't live close to me. And school wasn't my place of belonging. If anything, the US military base was a kind of place of belonging, but I couldn't go there often, so I felt like I didn't have any place. At home, if I was in bed pretending to be sleeping then no one would bother me, so maybe that was the closest, but I was crying in bed, and felt I had no place to belong to at that time. Even now, I don't feel belonging at home. School—well, it depends on who I'm with. When I'm with my closest friend, with whom I can be myself and be vulnerable, then I feel like school is where I belong. So to me it's school and not home which feels more like the place where I belong. But you can't stay at school forever. I have to start planning for the future before I graduate, since

> after that school will be no longer the place where I can belong. Shopping used to be my way of dealing with stress, and because of that I ended up mistaking shopping as my place of belonging. So I'm afraid I might go back to being a shopping addict again after school ends.
>
> I feel there is a disconnect between my self-image and other people's assessment of who I am. I know how easy it is to stick out in Japan if you're acting differently from other people, so I'm aware of that and act appropriately, because otherwise it would be a pain. I only reveal my true self toward those who are most close to me. I show only a small bit of who I am.

FINDING IT DIFFICULT TO LIVE

In her work *Precarious Japan*, Allison describes many of the social and economic issues that Japanese feel have been plaguing their country in recent years, leading to a general sense of "precarity."[27] She notes that many young Japanese nowadays suffer from *ikizurasa*, which she translates as "hardship of life" and "difficulty in life."[28] Japan's precarious economic situation, she argues, has resulted in young Japanese having lost hope for and optimism about their future.[29]

Like *ikigai* and *ikiru imi*, the word *ikizurasa* includes the term *iki*, meaning "life" or "to live." *Zura* comes from the Japanese word *tsurai*, which means "difficult" or "hard," and the final *-sa* is an ending that makes the word a noun. *Ikizurasa* therefore directly translates to "the hardship of living," "the difficulty of living," or "finding it hard to live." I use the last of these, as I find it closest to what an English-speaking college student might say.

Both Mie and Kaori used the term *ikizurasa*—notably, not a term I used in any of the interview questions—and spoke about finding it hard to live. As should be clear from the etymology of the word, *ikizurasa*, the hardship of living, can be seen as the dark alternative to *ikigai*, the worth or purpose of living. Indeed, the suicide website visitors I came across who lamented an absence of meaning in life expressed their *ikizurasa* in multiple ways, both explicitly and implicitly.

A final term worth exploring is *jibun ga nai*, which I used in one of my interview questions and which Mie spoke about at length. Since the most common translation for *jibun* is "self," most scholars of Japan have translated *jibun ga nai* as "not having a self" or "having no self." This very literal translation can be quite misleading, however, since the phrase "I have no self" is quite uncommon in English. It either sounds overly dramatic—as in the sense that a person feels completely dominated or invisible—or comes off sounding metaphysical or philosophical, such as in the Buddhist doctrine of "no self."

By way of contrast, *jibun ga nai* is a very common Japanese phrase and has neither a philosophical nor a dramatic connotation. Like *ikigai*, it does not have an exact equivalent in English, but this is not because it is a totally foreign concept. Rather, it is something Japanese think about more than their English-speaking counterparts in Western countries. Anthropologist of Japan Takie Sugiyama-Lebra notes that *jibun* in this usage refers to an ability to resist social pressure.[30] So in this reading, *jibun ga nai* is a way of saying that one cannot or does not stand up to peer pressure.

This certainly captures part of the meaning of the phrase, but to have *jibun* also means to have a sense of one's own views, opinions, preferences, and wishes, independent of what other people say. If we look at the usage of this phrase in context, we see that *jibun ga nai* is a way of saying that one does not assert one's own views and preferences and that one tends to simply go along with what other people are saying and doing. The phrase therefore does not mean a total lack of self, but rather not insisting upon one's independence of thought, opinion, and will. Understood this way, I do not think the term should be considered so foreign to non-Japanese-speaking readers.[31]

FURTHER STUDENTS

Space does not permit me to provide as many full narratives as I would like, so in this and the following sections I provide in briefer form a few illustrative statements made by other students whom I interviewed. Yuri was a twenty-three-year-old female student. She appeared friendly and cheerful when she showed up for the interview. When I asked about her opinions on suicide, and whether she thought suicide could ever be a "good death," she said:

> Purpose in life is very important to me. So to die for a cause or for one's purpose in life seems like a good way to die.

I was surprised, since I hadn't asked her any question about *ikigai* yet, nor had I mentioned the term. When I did later raise that question, her hitherto lighthearted demeanor changed and she became more serious, even concerned. She said:

> Purpose in life is very important, even though I haven't yet found mine. But even though I don't have one yet, I feel there is something. Maybe it's healthier not to think about such things, since we never know if we'll find it. But I think meaning in life and purpose in life are important. Whatever I'm doing, I always feel, "This isn't it."
>
> For example, I played basketball in the past, but even when I began playing basketball I felt, "This isn't it." And even though I kept playing for a while, that feeling didn't go away. It's the same with studying calligraphy. I felt the same way, "This isn't it." No matter what I do, no matter what I start, no matter how hard I keep trying, I feel, "This isn't it."
>
> So I wonder when I'll feel, "This is it." I'm still in the middle of searching for my meaning in life and purpose in life, although I fear that I may never find it in my life.

Hajime was a twenty-two-year-old male student who wasn't shy expressing his opinions. The first time I interviewed him, he said he was very much against internet group suicide. He thought it was "disgusting" for people to seek others to die with. Rather, he felt, they should die on their own and not involve others. Three months later, in our second interview, he said he had just read the novel *Suicide Club*. Reading about one of the characters in the novel had changed his views, he said, and he now felt he could not blame those who were attracted to internet group suicide. Thus while Mie could empathize with some cases of suicidal individuals on the basis of her personal experience, Hajime came to greater empathy through the reading of a work of fiction that explored the subjectivity of suicidal individuals. Of all the students I interviewed, Hajime made the most explicit connections between *ikigai* and being needed:

> I don't go through my everyday life consciously thinking about my purpose in life, but I do have a strong wish to be of help to others.
>
> After all, being needed by others is purpose in life (*ikigai*) and meaning in life (*ikiru imi*), isn't it?

Kanae was a twenty-seven-year-old student. When I asked her opinion on suicide, she said that she suffered from depression:

> It was before depression became commonly acknowledged, so I must have been depressed, but I wasn't diagnosed for a long time. It was probably around the beginning of high school. I didn't have any idea this was something that could be treated by medicine or that I was even suffering from depression at the time, so I thought I was going to break down (*kowareru*) and eventually lose control of myself. Three years went by and I had finished high school by the time I realized it.
>
> "Purpose in life" sounds pretty heavy and I can't yet think about that. But I do think it's important to have goals either for the near future or the distant future, or to have some things that you feel good at doing or that you enjoy doing. I think it's because I'm afraid of losing myself unless there is something there outside of me. Of course, it's possible that being completely absorbed in something might narrow my outlook, but I would like to have some goal, or something that could frame my world and myself from the outside.

Sanae, a twenty-one-year-old female student, had a response similar to Yuri's:

> Yes, purpose in life is very important. I think one must have purpose and I think people can't live without it. I don't have a purpose in life (*ikigai*), but I do think people must find meaning in life (*ikiru imi*).
>
> I mean I wonder whether there's anyone who can say with certainty that there's no such thing as meaning in life. If you ask me what meaning in life is for me, I can't tell you, but I do think meaning in life exists.

Emi, also a twenty-one-year-old female student, said:

> I think purpose in life is important. I don't like meaningless things, so I can't bear not having some sense of future goals, like what I'll do after I overcome my current hardship. I can't have hope unless I have something like work worth doing and purpose in life. It's something I'm going to look for, something I can manage to do in my life, like some kind of important work.

COMPARING THE STUDENT INTERVIEWS TO SUICIDE WEBSITE VISITORS

Having looked at some of the narratives of the college students I interviewed, let us now return to the questions I posed at the beginning of this chapter. First, to what extent do we see a reflection in the college students of the strong wish to be needed and to find meaning and purpose in life that we encountered with the suicide website visitors?

Out of the twenty-four students I interviewed, eighteen responded that they thought *ikiru imi* or *ikigai* was very important. In fact, several said that one could not live without *ikigai*—that life was meaningless without purpose. They also overwhelmingly responded that "being needed" was important, often even more important than having *ikiru imi* or *ikigai.* Moreover, several of them drew an explicit connection between being needed and purpose or meaning in life.

I was surprised that almost all the students told me that being needed was important for them. Some said being needed was the most important thing in life or was *the* meaning in life, while others were somewhat skeptical of the reality of being needed, saying that they were ultimately replaceable because other people could serve in their place. However, even the skeptical students told me that it would be nice to feel they were needed and that they were envious of those who did not doubt they were needed. The intensity of the college students' need to be needed was beyond what I had expected. Many students said that being needed, relationships, and activities that involved helping others was their *ikigai.*

In response to the question of whether they found *ikiru imi* or *ikigai* important, the majority of the students responded "Yes" immediately, but paused before responding to the next question asking what their *ikiru imi* or *ikigai* was. Several asked what I meant by *ikiru imi* or *ikigai*, especially the former. After I explained that *ikiru imi* was similar to *ikigai* and could mean something like purpose in life, what they found meaningful or valuable in their lives, or anything that mattered to them personally, these students appeared more comfortable responding to the question.

Those who said they had their *ikiru imi* or *ikigai* tended to more frequently use the term *ikigai* over *ikiru imi.* On the other hand, those who said they did not have *ikiru imi* or *ikigai* related to the terms in a more goal-oriented manner, rather than a relationally oriented way, using the two terms rather interchangeably.

Whereas suicide site visitors used the term *ikiru imi* (meaning in life) more often, usually to describe their lack thereof, the students preferred the term *ikigai* over *ikiru imi.* Some students said they were not sure what *ikiru imi* meant or that it sounded grand and lofty, but they found *ikigai* fairly concrete and down-to-earth, making it easier to talk about. A few, however, said that even *ikigai* sounded like a serious matter. I could not help but notice a pattern among suicide website visitors and students who said they did not yet have their *ikiu imi* or *ikigai*: both groups badly wanted *ikiru imi* and rarely used *ikigai* in their narratives. In contrast, students who told me that they had either meaning or purpose in life tended to use the term *ikigai* and not *ikiru imi*.

Even those students who did not say that *ikiru imi* or *ikigai* was important for them still talked about what they valued in their lives, such as being happy or doing things they enjoyed. They avoided calling these values *ikigai* or *ikiru imi* to avoid making things sound too serious, extravagant, heavy, or burdensome. For example, Mayu, a twenty-four-year-old female student, responded:

> I don't need such a serious thing as purpose in life or meaning in life. I am living because I want to do things that make me happy. I love food and when I am eating I feel that I am alive. Also sticking to one thing like my purpose in life rather than doing many other things seems pretty boring. I can't do that. Purpose in life to me is about providing meaning to one's life, like the process of making a story.

Akiko, a twenty-year-old female student, said, "I don't know what my purpose in life is, but if I have something happy to do then that's enough. The feeling of happiness is good enough and I won't feel like dying."

Only Kaori explicitly rejected the importance of *ikigai* or *ikiru imi*. She said she would rather die if she could, and that she was envious of those who had *ikigai* or *ikiru imi*. The only reason she kept on living was that her parents would be sad if she died, and she felt a sense of responsibility to them due to the money and tireless effort they had spent raising her.

Despite these important differences, there are clear resemblances between the student interviews and the posts of suicide website visitors. A recurring theme among the students was the importance of purpose in life, including the fact that most hadn't found theirs yet. Most of the students could not specify particular purposes in their lives at the moment, but they did think that it was important to find them, and they hoped to find theirs at some point in their lives. Indeed, they seemed to feel a degree of urgency regarding the matter, including some anxiety about possibly never finding their purpose. Alarmingly, several students spoke openly about needing something to guard against the wish to die.

Although some of the students did not explicitly say that they were having difficulties in their everyday lives, many told me that there were times when they felt they had no place where they belonged (*ibasho*). Three students explicitly told me that they had experienced *ikizurasa*—that it was hard to live—at some point in their lives. Kanae shared that she had been suffering from depression since she was a teenager. Mie shared her multiple suicide attempts. Kaori expressed pessimism about life in general. Akiko said feelings of happiness would help her to not feel like dying. I also noticed that those students who said they lacked purpose (*ikigai*) or meaning in life (*ikiru imi*) tended to use the terms interchangeably. Those who said they had one or the other did not.

Many students drew a strong connection between the question of being needed and the question of *ikigai* and *ikiru imi*. Several stated the connection explicitly, including Hajime: "I do have a strong wish to be of help to others. . . . After all, being needed by others is purpose in life and meaning in life, isn't it?" For others, the connection was stated implicitly: their *ikigai* was having people who were close to them, being in relationships, or helping others. As Aoi, a twenty-three-year-old female student, shared, "I think purpose in life is very important and the people around me are my purpose in life. Helping others and being helped by others is so important."

Reiko, a twenty-one-year-old female student, said, "Purpose in life, hmm, I have not thought about that so much, but there are things I need to do and there are things that I would like to do. . . . Also being needed is quite important." Aoi had a more intense response, emphasizing the importance of being needed: "It is incredibly important to be needed by others. To me, if I am no longer needed by anyone, there is no meaning in life or reason to keep on living." Akiko said, "I am not sure what my purpose in life is, but I feel content as long as there is something I can enjoy. So the sensation of feeling happy and laughing itself sustains me and I feel no need to die. Also doing what I want to do now could lead to purpose in life and meaning in life. This includes the sense of being needed by others and that others are counting on me, since such feelings also lead to purpose in life. Being brought up and loved by my parents is good by itself, and that is why I find suicide is not something I can allow." Although the first part of her response suggests that being happy is enough, she continued on to say that a sense of being needed also led to *ikigai.*

Many of the students intentionally downplayed their *ikigai* as being related to things that were simple, ordinary, yet still personally meaningful. Seiko, a twenty-one-year-old female student, told me, "I wonder what my purpose in life is . . . perhaps my family and my friends? . . . Having someone who is dear to me, something that is small and trivial might be most important thing. I don't need anything too special." Takako, another twenty-one-year-old female student, said, "Well, it is not anything special, but I would like to be of service to others. . . . Something small like listening to my friends' troubles or doing some helpful things for them."

CONNECTING THE NEED TO BE NEEDED AND LACK OF MEANING IN LIFE

The college student interviews shed light on the question of whether the need to be needed and lack of meaning in life are related or two distinct types of mental pain that lead to loneliness. As noted earlier, suicide website visitors made no clear connection between their strong need to be needed and their need for meaning in life. Although these were two of the most distinctive forms of mental pain described by suicide website visitors, I came across no instances in which they were explicitly connected by a visitor. They typically lamented their absence of meaning in life or any reason to go on living, raising questions such as, "What is the meaning in life?" and "Why am I living in the world?" At the same time, they lamented not being needed by anyone. For these individuals, it appeared to be a double whammy of not knowing what their meaning in life was and also having no one who needed, accepted, recognized, or loved them.

On the contrary, college students showed a fascinating correlation between these two issues, particularly among those students who said they had meaning or purpose in life. For many of them, they were one and the same thing, as shown in statements like, "Being needed is the purpose and meaning in life." Furthermore, the majority of students who responded that they had purpose in life listed things that were primarily oriented toward relationships and being needed. Yet among those students who lacked purpose or meaning in life, as well as among those who had struggled severely with their mental well-being in the past or present, this connection was not clearly stated. Their responses were closer to those of the suicide website visitors, relating to the question of meaning and purpose in life more abstractly and in a goal-oriented rather than a relationship-oriented way.

Students who said they lacked purpose and meaning in life also showed various levels of dissatisfaction with their current lives and signs of languishing. Like Sanae and Emi, they could not bear having no sense of future goals and finding things meaningless, so they felt purpose in life was important even though they did not have any. One student, Mayu, said that it was probably a healthier attitude to not think about purpose or meaning in life, because she felt she might never find any. Kaori, who rejected the importance of purpose and meaning in life, said that she would rather die if she could, but she kept on living because of her sense of obligation to her parents. Mie, who had made a suicide attempt in the past, said that it was easier to abandon her purpose in life while she was suicidal, turning to money and clothing. Now, her purpose was to get her life back. Kanae, who had been struggling with depression since she was a teenager, said she could not think about purpose in life, as it sounded daunting. However, she felt it was important to have a goal or she might lose herself.

As noted, suicide website visitors often express their lack of meaning in life and lack of a reason to keep on living, even wondering why they were born in the first place. It seems therefore that for those who are feeling lonely, suicidal, and languishing, the need to be needed and the need for meaning in life are two different issues. For suicide website visitors, meaning in life appeared to be something abstract, grand, and difficult to attain, but valuable. For languishing students, their understanding of purpose in life (*ikigai*) was much closer to the way suicide website visitors related to both meaning in life (*ikiru imi*) and purpose in life (*ikigai*), namely in a more abstract manner related to a life goal.

By way of contrast, those who felt that they *had* purpose in life tended to describe it in a highly relational manner, one that typically included being needed or being helpful to others. For these individuals, the need to be needed and the need for meaning in life were highly interrelated, or even one and the same. Therefore, with regard to the question of whether these two aspects are different, related, or the same, we can tentatively say that they were indeed interrelated among students who felt they had meaning or purpose in life, yet they were seen as separate among those who felt they were still seeking their meaning or purpose in life. This suggests that for those who have found purpose or meaning in life, they have found it through relational well-being, whereas those who have not found it are seeking it in goals rather than relationships, and may in fact therefore be seeking it where it is less likely to be found.

In short, the most important finding from my interviews with college students is that the presence of purpose and meaning in their lives was highly relational. It appears that those individuals who are embedded in positive relations either feel they have their purpose in life or do not even need to think about it, as they are already at some level of contentment with their lives. Those who said they had purpose in life often said that they did not have anything special, or they did not think much about it, but that they had small or everyday things that mattered to them, such as friends, family, helping others, and so on. In the examples students gave of their own and their parents' *ikigai*, a recurring theme was caring for and taking responsibility for another. They mentioned parents caring for them or their siblings, as well as friends who cared for them when they were in need. As in the quote from *The Little Prince* at the start of this chapter, what seemed to matter more than having many people around was the intentional choice of taking responsibility for another, even if it was just one person (the single rose). Similarly, students seemed to yearn to be that object of affection, to be the rose with intrinsic value who is seen not with the eyes, but the heart.

Listening to each one of these twenty-four college students for one to two hours, often for a total of six to eight hours a day, reinforced in me the idea that individuals who are desperately searching for meaning in life appear to be experiencing dissatisfaction with their lives or even languishing. Therefore, *having* meaning in life must be analytically distinguished from *searching* for meaning in life. If such people can make social connections or feel they belong to or are needed by others, this may drastically help them fulfill their search for meaning and purpose in life.

HAPPINESS, WELL-BEING, AND MEANING MAKING

These college students' sense of well-being, meaning in life, and purpose in life resonates powerfully with recent anthropology of Japan on happiness, well-being, the good life, and meaning making in neoliberal Japanese society.[32] Anthropologists of Japan Wolfram Manzenreiter and Barbara Holthus edited two volumes on happiness, well-being, and the good life in Japan, in which they argue that Japan in the twenty-first century is not a picture of a happy society, specifically pointing to social maladies such as death by overwork (*karōshi*), increasing fear of solitary death (*kodokushi*), and social withdrawal syndrome (*hikikomori*).[33] They write of the importance of exploring the positive sides of life—"making sense of happiness in unhappy Japan"—through exploring how different groups of Japanese perceive happiness and well-being despite Japan's social maladies.[34]

Research on happiness and well-being has expanded greatly in the past two decades, as researchers consider not only suffering and adversity, but also their more positive corollaries. While much of the focus in positive psychology has been on happiness at an individual level, initiatives like the United Nations World Happiness Report collect data from more than 150 countries to investigate the measurable causes and conditions of a society's happiness and subjective well-being. Such research suggests that trust and social support are major factors in determining self-reported happiness and satisfaction with life. This shift to looking into the positive sides of lived experiences rather than solely social suffering and social inequalities has been impacting recent anthropology as well.[35]

Despite this increase in research, it is challenging to find a single definition of happiness, and anthropologists Mathews and Caroline Izquierdo note, "Happiness is not one thing; it means different things in different places, different societies and different cultural contexts."[36] Nevertheless, precisely because happiness and well-being are closely related to physical, social, and environmental factors, they cannot be seen as having no cross-cultural dimensions whatsoever. The emerging science of happiness suggests that happiness, well-being, and satisfaction with life are connected both to affective factors (such as feelings and positive emotions; *hedonia*) and factors related to one's relationships, meaning in life, and psychological adjustment (*eudaimonia*).[37] Research also suggests that both loneliness and happiness, despite being universal human experiences, are inherently social and culturally shaped, yet both are still predominantly approached at the level of individual mental and subjective states, and research methodologies lack clear ways of examining how social and cultural conditions may be impacting subjective appraisals of loneliness and happiness.[38]

Manzenreiter and Holthus conclude, "Interpersonal relations therefore are a prominent feature of well-being throughout the life course."[39] Similarly, in his study of well-being among *buraku* youth in Japan, Christopher Bundy found that trust, place, and pride were crucial aspects of these students' sense of well-being.[40] *Buraku-min* are the largest minority group in Japan, and they have faced a long history of marginalization and discrimination in Japan that continues to the present day. Across the different groups studied in Manzenreiter and Holthus's volume, a recurring theme is the important role of relatedness and social networks.[41] As anthropologists Harry Walker and Kavedžija state, "Since Durkheim, anthropologists have recognized that people are generally happiest in those moments when they feel most connected to others."[42] Thus, there is a strong alignment between research findings by psychologists and anthropologists in this regard.

This chapter's focus on purpose and meaning in life among college students explored what these students value and think leads to the good life in order to avoid the lonely life. While the growing research on happiness and well-being points to the importance of meaning, relationships, and social support, the narratives collected here point to the affective dimensions of all these factors. The students interviewed spoke not only of the importance of *having* relationships, but of *feeling* needed, and they expressed their fears of feeling lonely and unneeded. Their expressions of meaning related not just to the presence of meaning or the cognitive ability to recognize meaning; rather, *feeling* they had a meaningful life was just as important as, if not more important than, being able to relate or describe their meaning in life in a cognitive way.

This primacy of affect may reflect developmental considerations. Economists Tim Tiefenbach and Florian Kohlbacher's study about a fear of solitary death (*kodokushi*) among older people in Japan, for example, found "young people being more vulnerable to feelings of loneliness and older people putting an emphasis on social support."[43] Nevertheless, I believe that attention to this affective dimension of meaning and relationships suggests that the division between *hedonia* as the feeling of being happy and *eudaimonia* as the presence of relationships and meaning in life may potentially be misleading if the two concepts are taken to be entirely distinct. Further attention should be paid to the subjectivity of individuals regarding how they experience the presence or absence of meaning in life, as well as the presence or absence of relationships and how this subjective experience conditions overall experiences of happiness and well-being.

What is the invisible that gives meaning, that allows one to look with the heart rather than the eyes, and thereby find the single rose, instead of searching among a thousand things and not finding anything worthwhile? For many of the college students I spoke with, it was mattering to others. But instead of hope and optimism for a future in which they would matter to society and have purpose in life, they often expressed doubt and anxiety about the future. Furthermore, as Mie mentioned when speaking of her mother, being needed by others can be a burden if it is not accompanied by mutual empathy and understanding. For her, the one thing that had meaning in her life beyond herself, and the place where she felt belonging, were the friends who empathized with her and with whom she could cry and show vulnerability without shame. In the next chapter we will continue to explore these themes of mutuality and human connection and the relationship between hope and loneliness, and how they can manifest even on the larger level of a whole community.

5 Surviving 3.11

We know a person can be lonely, but can a community be lonely?

In a North American context, our approach to loneliness, depression, and anxiety is so highly individualized that it may seem strange to think about a community feeling lonely. But the same factors that lead to loneliness on an individual level—feeling invisible, uncared for, forgotten, neglected, and a loss of connection—can be experienced by an entire community. Indeed, the experiences of communities that have been marginalized or oppressed bear many of these hallmarks of loneliness. It therefore makes sense to study loneliness not just on an individual level, but also on the level of communities. Similarly, we can study the resilience required to deal with loneliness and marginalization not just on an individual level, but on a communal or societal level as well.

Many insights can be gained by looking at loneliness on a larger scale—that is, as a social phenomenon and not just an individual one. This is the topic of the present chapter, which draws from fieldwork conducted in Ibaragi, an area of Japan affected by the March 11, 2011 natural and nuclear disasters (3.11 disasters), and the way these disasters and their aftermath affected the community there.

In the case of young Japanese suicide website visitors and college students, we find individuals who experience social isolation or who anticipate social isolation with significant anxiety. In the case of people living in Ibaragi and other areas affected by the 3.11 disasters, we see communities that have been forced into actual, physical isolation. People in these communities lost their homes, their towns, and their places of work. They lost friends and family members. Their whole way of life was taken from them. Thousands of them were placed in what were supposed to be temporary shelters, but where they were forced to stay for very long periods of time, often several years. And yet communities like Ibaragi, despite being heavily affected by the disasters, were not among those areas that were specially designated as primary disaster sites for national attention. This made many of those who lived there feel invisible, abandoned, irrelevant, and uncared for.[1]

Is the objective, physical isolation of being uprooted from and losing one's home greater than the perceived social isolation of a lonely individual surrounded by others? What are the differences and similarities between these two conditions? What role does loss play in the experience of loneliness, and what forms of loss are involved in cases of forced migration? These are questions with wide-ranging implications, as loneliness and isolation are not only the results of large-scale disasters, but also arise from the loss of friends, family members, spouses, and even children. Each of these scenarios can lead to profound loneliness.

Such losses, whether on an individual or communal scale, are not just sad and isolating. They can be traumatic and morally injuring as well. They are traumatic because they threaten our sense of safety on a fundamental level. They are morally injuring because they violate our sense of what is right and expected: our sense of life being just, orderly, and fair. Both trauma and *moral injury*—a term created to expand and depathologize experiences of post-traumatic stress—leave people and communities feeling alone, isolated, and lonely. For this reason, when the tragedies of 3.11 unfolded, many people, including me, were concerned that they would lead to a host of mental health issues and possibly a concomitant spike in suicides. But despite the magnitude of the disasters, there was no dramatic increase in suicide rates. On the contrary, the story of those who were directly impacted by 3.11 is a more variegated, complex picture that includes not only trauma, moral injury, and marginalization, but also incredible resilience; the re-creation and strengthening of community; and the importance of meaning making, human bonds, and connection in the face of adversity.

WATCHING THE TRAGIC UNFOLDING OF 3.11

Day 1: March 11, 2011

On the day of the terrible disasters of March 11, 2011, like so many other Japanese living abroad, I woke up to a large number of email messages from friends, former students, and colleagues asking whether I had heard the news about the earthquake in Japan, how I was doing, and whether my family was safe.

I am not an early riser, and it must have been almost 9:00 a.m. in Atlanta, Georgia. I immediately got out of bed and turned on the television, flipping to CNN. Thus began my indirect witnessing of the incidents that became known as "3.11" or the Great East Japan Earthquake and Tsunami. I immediately called my sister and brother, who both live in Yokohama, only about 160 miles from the disaster site, as well as my friends in the Tokyo area. But like many who were trying to contact loved ones in Japan, I could not get through to anyone. Phone lines and other lines of communication had been cut off by the earthquake.

Finally I was able to reach my parents. Since they live in Kagoshima in the south of Japan, their phone service had not been disrupted. After many harrowing hours of uncertainty, my parents were able to confirm the safety of my immediate family members, some of whom had gotten stuck at their workplaces overnight because of the halted train and subway services. My brother, I learned, had had to walk home from his workplace on foot, which took several hours.

During this time, I felt like I was in limbo. All I could do was try to reach friends and colleagues in Tokyo and wait to hear updates from other relatives in less affected parts of the country. I felt like one of the characters in Haruki Murakami's novel *After the Quake*, loosely based on the Hanshin Awaji earthquake of 1995, who is glued to the television news for five days without moving as it shows sites of collapsed hospitals, banks, and shopping centers covered in fire. I, too, was glued to my small Sony television screen for at least five days until the final explosion of the nuclear reactor in Fukushima. I had never felt so helpless. Like so many other Japanese, I was paralyzed by the unfolding disaster.

The earthquake took place at 2:46 p.m. Japan Standard Time (JST). It was a magnitude 9.0 earthquake, not only the largest ever recorded in Japan, but also the fourth most powerful earthquake in known history. Its epicenter was in the Tōhoku (Northeast) region of Japan, north of Tokyo on Japan's central island of Honshū. Its magnitude and power is nearly impossible to comprehend: it was so massive that it measurably shifted the earth on its axis and permanently shortened the length of each Earth day. Its aftershocks still continue now, over a decade later.

Within a quarter of an hour, the massive earthquake had caused a giant tsunami that began bearing down on the Tōhoku coast, a towering wall of water that swept away entire towns. The first tsunami took many people's lives. Thinking the worst had passed, some of those who had escaped the first wave went back to their homes to collect valuables or to find family members. They became the victims of the second tsunami. Then, relentlessly, a third tsunami followed. The tsunamis created over 340,000 evacuees and caused a severe shortage of water, food, medicine, and shelter throughout the region.

At 3:27 p.m., the first tsunami hit the Daiichi nuclear power plants in Fukushima, leading to the third of the disasters. Within twenty minutes, the second tsunami, forty-six feet high, easily bypassed the seawall that was supposed to protect the plants from just such an incident, causing serious damage to the facility. Late in the evening, the government declared a nuclear emergency and asked residents within 3 km (1.86 mi.) of the plant to evacuate. Residents within 10 km (6 mi.) of Daiichi Nuclear Unit 1 were asked to shelter in place. Meanwhile, even though the active reactors had automatically shut down, the subsequent tsunami disabled the emergency generators that would have otherwise kept the reactors cool.

This trifecta of disasters—earthquake, tsunami, and nuclear reactor meltdown—quickly came to be known as "3.11," chosen for the date on which they happened, and in clear reference to the tragic events of 9/11 in the United States ten years prior. But these three disasters were not the end, and only served as a further example that natural disasters are always accompanied by social disasters. The three major disasters of 3.11 were indeed followed by an entire series of social disasters, involving the displacement of peoples, mismanagement of relief efforts, a perceived lack of transparency from the government and nuclear power company, consequent loss of trust from Japanese society, and a protracted cleanup effort—still ongoing today—that has led to many Japanese temporary workers being exposed to very high levels of radiation.

So often, however, great adversity is also a proving ground for even greater resilience. The natural, nuclear, and social disasters of 3.11 also led, more encouragingly, to people from the afflicted regions coming together to deal with the tragic events and reestablish some of what had been lost. It led many to take a conscious stance regarding the importance of community and relational bonds (*kizuna*) in the face of tragedy, displacement, and neglect.

Day 2: March 12, 2011

The following day, all television stations were showing the sight of white smoke forming a mushroom-shaped cloud above the nuclear reactors. Reporters narrated breathlessly that one of the Fukushima nuclear reactors was exploding.

For any Japanese person, the visual image of the atomic bomb in Hiroshima and Nagasaki—the iconic mushroom cloud—is a haunting sight. The theme and images of nuclear holocaust have formed a key part of countless films, animated series, and graphic novels in Japan for decades, with some notable instances being *Nausicaa of the Valley of the Wind*, *Akira*, and *Evangelion*.[2] I personally grew up being repeatedly informed by numerous documentaries, movies, and history books about the danger of nuclear weapons and the crucial importance of never repeating the tragedies of Hiroshima and Nagasaki. It is important to recall this cultural history when considering the traumatizing impact that these televised images had on Japanese: the billowing smoke clouds emerging from the nuclear reactor and the concomitant fear of how many millions of people could be affected by the radiation. Indeed, some have gone so far as to call Fukushima Japan's "third atomic bombing."[3]

That morning, the government expanded the nuclear emergency area, asking residents within 10 km (6 mi.) of Fukushima Nuclear Unit 1 to evacuate. Within a few hours, a second nuclear emergency was declared, and residents close to Fukushima Nuclear Unit 2 were also asked to evacuate. At 9:40 p.m., the evacuation zone in Fukushima Unit 1 was extended to 20 km (12 mi.), while the evacuation zone around Fukushima Unit 2 was extended to 10 km (6 mi.).

Insufficient cooling resulted in the meltdowns of three reactors and hydrogen air explosions in Units 1, 2, and 3 within three days of March 12, 2011. The television networks repeatedly broadcast the sight of the massive hydrogen explosions. Later, the limited distance of the evacuation area would come under criticism, as high radioactivity was detected outside of the 20 km range.

Day 3: March 13, 2011

I don't know how much sleep I got over the several days that followed. My memory is vague from the third day on, perhaps partly due to the overwhelming amount of information coming in from news reports and the ongoing uncertainty about the state of the Fukushima nuclear reactors, which continued to explode on a daily basis.

The government expanded the area for evacuation to 20–30 km (12–19 mi.) on March 25, but only as a recommendation. High levels of radiation were being detected in the air, moving southward to regions such as North Ibaragi, Tokyo, Chiba, and Kanagawa. This was a major concern, as the greater Tokyo area, home to thirty-nine million people—roughly a third of Japan's entire population—is located less than 150 miles from the Fukushima power plants, or an eighty-five-minute ride on one of Japan's high-speed bullet trains. A strong wind could blow that radiation to Tokyo in a very short amount of time, to devastating effect.

News gradually shifted to include reports on the environmental damage the disasters had caused. On March 23, it was reported that highly toxic levels of radioactive iodine, cesium, ruthenium, and tellurium had been detected in the seawater near Fukushima. By April 4, it became clear that Unit 2 was leaking highly radioactive contaminated water into the sea. There were ongoing findings of radioactive contamination in the air, water, and dirt, leading to anxiety about fish, produce, and other food.

In the wake of a large earthquake, smaller—yet still powerful—aftershocks are common. People in the Tokyo and Tōhoku areas experienced these repeated earthquakes frequently for months and years following 3.11, retraumatizing many.

To make matters worse, many perceived the decisions and reporting from the government and the nuclear power company responsible, Tepco (Tokyo Electric Power Company), to be lacking in honesty, transparency, and sound judgment. The general attitude of trust toward the government in Japan appeared to be eroding. The discrepancy between the international media reports on the risk of the nuclear disaster and those by Japanese media became increasingly clear. Japanese news media reported based on information they received from the government, which appeared to be downplaying the nature of the disaster. The government, in turn, relied heavily on information from Tepco, which had extremely close ties to the government. But every few weeks the Japanese media would revise their assessment of the danger, and they grew increasingly closer to the reports of the international media.

As the cleanup efforts dragged on, international media reported that Tepco was turning to unskilled, destitute laborers to deal with the dangerous and radioactive situation at Fukushima. The *New York Times* reported that one online ad for workers read, "Out of work? Nowhere to live? Nowhere to go? Nothing to eat? Come to Fukushima."[4] The article continued: "A crew of contract workers was sent to remove hoses and valves as part of a long-overdue upgrade to the plant's water purification system. According to regulatory filings by Tepco, the team received only a 20-minute briefing from their supervisor and were given no diagrams of the system they were to fix and no review of safety procedures—a scenario a former supervisor at the plant called unthinkable. Worse yet, the laborers were not warned that a hose near the one they would be removing was filled with water laced with radioactive cesium."[5] Thus, the entire nation was not only traumatized by the disasters themselves, but experienced a state of moral injury as well, as it saw political and corporate interests undermining efforts to provide relief and protection to people in need.

At the same time, the earthquake and tsunami survivors were being forgotten, overtaken by the national and international crisis of the nuclear fallout. Once the nuclear reactors began to explode, news coverage shifted almost entirely away from these people. Despite being the first and most direct victims of 3.11, within days they were already objects of neglect.

As of 2018 the official toll of the 3.11 disasters was 15,895 deaths, 2,539 missing persons, and 6,156 injured.[6] In 2014, it was reported that there were over 400,000 evacuations and relocations following 3.11.[7] As of 2018, there were still over 58,000 evacuees remaining.[8] These numbers are low, because they do not include people who voluntarily evacuated from areas that were not officially classified as evacuation order areas but still experienced extremely high levels of radioactive cesium. Most of these 3.11 survivors were relocated to temporary housing, where they faced a murky future, uncertain of whether they would ever be able to return to their home areas, and in the meantime, where else they might be sent. As a result, the disaster and subsequent nuclear crisis not only caused an economic deficit, humanitarian crisis, and environmental concerns, but also mental health issues on a large scale.

A SINKING BOAT

It can be difficult for people who live in the United States and other large countries to grasp the small scale of Japanese geography and the island mentality of its inhabitants. If a disaster occurs in California, such as the terrible forest fires that have afflicted that state in recent years, people on the East Coast or in the South are sympathetic and concerned. However, they do not tend to feel the disaster personally unless they are from the affected areas or have loved ones there. After all, the distance from Boston to Los Angeles is around 3,000 miles, nearly twice the distance that London is from Moscow. Yet as mentioned, Fukushima is only an eighty-five-minute train ride from Tokyo, just 150 miles away. That is far less than the distance from my home in Atlanta, Georgia, to the city of Savannah, Georgia, some 250 miles away. Indeed, the geographical size of the state of Georgia is around 60,000 square miles, while the entire country of Japan is 146,000 square miles. No matter where people were in Japan, the disasters of 3.11 were not experienced as something far away in a distant part of the country; they were felt with immediacy.

A colleague of mine provided a good metaphor that puts this point across well: Japan is like a boat. If there is a leak on one end of the boat, and water is pouring into the vessel, people on the other side of the boat cannot watch in mute sympathy and then go on with their lives. A leak anywhere will lead to the entire boat sinking.

This is a very apt metaphor. Unlike the United States, which is in many ways a decentralized and geographically vast country whose people have widely diverse lifestyles and opinions, Japan is a small set of islands surrounded by the sea. Japan also feels small because it is centralized in terms of its government, its media, and its language. If something happens in one area, the impact is direct and immediate among the rest of the country. When something becomes a trend, it quickly catches on throughout the country. When something important happens, it is known everywhere. And when disaster strikes, its effects tend to be met with alarm by everyone. As a society of islands that is dependent on agriculture, people feel they have to stick together and think and act collectively if they are to survive. The idea that we are independent individuals who just happen to be in the same society is not very prominent in Japan.

This is not to say that there is no diversity in Japan. But as human beings and as social animals, we are naturally affected by scale, proximity, and immediacy. This holds true especially when considering how we experience threat and danger.

In the immediate aftermath of 3.11, there was a strong sense that the boat called Japan was shaken, and possibly even slowly sinking. There seemed to be a lack of good leadership, a lack of trust and transparency, and a deficit of good decision-making. The lengthy economic recession had already placed Japanese society in a state of "precariousness," shifting the tradition of lifetime employment increasingly to a neoliberal system of temporary workers with no benefits or job security.[9] In Japan, there is a sense that the natural world and the world of human society are not separate, but of one cloth. When natural disasters strike, they are not seen as something wholly other from the disasters afflicting society. Rather, they reinforce the sense of economic and social hardship, and the sense that in Japan—as a geographical, natural, social, and political entity—things are not going well.

RESEARCHING THE AFFECTED AREAS

Following 3.11, a number of researchers, including me, wished to visit the affected areas. I wanted to know how people in these regions had been affected, the status of their mental health and well-being, and how they were coping with the terrible things they had witnessed and everything they had lost. How were they experiencing enforced isolation in the temporary housing communities in which they had been placed? Would I see similarities with the other groups I was studying with regard to loneliness, meaning in life, and mental well-being?

Visiting the affected areas presented some difficulties, however. Prior to 3.11, the greatest natural disaster that had afflicted Japan was the Great Hanshin-Awaji earthquake of 1995, also known as the Kobe earthquake, which claimed 6,434 lives. Those who survived that earthquake suffered from high levels of post-traumatic stress disorder (PTSD), so there was recognition in the immediate aftermath of 3.11 that there would be a need for mental health services in the affected areas. Nevertheless, in the aftermath of the Kobe earthquake, there had been insufficient guidelines and protections regarding research and mental health-care services, and this resulted in a lot of negative experiences among survivors, many of whom felt that the outsiders coming in were not actually helping at all. Thus, after 3.11 there was a strong concern that visiting researchers and health-care professionals might retraumatize survivors and do more harm than good. As Ralph Mora has noted, "In Japan, medical personnel were discouraged from immediately counseling survivors as it was felt that this might increase a person's risk."[10] This held true even several years after the events of 3.11.

For these reasons, I judged that actively recruiting and seeking interviewees in the immediate aftermath of 3.11 would not be appropriate. Instead, I concentrated on journal articles, magazine articles, television news, and books that included the voices of 3.11 survivors, until the opportunity arose to conduct in-person fieldwork in an appropriate way. I also attended activities and gatherings that were held for 3.11 survivors and that were open to anyone. I did this for several months in Tokyo, from June 2011 until January 2012. During this time, I only interviewed one person, an individual who had attended one of these gatherings and volunteered to narrate his story.

I also visited a Kanagawa prefecture volunteer organization and interviewed a volunteer coordinator who had long-term experience supporting both survivors of the Kobe earthquake and survivors of 3.11. I also met with mental health professionals at the National Center of Neurology and Psychiatry (NCNP) who were involved in visiting the stricken areas and offering mental health-care there.

Through the recommendation of a NCNP colleague, I became connected to a group of researchers, mainly psychologists, that included Dr. Tetsuji Ito, a professor of psychology at Ibaragi University and a survivor of 3.11. This group organized a three-day workshop about 3.11 from October 8 to 10, 2011 that included a one-day visit to a temporary housing community in North Ibaragi not far from the Fukushima Daiichi plant. The trip also included numerous site visits and gatherings with local people who had experienced 3.11. Dr. Ito's position as both a local and a survivor of 3.11 allowed this group to have access to local communities in Ibaragi that would otherwise have been unlikely. This provided a unique opportunity for me to visit some of the affected areas.

A ZONE OF SOCIAL INVISIBILITY

North Ibaragi adjoins the south of Fukushima only forty miles from the nuclear reactors. The region suffered severely from the earthquake and tsunami, with the coastal areas being especially damaged by the tsunami (see figures 1–3).

The three-day workshop on the earthquake, tsunami, and nuclear disaster with this group of survivors was held in Ibaragi, not in the north but in the middle of the region along the coastline. It was hosted by Matsuda-san, the young owner of a newly constructed local inn. The small inn surprised me with its traditional Japanese style, elegance, and high-end appearance. It included hot springs baths (*onsen*) overlooking the sea and traditional tatami-floored rooms—not at all what I had expected as the site of our workshop.

Matsuda-san greeted us in person when we arrived. The inn had been opened just prior to 3.11, he told us, and it hadn't been thriving since the disaster. No one wanted to visit Ibaragi anymore.

Figure 1. North Ibaragi City, October 10, 2011, seven months after 3.11. Photograph by Ichiro Yatsuzuka.

Figure 2. North Ibaragi City, October 10, 2011, seven months after 3.11. Photograph by Ichiro Yatsuzuka.

Figure 3. North Ibaragi City, October 10, 2011, seven months after 3.11. Photograph by Ichiro Yatsuzuka.

The workshop was organized by the Qualitative Methods Working Group on 3.11. It consisted of eleven researchers, mainly psychologists from various universities and the Japanese NCNP. The workshop began with the issue of disparities (*kakusa*) among the so-called stricken areas, which had been erroneously lumped together into a single category. Many participants of the workshop had experienced relief efforts from support groups from the Ministry of Health, Labour and Welfare and had recognized an uneven distribution of the support groups among the areas. A particular region would gain recognition as being severely damaged. Then the media would report widely on that area, and the area in question would suddenly receive a highly concentrated amount of government- and volunteer-based support. Meanwhile, other equally damaged regions would be unnoticed, neglected, and invisible.

The local participants of the workshop all expressed that they felt neglected by the government, the media, and regional volunteer support groups. One shop owner vented his frustration:

> We all feel that there are huge disparities among the stricken areas, such as Fukushima, Miyagi, Iwate, and Ibaragi. People in Ibaragi, especially in North Ibaragi are now suffering from ever-widening disparities (*hasami-jō kakusa*). Unlike others, who are on a path to recovery, we are still stuck at the bottom and still struggling. Ibaragi has hardly received any recognition by the government or media as an area in need of financial support. As a result, we have received little material support compared to other regions. This is secondary damage on top of the earthquake and tsunami!

Matsuda-san the innkeeper expressed concern as well:

> The media only spreads negative news on Ibaragi, saying it's close to the Fukushima nuclear reactors and therefore dangerous. Even though the city has been cleaned up a lot, we've lost visitors. People like us who run tourist businesses are trapped. But these are nothing but harmful rumors (*fūhyō higai*).

Matsuda-san said he felt devastated by the way the media had reported on Ibaragi and gave an illustrative example:

> On our city's beach opening day, the weather was bad. It was drizzling and cold. So very few people came out for it. But the media then went and reported that no one came out to our beach because of fears of radiation. That was completely untrue! The media should stop reporting in such an irresponsible way, so devoid of truth. Our city has been rapidly recovering from the earthquake and tsunami, but telling that story isn't appealing to the media. So they distort the picture of our reality.

One participant who had been involved in relief efforts after the Kobe earthquake said:

> Our support groups learned from our experience with the Kobe earthquake that narratives play an important role in the recovery process. Many Kobe earthquake survivors found narrating their stories very comforting. Laughter was also key to their positive mental health. People in the west (Osaka and Kobe) are known for their sense of humor. Laughter and stories—these were two pillars to successful recovery. So since we had learned such lessons, members of our group who had been in Kobe reached out to people in the northeast—Miyagi, Iwate, and Fukushima. But we realized that people there, in the northeast (Tōhoku), don't talk much! It's a well-known saying that people in Tōhoku don't talk and are tight-lipped, and this is so true. So we kept trying to encourage them to tell their stories, but it was a disaster. And they didn't laugh either.

Thus, some methods used by mental health support groups that had worked elsewhere were falling flat due to regional cultural differences. Dr. Kenji Kawano, a psychologist and researcher at the NCNP at the time, reinforced this idea when he noted that some areas were overflowing with *kokoro no kea* (mental health-care) support groups, to the point that survivors would greet strangers by asking them which support group they came from. Hardly any survivors welcomed them, he said. Rather, he said, the local people far preferred visitors who offered them free cigarettes and drinks.[11]

As the discussion wore on, the term *hasami-jō kakusa* resurfaced several times. Literally meaning a "scissors-like gap," it refers to the widening disparities between communities that were doing well post-3.11 and those that were not. Many communities, each struck by the 3.11 disasters, began on the same footing. Now some were recovering well and receiving adequate assistance, thereby slowly recovering. Others were being ignored and neglected. These invisible communities were struggling along not much better than before, and in some cases languishing in a downward spiral. Despite having the same initial starting point, the gap between these two trajectories kept increasing over time, creating a graph shaped like scissors.

The anthropologist João Biehl uses the phrase "zones of social abandonment" to discuss institutions that hold abandoned elderly and sick people away from their families, isolated and alone.[12] Adapting this phraseology, we can say North Ibaragi and other areas like it were "zones of social invisibility."

MEETING THE LEFT BEHIND

The day finally arrived for our group to pay a visit to one of the temporary housing communities in North Ibaragi. This particular community was unusual in that it was an apartment complex that accommodated displaced natural disaster survivors alongside regular residents. It was an old building that had been slated for demolition and had therefore been relatively empty at the time of the disasters, with only 14 families remaining (see figure 4). An additional 107 families had been placed there due to the disasters. The complex was only designed to accommodate 96 families in total, so it was now operating beyond capacity.

Figure 4. Temporary housing building complex in North Ibaragi. Photograph by Ichiro Yatsuzuka.

The complex was located in the middle of nowhere, remote from shops and the train station—hardly an ideal location for the survivors, who had lost not only their homes but also their cars and means of transportation. The displaced residents wanted very much to be somewhere more convenient, close to a station, but nothing like that was available to them. Moreover, they had no idea when they might be able to return to their home areas.

The diversity among the residents in the complex created obstacles to building a sense of unity and connection. Due to this, the evacuees created a local association for gatherings and group activities. The association had forty-three members, just under a quarter of the people living in the complex.

We met the residents in a small one-story building designated for communal meetings. There we were greeted by Fujiwara-san, head of the

Figure 5. Words of encouragement on a community meeting room bulletin board. Photograph by Ichiro Yatsuzuka.

association and director of a local nonprofit.[13] He had become a leader-like figure at this temporary housing community since he had started visiting and supporting the community. When we arrived, he was the only one present. The gathering space was small but cozy, with a small kitchen adjoining the meeting room (see figure 5). Several long tables had been pushed together to make a large combined table space that we could sit around.

Fujiwara-san had started his regular visits to the community on June 1, 2011, although he had also provided support in the immediate aftermath of 3.11. After he introduced himself, I asked if I could audio record the meeting, and he said quite openly:

> Please excuse me for being so blunt, but we do feel a bit of distance to academia and academics. We've had many such visits already. Many people from Ibaragi University have visited us. NHK has reported our situation twice already, and we were in the Ibaragi newspaper and also in Ibaragi

> University's news. So we do have some media attention being paid to our community. What can you do for us, though?

Dr. Ito responded that he wished to learn more about the current situation and what kind of support the community needed. To this, Fujiwara-san replied:

> I really felt that establishing *kizuna* (bonds) and community was most necessary. So I thought: What connection could people here establish among themselves? And what they all share in common is that they experienced the Great East Japan Earthquake, Tsunami, and Nuclear Disaster of 3.11. So I thought we should talk about the earthquake and tsunami. But even after trying that, I felt like the group hadn't established *kizuna*. . . . So then I thought perhaps we should talk about radiation. This place is only 85 km (53 miles) from the Fukushima Daiichi No. 1 Nuclear Reactor. Some areas in North Ibaragi are only 70 km (44 miles) away from it. In the end, we did feel that we had established a sense of *kizuna* among us.

In July, the community had organized a summer festival. They tried to take care of each other to prevent *kodokushi* or "solitary deaths." The community also paid particular attention to preventing people from suffering from the heat. The conditions of the temporary housing were poor, and residents were often boiling in the summer and freezing in the winter. Moreover, in the aftermath of 3.11, the national government and Tepco strongly encouraged the whole nation to conserve electricity, meaning that buildings throughout Japan turned down or turned off their air conditioning in the summer. Temporary housing units rarely had good insulation and had thin rooftops, allowing them to overheat easily.

Fujiwara-san continued to emphasize that he and the locals did not tend to welcome visitors who came merely out of curiosity:

> We have had many visitors; it's not like we need more. And we are not victims forever. We can give our all (*gambaru*), since we share the same circumstances. We share the attitude that we will help each other. We've thought about things like starting community businesses, such as growing and selling vegetables.

This raised questions in my mind about how people elsewhere would perceive the safety of vegetables grown within fifty miles of Fukushima. When I looked outside our meeting space, I could see elementary school-aged children riding by on bicycles wearing face masks. In the seven years following 3.11, over two hundred children around Fukushima were diagnosed with thyroid cancer.[14] These factors typify the complexity of the challenges facing 3.11 survivors in these areas.

As I was looking at the children through a window, several women appeared, looking rather shy and reserved. First, four women from their thirties to sixties came in and sat down. Of the four, three were wearing large face masks. They did not look chatty or cheerful, and with masks covering their noses and mouths completely, it was hard to get a read on them.

Fujiwara-san said, "Why on earth are you all wearing facial masks today? We can hardly see your faces!" in a jovial manner, as if to make light of it. I felt a slightly tight and nervous energy from the women, and I felt uncertain whether our group was welcome. A few of the women responded that they had a cold and didn't want to spread it to others, hence the masks. They sat in silence while Fujiwara-san continued; they were soon joined by two more women.

Fujiwara-san next turned to the topic of the government's policy of protecting individual information. Because of this, even he could not identify all the residents' information in the temporary housing community. Some natural disaster survivors had been relocated to housing specially designated for survivors. This made it easier to connect with one another. Other survivors, however, had been relocated to mixed complexes. They didn't know who among them was a survivor, and they were prevented from finding out due to the privacy regulations.

When Fujiwara-san again began sharing that volunteers were often more bothersome than helpful, the women began to speak. The *kokoro no kea* (mental care) support they had been offered was a mixed bag. There were some volunteers the survivors simply did not or could not welcome. Some came assuming they'd be able to stay in the temporary housing alongside the survivors, but this was impossible as the housing was already stretched to capacity. They had recently received an invitation from an organization that wanted to send 130 volunteers for mental care. It was a nuisance, the women said; there was simply no way they could accommodate that many people.

The women began to talk about how difficult their situation had become. This difficulty was exacerbated by the high degree of uncertainty regarding their future. One woman noted:

> If they told me whether I could ever return to my hometown, then I'd be able to plan for my future. If I knew I could return, I'd be able to work hard with a sense of hope. Or if they told me I can never go back, I could plan accordingly and work towards a new future. But the government has been postponing this information every six months. So I have no idea regarding my future. And I have no hope.

Fujiwara-san said:

> There's a difference between just living and having *ikigai* (purpose in life) or having the hope to live. I wanted to give people here *ikigai* or some hope to live. So that is why we named this association "Hope Tree."

The group talked about how they could not remain victims forever. Fujiwara-san emphasized how important it is for people to become active members of society and not remain merely victims. He shared that people had started discussing the idea of becoming *jidai no kataribe* (narrators of the era). By narrating their experiences to those who had not experienced this earthquake, the Great East Japan Earthquake and Tsunami victims might be able offer help for future generations. Many people at the association felt a strong need to share their experiences with future generations to warn about the danger of natural disasters and what to do when a tsunami is approaching. Taking active social roles and becoming productive members of society was one goal they shared, something that could serve as *ikigai*.

"We were in a period of individualism until recently. But after 3.11, we've been shifting to an era of connection," Fujiwara-san said. "I am not sure whether that is an evolution or what."

Kura-san, a woman in her early sixties, replied, "This isn't new. It's basically mutual support, isn't it? We help each other when we are in trouble."

Tateno-san, a woman in her early sixties, then shared her story of joining the temporary housing on March 28:

> I started planting flowers on April 11 in front of Building No.3. Then I got to make friends, since the people who saw the flowers often chatted with me. So that was a bonus for me. Then there was this huge scary aftershake one day. It was so terrifying, but we could comfort each other by rubbing each other's backs.

Uchida-san, another woman in her sixties, said:

> We hear that we can stay here two more years, according to the government, but we don't know what will happen after that. I hope the city of Ibaragi can inherit this apartment complex from the government and manage it as a municipal dwelling house, so we can continue to stay here by paying this low rent.

TATENO-SAN'S STORY

After the meeting, I had the opportunity to speak with some of the committee members individually, including Tateno-san, whose story about planting flowers had moved me significantly.

"Thank you so much for your time and your story about planting flowers," I said. "My mother loves flowers, and your story made me think of my mother and that she might do something like that, too."

"I had to do something, you see. If I didn't have anything to do, I'd go crazy." With that, she almost broke into tears, which prompted the women around her to hug her and nod their heads in agreement (see figure 6).

Uchida-san, another of the women, stepped in to say:

> The aftershake on April 11, 2011 was remarkably scary. It was seriously scary, wasn't it? While I was rubbing other people's shoulders and backs to comfort them, I was very scared. Then that night, I was so scared that I went over and stayed at Tateno-san's room. Normally, no one would do such a thing as allowing someone else to overnight with them. Who knows what they might do to you.

Her point was that it was highly unusual in Japan for someone to simply allow a stranger to stay overnight at one's place so soon after meeting. It was a sign of how quickly people bonded after 3.11.

"What are you talking about? It was nothing," said Tateno-san, and patted Uchida-san's shoulders gently and warmly.

"Also, we were all comforted by Tateno-san's puppy," Uchida-san said, smiling. Tateno-san smiled also and showed me pictures of her puppy on her mobile phone.

"I cannot tell you how much I was comforted by this puppy," Tateno-san said. "She really cheered me up and comforted me. I was really hurt when someone who is also from North Ibaragi told me that I had already received a lot of support and that should be enough, and I should be satisfied with the support I had received."

Figure 6. Tateno-san and Uchida-san with the author, crying and laughing after telling the story of the flower garden. Photograph by Ichiro Yatsuzuka.

"We've lost everything," Uchida-san said. "Our houses, our jobs, everything. I'm living on my pension of $500 a month and now I don't even have a job. I have nothing. If you want to talk about the so-called 'support' we received, it was just supplies of food and so on, which we got three times. That's all we got."

Although people in Japan knew about areas such as Fukushima and Iwate, not many were aware that North Ibaragi had suffered from the earthquake and tsunami. Within Ibaragi, not all the areas were damaged. As a result, many thought that Ibaragi hadn't been damaged severely.

Uchida-san and Tateno-san went on to stress that "flowers and pets play a significant role" for them, and that "North Ibaragi women are strong and resilient" (see figures 7 and 8).

Figure 7. The flower garden created by Tateno-san. Photograph by Ichiro Yatsuzuka.

Figure 8. Another view of the flower garden created by Tateno-san. Photograph by Ichiro Yatsuzuka.

A SURVIVOR OF 3.11 FROM ISHINOMAKI

The people at the North Ibaragi meeting emphasized again and again that a strong bond had been created by sharing their experiences of 3.11. Many said that this bond was stronger than a blood connection.

These women's narratives resurfaced while I was interviewing another survivor. He was a retired gentleman whom I had met at a gathering for 3.11 survivors in Yokohama in Kanagawa prefecture. The Kanagawa Prefecture Residents' Activity Support Center had held a gathering for those who had been relocated from the severely affected regions to Kanagawa. At such gatherings, I heard many distressing stories. Person after person related witnessing the tsunami swallow up people they knew. They spoke about suffering from insomnia and anxiety about the future, and how alone they felt after being relocated so far from their native areas of Miyagi, Fukushima, and Iwate.

These gatherings were open to the public, and I attended several of them. That was how I met Oda-san, who ended up in the same small group I was assigned to for a discussion breakout session. Oda-san kindly volunteered to narrate his experience after the meeting.

At the time of our interview, Oda-san was sixty-nine. He had retired at sixty-one. He was from Ishinomaki, in Miyagi prefecture. Along with Fukushima and Iwate, Miyagi was one of the three areas designated as being most severely damaged. In Ishinomaki, the tsunami claimed almost 3,500 lives. It also destroyed some 54,000 houses and forced the evacuation of 50,758 people.[15]

Because he came from Ishinomaki, Oda-san did not experience the suffering associated with not being recognized as a person who had been badly impacted by the disaster. In this way, he differed from the group I had met in North Ibaragi. Nevertheless, he had clearly been badly impacted. His account shows the same themes of alienation, anxiety about the future, and a strong desire to belong to a community again. It also speaks powerfully to the fact that loneliness need not only be about human relations in a narrow sense; it can result from displacement, exile, and the loss of a place or environment where one felt meaning, belonging, and a feeling of being home (*ibasho*).[16]

Oda-san's Story

After the earthquake and tsunami, I lost my house. I went and stayed at my neighbor's house for five nights from March 11 until March 16.

Then from March 16, my wife, daughter and I moved to the Ishinomaki high school. It was being used as a shelter. At the time, the school's gymnasium was completely flooded, so we stayed in various classrooms.

I recall there were about 340 people or so at the shelter. Nineteen of us stayed in one classroom. There were nine people from my neighborhood. There was one blanket space for three of us, and we had to share one ball of rice and a half-bar of chocolate among the three of us. There was also one banana per person, and 1 liter of water or tea per person.

In any case, there were 70 pieces of bread and 40 balls of rice for some 366 people. But we didn't fight over food. I think we were lucky with our group leader. He was very good and our group was tightly united. The conditions weren't easy, but it was nice to bond with other people. I felt bonded with them.

We stayed at this shelter until March 29. The entire city was still flooded with water for two days after the tsunami. By March 13, the water had started subsiding, and we were able to walk a bit. On March 14, I began searching for people I knew. I also went back to my house. Unfortunately, the water was at the level of my neck at my house when the tsunami struck. So when I got back to the house, I saw that only the roof and pillars were still usable. Mine was only a one-story house, so it had to be demolished. None of the furniture could be saved, with the sole exception of my deceased parents' mortuary tablet and three sets of blankets that had been at the dry cleaners.

When the tsunami attacked, the three of us—my wife, my daughter, and myself—were all at home, inside our house. That morning, my wife had gone to the hospital. She has a leg problem and can't walk well. On the way back from the hospital, she went grocery shopping with my daughter. That was when the earthquake struck. Fortunately, they were able to return to home safely. That's why the three of us were there together in the house when the tsunami hit.

My daughter and wife drove the car out only to find out that the designated shelter was completely flooded. So, there was nothing for us to do but walk in the flood water. It came up to my thighs. Even today, my daughter says that she is sick of water because of that.

Eventually we found a two-story house. Our neighbors welcomed us in and we stayed there for five nights. Around March 29, the water had receded enough that people could go back to their homes, if they still had homes.

Once the water had subsided and the gymnasium became available, 130 of us moved into the gymnasium on March 31. Those who were fortunate enough to be able to return to their houses returned home that day, and some people moved to their relatives' places.

Many people were afraid of being alone at nights, including myself. The aftershocks were pretty bad, so I couldn't sleep well. 9:00 pm is lights out at the shelter, but I would wake up around 3:00 or 4:00 am. I used to wander around then. It got very chilly in the early mornings. 6:00 am was the time to wake up, and then we'd have breakfast at 7:00.

On March 29 we visited my son's place in Yokohama. We stayed with him for one month. Then this current temporary housing unit became available, and I drew a lottery to get in. I got my keys on April 20. So then we moved in. It's Kanagawa prefecture's public housing. I didn't feel comfortable depending on my son.

It's a five-story public housing building, and it accommodates 77 households in 50 units. Even though it's public housing, it became available as temporary housing, so I don't need to pay any rent for two years. But I have no idea whether there are other 3.11 survivors like myself in this building, because it is a mixture. It's predominantly regular residents along with a few people like myself from the 3.11-stricken areas. Because of privacy protections, I have no way of learning whether there are other comrades I could connect with here. So I felt alienated and lonely, especially for the first few months.

One day, I saw a flyer in my mailbox about a walking club. I thought I'd be able to make a connection and some human bonds if I joined this activity group. So I called the number. Oh, the person who picked up the phone was so kind! It's once a month, walking to Mt. Oyama, and then to Eno Island. And there are three members in it from the district I come from, and five people from the next district over.

Even now, I have a strong desire to go back to Ishinomaki. There are so many things I would like to do once I am back there! I was quite active in my local region and was serving in the local government. I'd like to continue being involved with the work there at the local government, and also to pass on this work and my experience to younger generations, because there will be a generational change inevitably. I want to make sure the generational change is smooth, and connect our current work to the next generation.

I still visit Ishinomaki regularly. I visit there once a month. I used to stay at the shelter. I'd stay at a shelter for two nights and then one night at my acquaintance's place. Now the shelters are closed, since they built enough temporary housing. You know, there aren't any vacancies at the hotels in Ishinomaki. And you know why? All the hotels are packed with all these volunteers! So I bring my camping sleeping bag and stay at my acquaintance's place.

I always take the night bus that leaves here at 10:15 pm, connects at Sendai at 5:00 am, and then reaches Ishinomaki at 6:00 am. I do the same on my way back to save from having to overnight somewhere in Ishinomaki.

When I arrive at Sendai, I usually take my breakfast there because there is hardly anything in Ishinomaki. So when I come back, I hop onto the night bus that leaves Sendai at 11:00 pm and I'm back in Kanagawa at 6:30 am. It costs 6000 yen ($60), so it's not cheap.

I think they need to establish a system to accommodate people like us back in our hometowns. I feel like every day goes by so fast. I'm completely preoccupied with Ishinomaki. Mentally, I am always turning towards the direction of Ishinomaki. But it's not easy to find a place to stay there.

Well, I still wake up in the middle of the night and I can't go back to sleep. This has been continuing since 3.11. While I lie there awake, I always think about the same things: the things I need to do, and so on.

I used to live with others in the local community. No one locked their front door, so if it rained, someone would pick up your clothing that was hanging outside to dry and they'd bring it indoors. Our doors were always open to each other. Here, I don't feel I can establish those kinds of bonds and human connections. I don't know my next door neighbors in this apartment building. Also, my health isn't that great, and I'm sure it's because of the stress. My blood pressure rose by 20, and my cholesterol levels became high, too. My bone density decreased, and I was told it suddenly dropped to only 69% of the average for my age. I used to drink a bottle of milk every morning when I was in Ishinomaki.

I also worry about my wife and daughter. I know they're not sleeping well either. But I don't have any complaints about our current living conditions or about our room. I'm grateful for all the kindness we received to be able to live like this. I am most grateful about still being alive. I feel that I have been sustained, given life (*ikasareteiru*). I feel that there must be some challenges or tasks I am supposed to accomplish with this life, since I was given a second chance. I really have a strong desire to help other people and wish to contribute to a society. I just want to do something.

6 The Anatomy of Resilience

My in-person visits, community discussions, and individual interviews proved valuable in providing a more personal and varied understanding of the aftermath of 3.11. While some of the things that individuals recounted were familiar to me from media reports, there were many things that were new. Most notably, I hadn't been aware of the variety of experiences among the stricken areas. In the media, these areas tended to be simply categorized as "the disaster-stricken areas" or "the 3.11 survivors." While the news provided a "master narrative" of the events of 3.11, my visits to North Ibaragi and support group meetings elsewhere in Japan provided a far more variegated understanding of the effects of the disasters.

I had also been completely unaware of "invisible" stricken areas like North Ibaragi—places that had been severely affected but largely ignored because they lay along the periphery of affected regions. The people in North Ibaragi described themselves as "invisible" precisely because they weren't seen or attended to in mass media accounts and were therefore ignored in the larger narrative around 3.11. Had I not gone personally to see them, they would have remained invisible to me as well.

Most importantly, I was able to experience the affect of the individuals and the community: their emotions and feelings, their experiences, their hopes and fears. The sense of uncertainty they felt about the future; their loneliness and sense of abandonment by the wider society; their resilience, manifested in simple acts of kindness to one another; and the broader impulse to form a new community and human connections that extended beyond kinship were almost wholly uncommunicated by television or newspaper reports. Yet these affective dimensions of the 3.11 disasters and their aftermath were loud and clear in the narratives of these individuals. Moreover, even in my limited interactions, I was able to listen to a range of experiences from different groups: those in temporary housing, those who were not in temporary housing but who had been affected by 3.11, and those who were scattered in different parts of Japan after their relocation and were therefore isolated from other survivors.

The various stories I heard revealed a few common themes. On the one hand were suffering, anxiety, missing home, and uncertainty about the future. On the other hand were the determination to make their lives worthwhile; the resolve to have agency and not be merely victims; and an emphasis on the strong need to establish human connections (*kizuna*), community, and belonging.

In this chapter I present a theoretical analysis of the experiences of the 3.11 survivors I interacted with by exploring a few concepts that shed light on such experiences and can more generally contribute to the anthropology of subjectivity. The first concept is moral injury, a term created to expand our understanding of PTSD. After introducing this concept, I go over the themes of adversity that emerged from the narratives of the previous chapter.

This is followed by a discussion of the theory of affordances, presented by the psychologist James Gibson, and its relevance for an anthropology of subjectivity. I explain this theory and then employ it to explore the themes of loneliness and alienation that I encountered among 3.11 survivors. Last, I turn to the aspects of resilience that emerged among the narratives of 3.11 survivors and discuss the importance of a broader conception of resilience that includes social and communal—not just individual—resilience. These conclusions align broadly with the work of other anthropologists such as Neely Laurenzo Myers, who has written on the importance of moral agency in dealing with mental illnesses such as schizophrenia, and Karen Nakamura, whose research on Bethel House, a small intentional community in Japan for people with schizophrenia, explores the role community, belonging, and sanctuary play in supporting resilience.[1]

By exploring these two dimensions of adversity and resilience, not only do we see the individual components of each, but we also see how they relate. Just as importantly, we gain clear insight into the ways in which the existing mental care efforts—especially state-sponsored mental care—either supported the resilience of survivors or failed to do so, and why. The purpose of this process is diagnostic, but not merely so; the more important aim is to support the exploration of better remedies and methods for supporting resilience and promoting moral repair.

MORAL INJURY

The previous chapter revealed some of the limitations of a mental health approach focused on individuals and trauma in isolation. Two aspects of such an approach, individualism and a deficit mentality, were rejected by 3.11 survivors. They did not deny that they had individual experiences of hardship or that they had suffered. But they strongly emphasized the wish for a communal focus and a strengths-based approach to resilience and agency.

The term *moral injury* was originally coined by the psychiatrist Jonathan Shay and his colleagues to refer to the injury of moral conscience suffered by military personnel and veterans, for whom the labels PTSD and mental illness were stigmatizing.[2] Since then, definitions have continued to evolve, but following psychologist Jacob Farnsworth and colleagues, I define moral injury broadly as a form of ongoing suffering caused by committing, witnessing, or being the victim of acts of violence that deeply violate one's moral beliefs or expectations of how people should behave.[3] By "acts of violence," however, we should understand that these can be acts of commission or omission. This is especially important in understanding the moral injury of survivors that took place in the aftermath of 3.11.

Moral injury literature often associates the term with a sense of betrayal that results in condemnation of others; a damaged sense of oneself as a moral agent; and feelings of guilt, shame, anger, and helplessness. The concept of moral injury expands our understanding of traumatic events by attending to triggering events that do not necessarily involve threats to an individual's life or physical safety. It also shifts the focus away from an often medicalized and stigmatizing understanding of PTSD as an individual affliction toward a consideration of the moral, social, political, and systemic causes of traumatic experience. Finally, moral injury is an example of what I call "afflictions of subjectivity," in that it reshapes a person's or community's view of themselves, others, and the world.

Moral injury suggests that solutions must lie in the restructuring of societies and institutions themselves, such that they no longer support moral injury and instead promote moral repair and the protection of individuals' moral consciences. On the surface, the language of moral injury may appear to be, like PTSD, a deficit-based, rather than a strengths-based, approach. However, its shift of focus to the social origins of such suffering means that it moves away from an individual-level treatment to structures of society that can be more or less supportive of resilience and healing. Also, by using the term *injury* rather than *disorder*, moral injury suggests that there is nothing fundamentally wrong with the individuals affected, and that they can heal.

While the immediate experience of 3.11 was clearly traumatic for those who witnessed it directly, what survivors in North Ibaragi and elsewhere experienced in the aftermath of the disaster seems to be a clear case of moral injury. This can be seen more clearly by looking at five major themes that emerged from the narratives of 3.11 survivors. Because they involve fear and a feeling of being separated and isolated from others, each of these are factors that I believe contributed to a sense of collective loneliness.

Distrust of Government and Media

The sense of distrust toward the government and media was particularly strong among people in Ibaragi, both the local participants in the workshop I attended and residents of the temporary housing community I visited in North Ibaragi. Ibaragi became a zone of invisibility and a zone of social abandonment and neglect, not counted among the three main areas that were termed the "3.11 stricken areas": namely Iwate, Miyagi, and Fukushima. Even the not so favorably perceived mental health teams were not sent to Ibaragi. The media hardly reported on Ibaragi as a place that had experienced 3.11 as a major disaster. In part, this was because the North Ibaragi coast had been severely damaged, while South Ibaragi had been less badly damaged. As a result, Ibaragi had not lost as many lives as the other three prefectures.

The natural disaster itself had been traumatic, but on top of that, residents felt that their area was neglected, unrecognized, and invisible to the government and media, in turn creating moral injury. Several of those in Ibaragi said that it was painful to hear nonresidents claim that Ibaragi had not suffered badly. It meant that their pain and suffering were not recognized, and this made them feel alone. This sense of alienation created a distinctive kind of loneliness, a feeling that no one understood them except those who shared the same suffering. It was almost as though Japan as a nation had abandoned Ibaragi.

Distrust of Mental Health Service Providers and Volunteers

The 3.11 survivors expressed a deep gulf between what they needed and what providers were attempting to give them. Volunteers and providers shared similar sentiments, saying that they would be more welcome if they only brought food, drink, and other basic supplies. From the narratives of those I met in North Ibaragi, the mental health groups organized by volunteers were seen as an imposition rather than as something the residents wanted or needed, especially given the fact that volunteers often wanted or expected housing and amenities for themselves.

The mental health-care groups were set up to provide services in the wake of trauma. They looked for disorders like PTSD and treated them. But this was not what many 3.11 survivors wanted. They did not appear to value the "top-down" approach to mental health-care that was being offered. This suggests that what they were seeking was not primarily mental health treatment, but moral repair and community care. Even the Ministry of Health, Labour and Welfare, which was responsible for organizing the mental health-care teams, consisting of psychiatrists, clinical psychologists, and other mental health-care professionals, admitted that such teams were not welcomed by local communities.[4]

In many ways the reactions of 3.11 survivors in the communities I visited reflect the history of the professionalization and medicalization of mental health in Japan. Kitanaka chronicles how the medicalization of depression in Japan was founded on the imposition of psychiatric language and disease categories onto patients, rather than on the basis of patients' agency and their own illness narratives (a key difference highlighted by Kleinman's landmark work, *Illness Narratives*).[5] Kitanaka writes, "Until relatively recently, psychiatry in Japan was able to maintain its authority not because its knowledge was accepted as cultural common sense, but because it was able to monopolize medical knowledge and exercise its jurisdiction for treating those diagnosed as mentally ill even without their consent."[6] She notes, "Indeed, one may even argue that the history of modern psychiatry in Japan is characterized by this radical disconnection with subjective pain."[7]

Indeed, much of the history of medical anthropology has been dedicated to making the case for the importance of attending to, rather than ignoring, the subjective experiences of those who are suffering, with the belief that this will support the provision of effective health-care and healing. In her ethnography of Bethel, a home for people with schizophrenia in Japan, Nakamura describes how health-care professionals would visit Bethel's chief physician Dr. Kawamura as "psychotourists" to learn "what Dr. Kawamura calls the 'Philosophy of Non-Support (*Hienjo Ron*)', which he [Dr. Kawamura] contrasted to the medical model that dominated psychiatric care in Japan." Nakamura explains, "In the non-support model, the goal is not to cure or even to 'help'—a position that too often is unilateral. In the non-support model the 'expert' takes a position of powerlessness. Their goal is to help heal and recover, to encourage, and to help people get a better understanding of themselves through self-directed research. . . . People are encouraged to talk with other people in similar and different situations and make their own connections."[8]

On the other hand, 3.11 survivors did greatly appreciate workshops on creative arts. One participant excitedly said that she loved the workshop led by a Japanese paper-collage artist on how to create collages using pieces of colored paper. Arts activities empowered residents. They were communal in nature, rather than one-on-one psychotherapeutic interventions. Residents welcomed group activities, and they appreciated the ability to create things for themselves. These were forms of care that helped people feel like active agents and a community. The loss and lack of community care was central to their suffering and their experience of loneliness and abandonment. Therefore, the establishment of community care came to be seen as essential for their resilience. They seemed to want and need to "share a world" again.

Harmful Rumors

A further double-bind arose from what survivors called *fūhyō higai*, or "injury due to harmful rumors." On the one hand, the people of Ibaragi wanted to be legitimately acknowledged as being in a disaster-stricken area so that they could receive recognition and material support. On the other hand, they did not want Ibaragi to be viewed as a dangerous area contaminated by radiation.

I found Ibaragi to be doubly unfortunate in this regard. Although it was not recognized as a central, legitimately stricken area, the media focused on Ibaragi's proximity to Fukushima and the nuclear reactors, as well as the higher levels of radiation contamination in its fish and vegetables. As a result, people did not want to visit Ibaragi during the tourist season, which badly affected the important tourist industry there. This led to a lot of complaints about *fūhyō higai*; individuals felt that they were being injured by unfair and harmful rumors. This created a further sense of moral injury and sense of distrust, distance, and alienation from the media and those outside Ibaragi.

The Scissors-Like Disparity and Differences in Temperature

On top of feeling abandoned by the government and media, a rift was growing among the 3.11 survivors. Two terms were used repeatedly: *hasami-jō kakusa*, meaning a widening or "scissors-like" disparity, and *ondo-sa*, meaning a "difference in temperature" or "viewing things differently." Among the residents in inland Ibaragi, some had quickly recovered from the 3.11 damage and resumed their normal lives, while others were still struggling with a precarious future. Within six months, the sense of unity among survivors in the immediate aftermath of 3.11 gave way to this widening gap between those who were steadily on the path to recovery and those who felt left behind, still stuck in temporary housing and without employment.

Ondo-sa (temperature) also pointed to a similar phenomenon: people felt differently about 3.11 and its aftermath. Using the term *temperature* to suggest this difference is particularly interesting, as temperature is something that a group of people should all feel together; it should either be very hot or very cold. When this is not the case, it causes problems. If people are indoors and some find it too warm and others too cold, the heating or air conditioning can't be made to accommodate everyone. Feeling the temperature in different ways creates not just practical problems, but emotional ones as well, namely a sense of disharmony. Elsewhere I have written of the importance of "sharing a world"—that as social beings, we naturally want to feel that we resonate affectively with others.[9] It is generally disturbing to us when this does not happen, like when we are deeply moved by something that another person harshly criticizes, or when we find beauty in something but others find only ugliness. This aspect of "sharing a world" is certainly emphasized in Japanese society. The strong sense of *not* sharing the world in Ibaragi—both among residents and with outsiders—appeared as yet another component in people's experience of alienation, abandonment, loneliness, and not being understood and empathized with by others.

A Precarious Future

All the groups I encountered expressed anxiety over a precarious future. Those in temporary housing had been told they would only be able to stay there for two years; beyond that it was murky. Like Oda-san from Ishinomaki, whose narrative I related in the previous chapter, many were desperate to return to their hometowns and rebuild their houses and lives. Many people recounted that they did not know what their future would look like, especially because they didn't know when or whether they would be able to go home. This kind of precariousness prevented them from having hope, future plans, or a sense of direction.

Tōhoku is not a typical urban area like Tokyo, Osaka, and Kobe. It had a strong community life. I was surprised to hear that people didn't lock their front doors, and that their houses were left open to their neighbors. I had never experienced life that way. For those who had been so used to being in a close community where everyone knew their neighbors and helped one another, being uprooted from that community would be doubly challenging. Some in temporary housing were able to re-create a sense of community, but many experienced lasting loneliness. The importance of close community for many in Tōhoku made this precarious future and uncertainty around returning to one's community all the more poignant.

SOCIAL AFFORDANCES FOR LONELINESS

It was alienating and morally injuring for those in North Ibaragi to not receive sufficient material supplies, attention, and recognition from the wider Japanese community. On a micro level, North Ibaragi people also felt that other Ibaragi residents in less affected areas did not recognize their suffering and need for support. They were thus doubly rejected by the larger community of Japan and their smaller community of Ibaragi.

The psychologist Gibson developed what he called "a theory of affordances," which suggests that aspects of an environment "afford" certain perceptions and behaviors.[10] A strong enough flat surface affords standing, whereas a chair of a suitable height to one's body affords sitting. Affordance theory suggests that there is a complementarity between the environment and one's subjective experience that makes certain perceptions and behaviors easier than others. Gibson writes, "The *affordances* of the environment are what it *offers* to the animal, what it *provides* or *furnishes*, either for good or ill."[11]

Although Gibson focused mainly on perception and behavior, and therefore his theory might seem ill suited for the study of society and culture, much less subjectivity, I believe this is in fact far from the case. He himself recognized that his theory included a "radical hypothesis, for it implies that the 'values' and 'meanings' of things in the environment can be directly perceived. Moreover, it would explain the sense in which values and meanings are external to the perceiver."[12] I believe this observation takes on additional significance when we consider, as Gibson did, that society and culture are, at least in large part, the product of a long process to establish affordances supportive of human flourishing. This is because affordances can be social as well as physical. Gibson writes, "It is also a mistake to separate the cultural environment from the natural environment, as if there were a world of mental products distinct from the world of material products. There is only one world, however diverse."[13] In fact, since it is obvious that many behaviors require the presence or participation of others, it is clear that other people offer affordances just as the physical environment does. He notes, "The other animals afford, above all, a rich and complex set of interactions, sexual, predatory, nurturing, fighting, playing, cooperating, and communicating. What other persons afford, comprises the whole realm of social significance for human beings."[14]

In this reading, society itself is the product of human beings' efforts to establish affordances more suitable to what helps them survive and thrive, and less suitable to suffering and death. This aligns closely with my arguments in chapter 1 for seeing society as in large part the external manifestation of subjectivity. But is everyone within a given society exactly the same? Is any individual replaceable with any other individual, or any community replaceable with another? Gibson's concept of niche is useful here and closely related to the Japanese concept of *ibasho*. He writes, "In ecology a niche is a setting of environmental features that are suitable for an animal, into which it fits metaphorically."[15] A niche is a place where the affordances of the environment (both physical and social) suit the individuals who reside in that niche (both physically and mentally), contributing to their survival and well-being. Those who can't find their niche are at risk.

The many suicide website visitors whose posts I examined were searching for their niche, their *ibasho*, and they saw it as crucial for their ability to survive. When residents were displaced from their communities due to 3.11, they lost their niches. By losing those environments that afforded their form of existence, they lost their way of life. They lost certain ways of being that had become impossible without the affordances of their niche. When I encountered them, I saw them struggling to re-create that niche, either by trying to reestablish forms of life that they had lost or by trying to return to their hometown, the physical location of their niche. As Gibson writes, "The natural environment offers many ways of life, and different animals have different ways of life. The niche implies a kind of animal, and the animal implies a kind of niche. Note the complementarity of the two."[16] He also notes, "We all fit into the substructures of the environment in our various ways, for we were all, in fact, formed by them. We were created by the world we live in."[17]

If we expand Gibson's theory of affordances to include not just perceptions and behaviors, but also ways of feeling, thinking, and believing about the world, then the theory has significant value for anthropologists of subjectivity. Japanese society has affordances that support certain ways of being, certain ways of perceiving self, other, and society. If society repeatedly sends signals indicating that individuals don't matter, such as denying, ignoring, or even actively rejecting subjective experiences of suffering, then such a society has high affordances for loneliness.

In the case of 3.11, we see that affordances in Japanese society allowed for systemic inequality and neglect. Natural disasters are unavoidable, but the social and governmental responses to them can vary. The highly centralized and standardized way the Japanese government operates was inadvertently conducive to creating zones of neglect, abandonment, and invisibility. Forms of government shape forms of affect; forms of society shape forms of experience.

If we return to the way internet group suicide was initially handled by the Japanese media, we recall that the suffering of those who committed suicide was actively rejected. They were seen as thoughtless, careless individuals who didn't understand the value of life. This narrative negated their subjective experiences, and it sent a signal to others that if they felt a similar way, they were wrong. This rejection of the value of individual suffering is again a social affordance for loneliness.

At the same time, people are not merely victims. They seek out well-being and seek to find places and communities that support their survival. The 3.11. survivors I met had lost their *ibasho*, but they were seeking to find it again, either by establishing a new *ibasho* or by returning home. As humans, we are not just created by the world we live in; we also seek to have the agency to co-create the world we live in.

ASPECTS OF RESILIENCE

If structures of government and society provide affordances for subjective states such as loneliness, then by definition they can also serve as affordances for resilience, such as by supporting human connection, a sense of belonging, being seen, and mattering, and by facilitating places of belonging (*ibasho*) for those who would otherwise lack it. These affordances should not be seen as either-or situations, but as complex circumstances existing along continua. Once we have identified social structures as important contexts for suffering and moral injury, we must also investigate the ways in which they can serve to promote resilience, moral repair, and healing.

In a study of 241 evacuees from 3.11 regions, nursing scholar Hiroko Kukihara and her colleagues concluded that "depression and PTSD are prevalent among the survivors of massive earthquakes, tsunamis, and accidents from nuclear power plants. However, the results also showed that some survivors managed to endure the traumatic events relatively well, and resilience was a significant protective factor in dealing with such events. Therefore, it is crucial to assist survivors in improving their resilience."[18]

The narratives of 3.11 survivors also displayed these aspects of resilience; they were clearly trying to reestablish aspects of social life that would help them cope with previous and ongoing difficult experiences. They spoke about what they appreciated in their current living situations, what they enjoyed, and what they had been doing to ease their loneliness and anxiety. Just as themes of adversity emerged from their narratives, so too did themes of resilience. The first was agency: the importance of being independent with active social roles, and not being treated as mere helpless victims. Aligned with this was a theme of community care and mutual support among survivors. Additionally, there was a strong theme of the importance of establishing human connections and bonds among survivors and establishing or returning to places of belonging (*ibasho*).

Although resilience is often defined as the capacity to "bounce back" after suffering adversity, much in the way that a piece of metal might bend back to its original shape after receiving a blow, I draw from a broader and multidimensional model of resilience. Unlike inanimate objects, people rarely return to an original state after significant adversity. Significant wounds to the mind or body do not leave a person exactly the same as they were before, even after healing has occurred. Our experiences change us, sometimes forever. And unlike inanimate objects, we human beings can become stronger and more resilient over time. We are also supported in our resilience by the presence and support of others, as well as by the structural and cultural systems we inhabit.

In her book *Spacious Minds*, which examines the resilience of the Tibetan community in exile, anthropologist Sara Lewis writes,

> Resilience is not a mere absence of suffering. Rather, it is the way a person copes with adversity that is evidence of resilience. Like suffering, resilience is also culturally shaped and defined. In the United States, for example, we tend to think of resilient individuals as those who can withstand pain and injustice. But for Tibetans, those considered most resilient are often those who are deeply affected and transformed by adversity. Resilience here is not defined as the ability to "bounce back," like a physical material that can withstand brunt force. It is not grit. Instead, those who are most resilient use their vulnerability as a way to deepen compassion. In this way, compassion is both the result of resilience and a method to train in resilience. Similar to what researchers call "post-traumatic growth," Tibetans in their practice of resilience use suffering as a transformative opportunity. Because suffering is seen as an unavoidable aspect of everyday life, this approach is not limited to remarkable individuals.[19]

I draw from work on resilience that examines its multiple dimensions, including how resilience manifests and can be cultivated on personal, interpersonal, and systems levels.[20] I also, like Lewis, see resilience as involving not just coping and adaptation, but also the possibility of transformation: turning one's past survival from adversity into something positive for the present and future. I also see resilience as something that does not exist just within individuals, but can exist between and among individuals, and that can also be a feature of communities and society itself. We see this, for example, in the support sought out by suicide website visitors and even, one could argue, in the wish for strangers to find others to commit internet group suicide with. The working definition of resilience I use, therefore, is the enduring capability of a person, a group, and a community to cope with, adapt, and transform adverse circumstances in order to survive and flourish. The word *enduring* here refers to the fact that resilience is a lifelong process and also to the fact that it exists along a continuum. Rather than viewing people as having or not having resilience, we should see that people can have more or less resilience to specific forms of adversity. In this way, we can consider those who commit internet group suicide as having and seeking resilience, even if we wish to promote changes in society that enable such individuals to experience different kinds of resilience so that they might have less reason to choose to kill themselves.

ACTIVE SOCIAL ROLES AND COMMUNITY CARE

Along with the rejection of the mental health-care teams, there was a strong sense that only North Ibaragi survivors knew what kind of care people actually wanted. It was not that they did not want to receive any care or support whatsoever, but they rejected support that put them in the role of passive recipients and victims who could only receive, not contribute. They wished to receive support that would enable them to be more independent and self-sufficient. They wanted to maintain their independence, autonomy, and agency. They desired roles in which they could play a positive and contributory part.

One example was their suggestion to become *jidai no kataribe*, or storytellers of the era, so that they could be valuable assets in narrating their experiences of the earthquake and tsunami for the benefit of future generations. While altruistic, such storytelling is also self-beneficial. They had seen the destruction and loss of life from the earthquake and tsunami firsthand. Some had seen people drowning before their eyes, or being enveloped and washed away by the giant waves. When they slept, they said, these visions came back to them. They would reach out to try to save their drowning friends, neighbors, or family members, only to wake up just before they could save them. There would be some therapeutic benefit, they hoped, in being able to warn others of the dangers of natural disasters. Their grandparents, they shared, used to know such things from past natural disasters, but the younger people in Ibaragi had never experienced a tsunami and therefore didn't know even the most basic facts about them. They had the ability now to confer such information and play an active and constructive role in society.

One individual said, "There are things we need to share and pass on to the next generations and those who haven't suffered from this natural disaster. We also need to take on social roles. It is a necessity. *There is a general rule* about the spirit of helping each other."

The women talked about growing their own vegetables in their gardens and eventually having the means to sell them as merchants. Some of them were fishers. They jokingly told me, "We North Ibaragi women are strong! We fishers are strong, aren't we?" They were half-laughing and half-crying; their words of self-praise were a form of comfort to them.

This need to assert one's autonomy and to find an active and constructive role for oneself revealed itself on multiple occasions. It was intimately connected to the path to recovery, happiness, and moral repair. This was combined with a strong reluctance to become a burden on others, an eternal victim. As we saw in the case of Oda-san, he was unwilling to stay at his son's place in Kanagawa, despite not having a stable residence for himself. He combined a strong desire to return to the community he had in his hometown of Ishinomaki with a reluctance to move into his son's place, where he would feel like a burden.

BONDS (*KIZUNA*)

After 3.11, *kizuna* (bonds) became a very popular term in Japan. Even those not directly affected by 3.11 seemed to momentarily reassess their priorities in life. Reports indicate that nationwide more people started visiting their families and elderly parents rather than going abroad for the holidays. Television reports noted that people found human bonds, *kizuna*, to be the most important thing since 3.11.

Kizuna was used frequently by the survivors I met and spoke with, but it wasn't restricted to family. Instead, the human bonds among survivors were based on having shared the hardships of 3.11. The survivors I spoke with in North Ibaragi had a strong sense that only those who had shared in the experience of the natural disaster could understand and help each other. As several of the women noted, they felt a strong bond among themselves, "much stronger than connections of blood." Traditionally, blood ties are considered the strongest type of bond in Japan, followed by the ties created through one's corporate or company "family," but 3.11 showed that the sharing of an experience could be just as strong. This connects with a broader trend in Japanese society, where human bonds created through common experience trump more traditional connections of workplace and family.

North Ibaragi survivors sought genuine bonds (*kizuna*) instead of the instrumentalized services they were receiving from mental health providers, despite the fact that the latter were more professional. Indeed, widespread interest in *kizuna* across Japan may be correlated with an increasing professionalization of care and service, another possible unintended consequence of neoliberalism. This suggests that it is not just any kind of social bond that is supportive of recovery. Anthropologist Cheryl Mattingly writes of interactive social spaces as "moral laboratories."[21] Myers draws upon Mattingly's work to suggest that the types of bonds supportive of recovery are those that allow for and promote moral agency.[22]

Interestingly, in my own ethnographic work presented here, the questions of moral agency and being a good person (or being seen as a good person) are subsumed under the larger categories of human flourishing and meaning, as noted in the terms *ikigai* and *ikiru imi*. This suggests to me that an anthropology of the good and the anthropology of ethics cannot be tied solely to a Western conception of ethics, but should be expanded to include diverse cultural frames of what makes a meaningful or good life. While being seen as a moral agent can be important in many circumstances, it may only be one possible source of meaning. After all, not every type of human being can be recognized equally as a moral agent, and to be recognized as a moral agent is not the same, nor as fundamental, as being recognized as a human being worthy of respect, worthy of value, and worthy of care. Regarding the issue of moral agency, we can ask the same question: What about those who are prevented from doing the moral work that would lead to others granting them moral agency or recognizing them as moral agents? Many of the same categories apply: children, those who are cognitively or physically disabled, and those who are prevented through other means such as incarceration, but also those who have suffered moral injury. Indeed, my research on Naikan suggests that healing can come from a sense of having been recognized and loved despite not having been a moral agent.[23]

The work of Mattingly and Myers therefore offers us powerful tools for assessing the resilience shown by the North Ibaragi communities I visited and for thinking about questions of moral agency, meaning, and value in the establishment of an anthropology of the good. But what happens when the need for intimate relationships is not sought out or provided in a community form, but rather through the forces of the market economy? The question then becomes whether such manifestations of commercialized and commodified intimacy are supportive of recovery and moral agency.

THE COMMODIFICATION OF INTIMACY

In a room a few women are seated around a table, watching a video on a small portable screen. Seated with them, and also watching the video, is a good-looking man with a very stylish haircut. The video plays back a number of terrible things happening: children dying, people being separated from loved ones, small pets in distress, and other emotionally charged scenes. The man starts to shed tears, and soon the women follow. As they start to cry, the man gets up and walks around the room, slowly and respectfully wiping tears from their cheeks with a handkerchief.

This is a session provided by Ikemeso Danshi or Handsome Crying Boy, a company that was set up to provide this service of allowing Japanese women to cry in a safe, carefully cultivated environment, for a fee. The founder of the company, Hiroki Terai, came across the idea while writing a book on divorce in Japan. He came to realize that many Japanese women failed to see their divorces through to conclusion because of the many legal and practical obstacles they faced; these women also never got the chance to cry and let their emotions out. So he came up with the idea of providing a service that would allow them to experience the catharsis of crying in a shared space.[24]

Japan has a large and well-known sex industry, called by the euphemistic term *soapland*, but what is interesting about new phenomena like the "crying boy" service is that they involve the commodification not of sex, but of intimacy and companionship. This too has a long history in Japan. An obvious example is the numerous "host" and "hostess clubs," where young men and women provide an open ear and companionship to patrons, who in turn pay far higher than normal prices for their drinks. Allison wrote her first book on Japan on these clubs and this phenomenon, and they remain popular to this day. But recent years have seen a proliferation of new forms of the commodification of intimacy, enacted between strangers or sometimes with inanimate objects.

An example of the former is "co-sleeping specialty shops." This is featured in the film *Shoplifters*, which I discuss later, in which one of the main characters is a young woman who works at such a facility. At these establishments, customers pay by the hour or portion thereof to lie down with young women, such as with their head in the woman's lap or with her head in the customer's lap. Other services can include hugging or sleeping side by side, but no sexual services are provided.

An example of commodified intimacy with inanimate objects is the popularity of the *dakimakura* or "body pillow." These are long pillows roughly the size of a small person (fifty-nine or sixty-three inches long) that can be embraced in bed, akin to what was formerly called a "Dutch wife." Printed on the pillow, or on the pillowcase, is typically a popular animated character, such as a pretty boy or girl. These pillows can also be called "love pillows," and people form relationships with their pillows that are akin to real-life romantic relationships, even calling them their "wife" (*waifu*).

It is difficult to not see these phenomena as manifestations of loneliness. They are also, however, manifestations of a lack of availability of genuine human relationships. Commodified intimacy is easy; it can be bought, it is bounded, it is predictable. But it is also conditional upon an economic exchange. Reciprocal care and helping is a common feature of adult life, but in most societies its character changes when it is enforced or commodified.[25] Nevertheless, the wish for genuine care appears to result in a willingness to settle for something that looks like it. As we saw in the words of one suicide website visitor, "As I cannot believe in true love, I seek even just the words."[26]

This is not to say that paid care is necessarily devoid of genuine affection; the two can certainly go hand in hand. But the increasing commodification of intimacy may suggest that noncommodified forms of intimacy—again, those that depend only on genuine other-oriented feelings or on noncommodified reciprocity—are on the decline. The reduction of human kindness to a monetary exchange is the reduction of human value and worth to a price tag. Since intimacy—genuinely relating to one another in close and trusting relationships—is the very thing that lies at the core of and defines our humanity, the commodification of intimacy seems like the commodification of humanity itself.

SOCIAL AND CULTURAL RESILIENCE

The links between trauma, adversity, loneliness, and human connection may not seem obvious at first. To elucidate this, it will be helpful to turn to the work of psychological anthropologist Rebecca Lester, much of whose work has focused on eating disorders, trauma, and the essentially relational nature of healing. In an incredibly insightful passage, Lester explains that we must think of trauma not as the intrapsychic injury of an individual, but as a relational injury, a rupture that exposes our "ontological aloneness":

> People find ways to go on living—not just by resolving deep psychological conflicts or by reorganizing their experience to meet existing categories, but through ongoing, iterative, continuous processes of meaning-making that emerge *in relationship with others*, across a variety of levels and contexts, and through time. A traumatic event is traumatic precisely because it sheers us off from our expected connections with others, from our perceived social supports, from our basic sense of safety, however locally construed. Whether this happens in sexual abuse, war, death, torture, natural disasters, spirit attacks, soul loss, or any number of other things, experiences that radically sever regular, everyday modes of basic human connection and relationship bring us face-to-face with the limits of our own existence. We glimpse the edge of our very being, and we feel our ontological aloneness. If we think of "trauma" as a relational injury rather than a purely intrapsychic or structural one, we can see even more clearly that, however it is locally defined, [it] is hardly over once the immediate danger has passed—it simply enters a new phase. Through human relationships, a traumatized person retethers to the world.[27]

As I have argued, this dimension of ontological aloneness is built into the very nature of our consciousness and subjectivity as human beings. It is tied to the fact that we always experience the world from a first-person perspective, from a dualistic consciousness that fundamentally separates self from environment and other: one that constitutes the self through its differentiation from what is not-self. At the same time, I have spoken of our social nature, the fact that we are also ontologically interdependent and interconnected, that our very existence—including the existence of our self, consciousness, and subjectivity—is inseparable from, and dependent upon, others. Self is always not-other, but without other, there is no self. What Lester points to is that this fundamental condition is at play in the living and reliving of trauma, but also in the healing of trauma and the strengthening of resilience.

On that notion of healing, Lester makes another important point:

> If trauma is a discrete event or set of events that happened in the past, predicated on a clear dichotomy of agency between doer and done-to, we are significantly constrained in how we understand recovery. We cannot go back in time. We cannot undo the event. It is over and done with. The best we can do is try to lessen the impact, reduce the intrusion of memories, calm the "what ifs" and the ruminations about "what could I have done differently?" If we broaden our understanding of what trauma is from the event itself to the event *plus* its ongoing psychic, emotional, embodied, interpersonal life . . . then we have a different story. One may no longer be in imminent danger, but we could say that one is still in the midst of the trauma. Far from being a descent into victimhood . . . such a revisioning allows for a different ending.[28]

If trauma is fundamentally relational, we would expect recovery from trauma to be as well. Lester affirms this: "Far more important than the internal cognitive and emotional work of how one relates to the *trauma* is the interpersonal and social work of how one relates to other *people.* In other words, they illustrate that trauma is not simply a response to a particular *event* but is more productively understood as a rupture in the social fabric that becomes manifest *in* the event—both as a context that produced the trauma and as the individual and social responses to the aftermath."[29] Thus, Lester notes that "the rebuilding of social connection is [critical] to recovering from traumatic experiences. We might go so far as to say this *is* the work of recovery."[30]

If the rebuilding of social connection—*kizuna*—is critical to recovery from trauma, then the commodification of intimacy in a society becomes a more serious issue. The rise of this industry indicates that people are seeking human connection as a means of healing, but the fact that it is an industry at all, driven by market forces, is problematic. As we saw in the case of North Ibaragi, healing is unlikely to happen through just any kind of relationship, especially an economic relationship that instrumentalizes the value of a person based on what they can afford. And as we saw in the case of suicide website visitors, dependency on online social connections can be helpful, but they are also often viewed as surrogates for deeper relations. There is little doubt that healing and resilience in face of trauma can be cultivated at the individual level, by teaching individuals not only contemplative practices but also skills of body awareness and the regulation of the nervous system.[31] But what we are exploring here—as the case of 3.11 survivors illustrates—is how resilience can be cultivated on interpersonal, communal, and systemic levels.

Anthropologist of Japan Isaac Gagné participated in *keichō* (active listening) volunteer groups to promote social healing in 3.11 survivors.[32] The groups include self-identified "average citizens" who are trained in active listening. This active listening is a nonclinical practice; the members' job is simply to be there, hold hands, cry together when appropriate, and so on. Over time, survivors eventually come to accept reality as it is. Gagné argues that this creates a non-structured para-therapeutic space of empowerment where "people feel more comfortable and open with someone whom they feel has also suffered, but not necessarily suffered more; the shared ground of empathic solidarity becomes the foundation of a trust relationship."[33] This is similar to group narrative sessions proposed by Wada, who notes that natural disaster trauma victims benefit if their support system creates opportunities for them to take part in activities in which they can find positive meaning and joy.[34] A popular method for 3.11 survivors was the creation of elephant-shaped hand towels, which they sold in Japan and around the world, with proceeds going to recovery funds for survivors.

Systems-level changes also need to be considered. One of the characteristics of moral injury in the context of war veterans, the incarcerated, refugees, and others is its large scale. Moral injury is not just about an individual being traumatized and suffering a threat to their moral conscience; it is also about systems that enable and perpetuate such infractions. If we are to look from the other perspective and ask about moral repair and resilience, are we able to also identify systemic-level forms of resilience? These would be institutional, cultural, or social forms of resilience that would protect against moral injury and that would facilitate healing and moral repair. As many have recognized, it is not enough to ask individuals to be resilient as long as they live within systems that continue to be oppressive. It is therefore important that we not only study structures of oppression on a systems level, but also look at the way institutional, social, and cultural structures support and foster resilience. I include under "structural resilience" the manner in which social structures, such as laws, policies, and institutions, support resilience, whereas "cultural resilience" consists of the beliefs, practices, and values that underpin those structures.

Another way of framing systems-level changes is one I proposed earlier in this book. The external structures of society, such as its laws, institutions, and forms of government, are reflections of the internal subjective, cognitive, and affective states of the members of that society. In the same way, the internal subjective states of individuals are reflections of those external structures, which serve as affordances for such subjective states. This interdependence and mutual reflection must be accounted for when considering forms of social suffering like loneliness and the ways they can be addressed. Change can happen both on the individual and the social levels. Indeed, the most effective forms of change will likely be those that address both levels and their interdependence.

This is fully in accord with affordance theory and is, in fact, anticipated by it. Gibson writes:

> An important fact about the affordances of the environment is that they are in a sense objective, real, and physical, unlike values and meanings, which are supposed to be subjective, phenomenal, and mental. But, actually, an affordance is neither an objective property nor a subjective property; or it is both if you like. An affordance cuts across the dichotomy of subjective-objective and helps us to understand its inadequacy. It is equally a fact of the environment and a fact of behavior. It is both physical and psychical, yet neither. An affordance points both ways, to the environment and to the observer.[35]

Gibson's statement here echoes what I called the "Janus-faced structure of subjectivity" and the interdependence of subjectivity and environment. He is careful to point out that affordances are "*relative* to the animal. They are unique for that animal. They are not just abstract physical properties . . . so an affordance cannot be measured as we measure in physics."[36] In a similar way, if we consider that human beings have diverse subjective dispositions and exist in diverse environments, we will be less inclined to think that the social structures that afford human connection are universal across societies and cultures. We will expect diversity. But we will also expect a degree of similarity, because the diversity of human beings and their environments exists alongside a strong set of commonalities.

One of those sets of commonalities must be dwelt upon here, as any discussion of the social structures that afford loneliness and/or resilience would be incomplete without acknowledging the powerful force of political economy. Political economy shapes society and culture and establishes a common set of values and social affordances that are inextricably linked with loneliness and other forms of social suffering. I return to this in the following, concluding chapter.

The 3.11 survivors did not accept characterizations of themselves as victims or passive recipients of care. The international media widely reported on a "Resilient Japan!," and it is easy to reduce such endurance and resistance to a kind of Japanese or Tōhoku mentality of resilience. But I think this misses the point. When people lose their houses, communities, and family members and become disconnected from their neighbors, acquaintances, and jobs, they become similarly deprived of autonomy, self-reliance, and social belonging as they face grief, sorrow, and anxiety about their future. The 3.11 survivors' resistance to being treated as passive victims and their strong desire to become autonomous and independent contributors to society were not just signs of a resilience unique to their community, but necessary aspects of the process of moral repair, healing, and recovery. They rejected a highly individualistic approach to mental well-being that lacked any sense of community care and instead gravitated toward group workshops, communal and sharing activities, bonding, and the creative arts—activities that would help reestablish a dimension of social belongingness and an ability to be productive members of society. It was these forms of communal care that they found necessary and useful. For these communities, recovery from trauma and moral injury could not merely be addressed at the individual level. They had lost their *ibasho* and community; their *ibasho* and community had to be reestablished.

Moreover, the widespread commodification of intimacy in Japan suggests that society is beginning to provide through market forces affordances for those who seek intimacy. At the same time, it suggests that such individuals lack affordances for noncommodified intimacy, one clear sign of a lonely society.

7 What Loneliness Can Teach Us

> There's no simple answer of course. But if we could through television programs as well as every other imaginable program let people know that each one of us is precious. Let everybody know that we have value in this life.
>
> —Fred Rogers (Yang 2013)

The preceding chapters each give us an angle from which to examine the anatomy of loneliness in its individual and social dimensions. At the beginning of this book I raised the question, posed by political economist Ritu Vij, of whether there was evidence of a crisis of subjectivity that paralleled the neoliberal political and economic transformations that Japan has undergone due to the stagnation of the Japanese economy. Thus far we have looked at cases of internet group suicide and the statements and narratives of suicide website visitors on loneliness and lack of meaning in life, as well as responses by young college students, to see how generalized these sentiments and experiences might be. From this research, it appears that a great many young Japanese do appear to be experiencing a crisis of subjectivity. Moreover, the deleterious effects of neoliberal market forces, which we would expect to see having an outsized impact on those who are unable to be "productive" according to the conventional standards of society, do indeed appear particularly prevalent among younger Japanese and those who are not yet in conventionally productive roles, whether in work or in a household.

What this means is that the traditional account of the rise of suicide in Japan that I presented—and rejected—in the opening chapter of this book is actually true in some respects, but not for the reasons its proponents have tended to think. I noted that within Japan, the typical explanation for the sudden rise in suicide was the economy: because of Japan's long-term economic stagnation, job prospects were poor, and people were depressed and committing suicide more frequently. I now recast this explanation in a different way. Since the Meiji Restoration in 1868, Japan's political economy has been established around a model of collective success and flourishing. The sacrifice of the individual and the individual family was justified if the group's flourishing was enhanced—measured prior to World War II through the military and economy, and then almost exclusively in economic terms in postwar Japan. The military defeat of Japan in World War II did not signal an abandonment of collective flourishing; it just shifted it away from geopolitical ambitions.

In this way, there was no need for a "liberal turn." The aspects of liberalism conducive to collective success could be adopted while retaining traditional notions of hierarchy, loyalty, and a centralized national consciousness. Moreover, as Maruyama chronicled so insightfully, the state retained primary influence not only in political economy as understood in Western terms, but in values as well. This meant that meaning making would take place not just individually—as is the traditional norm in liberalism—but collectively.

In such a structure, *ikigai*, one's purpose in life, as well as *ibasho*, one's place to belong to, are provided externally through society, namely the structures of political economy and the values around which and through which those structures were established. *Ikigai* is of central importance, but it is provided for oneself. But what happens when society fails to deliver on its promise of success as it has defined it: economic rewards, prosperity, growth, stability, and reliability? What is left is the abiding sense of a need for *ikigai* and *ibasho*, but nothing provided externally. Instead, society shows only dead ends: a lack of jobs and opportunities and an aging society whose health-care benefits are dependent upon a shrinking younger generation who are unlikely to enjoy the same level of benefits when they reach retirement—assuming that they first secure a full-time job. Furthermore, because Japan's society and political economy has been so totalizing and uniform in its approach, it has lacked the affordances for alternative or nonstandard roles and niches found in many other capitalist democracies, or else has stigmatized them as subcultures, making this struggle even more difficult.

This crisis of subjectivity is therefore also a crisis of meaning and purpose. It is logical that such a crisis would most strongly affect those Japanese who are the most vulnerable in the system: those who are young, not yet in full-time employment, and not yet married—not yet occupying two of the stable *ikigai* roles of work and family prescribed by society.

The role of the economy is therefore important, but not because a reestablishment of economic growth would restore optimism and end the emptiness that leads to loneliness and suicide. Rather, Japan's economic stagnation has revealed the emptiness of the promise its political economy was built on, the promise that justified sacrifice. The emptiness left behind is now being seen by young Japanese, who are provided with few societal resources to make meaning and find a place of belonging. Within such a context of failed promise, the demand for sacrifice turns sour, unpalatable.

When Tepco allowed its contractors to hire younger, poorer Japanese as temporary workers to clean up the radioactive waste of Fukushima, the Japanese government looked the other way, despite the fact that the levels of radiation were far above the legal limit (even after the government raised that limit), placing them at terrible risk for health complications. Several of these workers later contracted cancer from their radiation exposure.[1] Such sacrifices might be justifiable in war, or when the country is advancing toward a goal, but within this context, experiencing or even witnessing such events became moral injury. The government, and large companies like Tepco, were seen by many as having failed in their role to protect people.

The picture is not entirely bleak, however. We have seen examples of resilience, resistance, meaning making, and community building. Indeed, the purpose of diagnosing a problem is to find a solution, and exploring the crisis of subjectivity in greater detail with greater theoretical sophistication provides many clues for possible solutions. That is the aim of this concluding chapter. I argue that if the structures of our society are the external manifestations of intersubjectivity, we must approach them consciously in this way and transform them into structures of empathy and compassion that promote individual and collective flourishing on a human level and not merely on a market or economic level. In such structures, both individual and collective welfare must be preserved, and human beings must be seen as subjective and affective beings—that is, beings who feel and experience the world and whose feelings and experiences matter: to themselves, to others, and to us.

SHARING A WORLD AND THE SELF THAT IS SEEN

The idea that Japanese psychology is characterized by a sociocentric or interdependent construal of selfhood and that Western psychology is characterized by an individualistic construal of selfhood has been a topic of investigation and debate for several decades in both cultural psychology and anthropology.[2] It is important to acknowledge different cultural conceptions of selfhood and the different ways selfhood is dynamically shaped, while avoiding a reification of differences between a Japanese interdependent "self" in contrast to a Western individualistic "self," as though these were distinct ontological realities. In the twenty-first century, scholars have pointed out the need for a more differentiated understanding of selfhood that acknowledges individual differences as well as the degree to which individuals may share both individualistic and interdependent notions of selfhood in complex ways.[3] For example, cultural psychologist Hidetada Shimizu points out that individualistic and sociocentric notions of selfhood should be acknowledged as "mutually and dynamically constituting elements of the individual's personal experience."[4]

This approach resonates with the model of subjectivity I have presented in this book, which emphasizes the Janus-faced nature of subjectivity as simultaneously looking out to interdependence and shared experience and looking inward to independence and private experience. In this section I explore one consequence of this dynamic, namely the conception of selfhood that is constructed through the perceptions of others, or what I call "the self that is seen." This is in contrast to the conception of selfhood that is constructed as an unseen interiority: "the self that is not seen." The twin processes of subjectivity result in an objectification of the self in these two ways. It can be constructed largely through the perceptions of others, as a public self. At the same time, it can be constructed as a private self on the basis of experiences the individual believes are unknown to others or differ from the views of others. I argue that selfhood in both North American and Japanese societies is constructed in both ways among all individuals, and that culture promotes varying construals of selfhood in this dynamic that are more or less conducive to flourishing and to afflictions of subjectivity, such as loneliness, particularly as conditions of political economy change within that society.

The "self that is seen" is not, therefore, a uniquely Japanese concern and appears in various ways throughout work in psychology and anthropology. In terms of its developmental origins, it may stem from what Rochat calls "the basic drive to be acknowledged in one's own existence through the eyes of others," or, more simply, the "basic affiliative need" for recognition and acknowledgment.[5] In his words, "We essentially live through the eyes of others. To be human . . . is primarily to care about how much empathy, hence acknowledgment and recognition of our own person, we generate in others—the fact that we care about our reputation as no other animal species does."[6] Rochat writes that from very early on developmentally, "sociality or the quality of being sociable is inseparable from the elusive feeling of being included and having a causal role or impact on the life of others. It is about being 'connected,' ultimately about being visible rather than invisible, recognized rather than ignored or ostracized. . . . In this view, sociality rests on *mutual recognition*."[7] He goes so far as to say that "the need to be recognized ultimately drives social cognition."[8]

Like myself and others, Rochat sees the self as something that emerges through a process. For him, knowledge about the self comes largely from interaction with others, and the self is constituted through relations with others. The mere fact that foundational scholars including Charles Cooley, G. H. Mead, and Martin Heidegger, as well as contemporary scholars like Kitayama and Rochat, have gone to such great lengths to show the importance of sociality in the development of the self indicates that this line of thinking is something that is not taken for granted in Western thought.[9] This idea of an individual self that exists apart from others, and of a society that is the coming together of such originally free individuals through a form of social contract, is a culturally and historically specific development, given voice in the writings of Rousseau and Locke.[10]

In contrast, Takeo Doi writes of the importance of *amae* or "dependency" in Japanese social relations, a wish to be indulged and loved.[11] Although Doi concluded that *amae* exists cross-culturally and is not specific to Japan, he thought it significant that Japanese had a word for this mode of social interaction, whereas English did not, and he felt that Japanese used and related to *amae* differently than "Westerners."[12] Chie Nakane uses the phrase "vertical society" (*tate shakai*) to capture the structural principle behind group cohesion in Japan and to point to the way in which individuals' sense of self is rooted within a group.[13] Similarly, psychiatrist Bin Kimura develops the related notion of the "space between people" (*hito to hito no aida*), and sociologist Eshun Hamaguchi uses the concept of "interpersonal relationships" (*kanjin shugi*) to capture the highly interdependent nature of social interaction in Japan.[14]

Each of these concepts articulates in its own way the basic affiliative need and fear of social rejection. Thus, Mead's observation that "the individual mind can exist only in relation to other minds with shared meanings" and Rochat's insistence that "within months of birth, the self is increasingly defined in relation to others, not on the basis of an interior subjective experience" have a particular resonance within Japanese culture.[15] The greater emphasis on the socially constructed nature of selfhood evident in Japan results in a correspondingly greater emphasis on the importance of intersubjectivity and what might be called "sharing a world." This is a dynamic process of mutual interaction that is deeper than mere surface level imitation or mirroring; it is participation in the collective dance or ritual that forms the foundation of sociality and society itself.

If we put together the developmental model offered by Rochat and others, which shows that the self emerges from the very beginning already with a dual nature of being both individual and interdependent, with our understanding of cross-cultural differences between Western and Japanese societies, then we see more clearly how cultural processes are emphasizing and making salient different aspects of the dual-natured sense of self. This enables us to appreciate and recognize cultural differences while refraining from making the mistake of positing a fundamental ontological difference in selfhood between Japanese and "Westerners." The difference here is one of emphasis and deployment, not a fundamental difference in ontological selfhood.[16]

Ironically, awareness of the relational nature of self and the importance of "sharing a world" does not necessarily lead to only positive effects. This is because whether the self is objectified in dependence on internal or external perceptions, it is still a reification of self-concept that can lead to all the disappointments, disillusionments, tensions, and fears that accompany such a rigidly adhered to notion of "who I really am." Rochat notes that the basic affiliative need and other-dependence of self-consciousness results in a fear of social rejection that he labels "the mother of all fears."[17] It is possible that the more the self is objectified on the basis of the perceptions of others, the greater this fear of social rejection would become. Indeed, the fear of social rejection seems particularly prevalent in Japan, where a proscription or prohibition of individual experience, choice, and preference translates into the fear and felt intolerability of being "left behind" or "left out," of being seen as selfish (*wagamama*) or a "free agent" (*jiyūjin*), and where the primacy of maintaining shared experience takes priority over, and downplays, individual experience and autonomy. One way to avoid being stigmatized, censured, and left out in such a society is to suppress one's individual wishes and experiences and just "go along with others," which as I explained is the basic meaning behind the popular Japanese phrase *jibun ga nai*, literally "not having a self."

Drawing from his interviews with Japanese adolescents, Shimizu notes how even slightly critical comments can be seen as taboo because they are a potential danger to group collectivity. He notes that one teenage boy explained it this way: "When I had this person I didn't like and told my friend A how badly I think of him, he said, 'I didn't know you were the kind of person to say such things.' Then I felt that I lost A's trust in me."[18] In another interview with an adolescent girl, Shimizu asks her, "What's the most important thing to do in interpersonal relationships?" She responds: "To go along with others (*hito ni awaseru*)."[19]

This dimension of selfhood and the effects it has on interpersonal relations are important factors in understanding group suicide. In a society where autonomous action is denigrated, collective action is needed to avoid the shame of being alone and being selfish. The intolerability of being "left behind" is something that can even be projected onto others, as seen in forced suicides, when a father commits suicide and kills the remaining family members or a mother commits suicide and kills her baby at the same time (*shinjū*).[20]

It is encouraging that suicide research is starting to converge on the most important themes found in the subjective experiences of suicidal individuals. The Japanese psychiatrist Yoshitomo Takahashi has called the establishment of *kizuna* (bonds) essential to suicide prevention and considers its absence to be highly dangerous.[21] Recalling our discussion of the importance of *ibasho*, psychologist Thomas Joiner considers a sense of isolation or "non-belongingness" to be one of the three strongest risk factors for suicide.[22] The anthropologist Ronald Niezen argues along similar lines in his study of suicide clusters among Canadian Aboriginal youth when he writes that they are "driven by profound loneliness, neglect, or a sense of being unimportant and invisible, while, at the same time, this condition of loneliness becomes directly or indirectly shared with others."[23] This convergence suggests that we may be reaching a point where interventions can be developed that will prove more effective than those in the past.

The posts from suicide websites analyzed here underscore Rochat's argument that a lack of recognition—one could say *regard*—from others is a lack in the fundamental basis of what it means to be a human being and what it means to be a person, a "self."[24] As he writes, "Social comfort thus consists in the experience of being recognized as much as we recognize the other. Inversely, social discomfort is the experience of being transparent or invisible for others, the experience of not being acknowledged, hence socially disconnected."[25] This perspective enables us to consider that the question of *ikigai*, which I discussed elsewhere in connection with internet group suicide, is not itself a primary existential question, but rather the symptom of a decrease in the sense of affiliation and connectedness with others.[26] It is this loss of affiliation and place (*ibasho*) that leads to a loss of meaning that itself becomes the cause for a questioning of one's *ikigai*. The relational theory of meaning presented here suggests that as long as an individual experiences belonging, affiliation, and connection, questions of meaning are less likely to arise, because a key source of feeling meaningful (*ikigai*) is feeling that one is meaningful to others. The dependent nature of the meaning of the self is not something that can be escaped, even in suicide. As strange as it may seem, even internet group suicide is a way for two or more suicidal individuals to share a world and participate in a shared death, a transition from this life of suffering to the next life.

PERMISSION AND COURAGE TO DIE

I believe the theoretical arguments presented here are echoed in the ethnographic data collected in this book and help to explain a significant part of the subjectivity presented in the statements I have collected and presented. One key insight I want to explore in this section is the idea of "permission to die" and being given the "courage to die."

We have seen that every successive "wave" of suicides in Japan throughout the twentieth century included cluster suicides, and that this is a characteristic of the current suicide wave since 1998 as well, with many suicides imitating the exact manner and methods of previous ones. Why does a single visible suicide spark a chain of other suicides? And to return to an earlier question that we began with, why are Japanese seeking others to die with?

I believe part of the answer lies in the statements we have read in this book, specifically those that speak of the relief that many suicidal people in Japan feel when they are given "permission to die." We've seen the statements of those who felt encouraged and empathized with upon receiving or reading *The Complete Manual of Suicide*. They felt that many people were telling them to persevere (*gambaru*) in the face of life's difficulties, but when someone finally told them it was okay to die, and even showed them how, they felt their experiences were being authorized as legitimate. They received it as an act of empathy.

Similarly, in posts on suicide websites, the overwhelming internal pain of individuals was not being legitimized in the eyes of others, compounding their already severe feelings of loneliness. The emphasis on "going along" in Japan and the denigration of individual, private experience seem to only intensify such feelings.

Thus, when another person comes along and says, "I understand your feelings. It is okay to feel that way. I feel it too. And it is okay to die. It is okay even to commit suicide. Here is even a way you can do it," this is often met by feelings of relief, endorsement, and even liberation. Now the experience is no longer private, and action is no longer selfish; it is collective and therefore legitimate.

I believe this perspective also sheds light on the question of cluster suicides and what is sometimes called "suicide contagion," although that is an unfortunate, stigmatizing term. When people who are feeling alone in their pain see another person like them committing suicide, they recognize that they are not alone. The suicide of that person shows a way out, and the courage of that person to act can give others the courage to follow suit. For those who follow, their action is no longer private and alone; it is collective. Committing suicide is now not a selfish, independent act, but can also be a way of "going along." As more and more people commit suicide, as happens in cluster suicides, it becomes easier to commit suicide as a "joining in" or "going along" rather than the action of a solitary individual. The same holds true for joining an internet suicide pact.

I have not seen this explanation offered in scholarship on suicide in Japan, and I would not have come to this conclusion if I had not decided to foreground critical empathy as a methodological approach in my research and focus on the subjective experiences and statements of suicidal and lonely individuals. Yet it is important to recognize that this very situation also points to the ambiguous nature of empathy itself. The idea of being seen, heard, and acknowledged in a way that endorses a person's wish to commit suicide is evidence of why it is problematic to treat empathy as if it is inherently or unproblematically always ethical. Those who were given copies of *The Complete Manual of Suicide*, who joined suicide websites, or who joined internet suicide pacts, reported the feeling of relief that came from finally being heard and seen, from finally hearing a peer or someone in authority (a book author, a librarian, a website moderator) say to them, "It's okay to want to die, and it's okay to die." Yet many might question the ethics of such actions—a librarian telling a student it's okay to commit suicide and giving them a book on how to do it, or the author of the book writing such a work—particularly if they contribute to people committing suicide.

In one of the online dialogues at the beginning of chapter 2 the moderator, Marcy, criticized one of the participants, not for expressing her wish to die, but for becoming an "ally" or "pal" for another person who wanted to die in a way that might give that person the courage and permission to die. Marcy noted that it is totally fine to commit suicide, but "disgusting" to prey upon a person who lacks the courage to die and instead wants to succumb to a "herd mentality." Thus we see that empathy can be expressed and received in various ways. Boiled Egg sought to normalize feelings of suicidal ideation while still encouraging site visitors to try to live until their mid-thirties. At the other extreme, Shiraishi (Mr. Hangman) preyed upon his victims' need for empathy to lure and murder them, yet claimed that his motivation was compassionate.

If there are indeed a large number of Japanese who feel alone and unseen, and who are in intense mental pain, the prevalence of group and cluster suicides suggests that Japanese society must find a way to allow for the expression of private experience in a way that is non-stigmatizing. Such people are yearning for empathy. But the specific forms that empathy takes in society and between people is of utmost importance if the long-term goals of suicide prevention are to be reached.

RELATIONAL MEANING IN LIFE

The preceding discussion connects closely to the examination of subjectivity I presented in chapter 1, where I argued that loneliness is fundamentally connected to the structure of subjectivity and is therefore a universal human experience. This does not mean, of course, that every individual is always experiencing loneliness as an affliction. Loneliness is varied and impermanent, meaning it is always involved in processes of change. To be stuck in the affliction of loneliness, however, is to be stuck in the liminality of what I called the Janus-faced nature of subjectivity that looks out and looks in, to feel locked in a place of desolation, as if the membrane between outer and inner had become ossified, and one were trapped in the middle. Borrowing the Tibetan term for "in-between state," *bardo*, we could say that chronically or severely lonely individuals are trapped in the *bardo* of loneliness. The solution is not to move outward or to move inward, but to regain the flexibility of that membrane that allows for both sharing a world and an acceptance of one's own individual existence as a solitary being, that allows for a healthier reconstitution of self and other.

As discussed earlier, loneliness is dual faceted: it prompts a desire for relationships and affiliation (belongingness, being accepted, being recognized), and it triggers feelings of threat and dread when it is experienced.[27] If loneliness promotes a desire for relationships, then it is not necessarily negative, but when it becomes a chronic or intense level of loneliness, then the threat and dread of feeling socially abandoned might become debilitating.

We have noted that one of the primary structures of subjectivity is its division between self and environment, and that another is its first-person nature. But while phenomenologists have stressed one aspect of this—the fact that phenomena appear *to me*—they have paid less attention to its corollary: namely, that phenomena that appear to me may not appear the same way to others. This is key to understanding both loneliness and empathy. Through early human development, we see stages of a growing realization that subjective experience is not necessarily shared, that in addition to shared experiences, we have private experiences. Research in developmental psychology on the theory of mind shows that this realization of a private interior world unknown to others does not occur all at once; rather, it occurs in stages. While infants already have a sense of self as something distinct from environment and others, infants and very young children do not yet realize that what they know and experience can be unknown and unexperienced by others. This process of differentiation continues alongside brain development throughout adolescence, and along with it comes the process of fear of social rejection and the need for social acceptance. In other words, the very nature of subjective experience as having both shared or intersubjective and private dimensions means that loneliness—or at least the very real potential for loneliness—is built into subjectivity as part of the structure of consciousness.

There is also a close connection between loneliness and meaning in life, which we have explored in this book in various ways. In psychology, especially in positive psychology, "meaning in life" and "meaningfulness" have been recognized as one of the most essential factors for positive mental well-being. Research has also suggested that the *search* for meaning in life is negatively correlated with well-being.[28] Psychology, however, has largely been dominated by two definitions of meaning in life: first, having a cognitive map of significance that helps individuals make sense of the world, and second, having purpose, goals, or worthwhile things to do. Individuals who have one or both of these, according to this view, have "meaning in life" and as a result, feel that they "matter."[29]

According to such theories, "meaning in life" or "mattering" as a human being depends entirely on having higher cognition (being able to make sense of the world in a highly complex and cognitive way) and also being able to perform certain productive tasks (being able to do worthwhile things).[30] This unintentionally renders the lives of a vast number of beings "meaningless": not only children, people with certain disabilities, and all nonhuman species, but also those who do not fit into a certain mold of productivity established by the norms of their society. In other words, this approach to the study of meaning in life already contains within it some of the biases of neoliberalism that are the very object of critique here.

The alternative is a relational approach to meaning in life. As my husband, scholar in psychology and religious studies Brendan Ozawa-de Silva, notes, "Social relationships are not a subset of possible meanings in life, they are the context in which meaning itself takes place."[31] And further:

> If my life has meaning, it has meaning first and foremost in the eyes of others, such as my parents or caregivers. Furthermore, that meaning is neither purposive nor a higher cognitive process of "understanding" the meaning of my life; rather it is first and foremost felt in the care I receive from others, through which I come to sense that my life has meaning to others. Only secondarily, and co-constructed within that social context, does my life come to have meaning for myself. The meaning of my life, therefore, even in my own eyes, cannot be separated from this social matrix. By ignoring it, and by concentrating on the cognitive, goal-directed, purpose-directed, and individualistic side of meaning, we are limiting ourselves to an evolutionarily and developmentally later, and therefore potentially more superficial—in the sense of its relationship to our deep well-being and happiness, the topic of positive psychology—layer of meaning. The socially and co-conscious construction of meaning can be seen clearly in its absence as well. It appears that when individuals feel a lack of compassion and care and worth in the estimation of others, their life loses meaning in their own eyes as well. Nothing exemplifies this more than in the suicides of those who are lonely or at risk of social isolation and rejection. It should come as no surprise that those who consider or attempt suicide exhibit both a lack of meaning in life and a lack of social support and social connection with others.[32]

The ethnographic data explored here strongly suggest that relational meaning of life is a more accurate theoretical approach for understanding the phenomena of loneliness and suicide in Japan. In my interviews, those who appeared content with their life tended to describe their meaning in life in a highly relational context. Those who appeared languishing or frustrated tended to respond that they were still searching for meaning in life. Similarly, among suicide website visitors we find laments about a lack of meaning in life and a strong desire to find one, including suggestions that finding such meaning would end their misery. Cacioppo's point that loneliness is perceived social isolation raises the question of why some people perceive certain situations as social isolation while others do not.[33] It also raises the question of what this subjective experience of perceived social isolation feels like.

I have tried to address these questions by pointing to the link between fear of social rejection and loneliness; indeed, I have noted that fear of social rejection is already a form of loneliness and a threat to meaning. Loneliness is social and spatial. It emerges through the interplay between individual and environment, but the membrane that separates the two is porous and dynamic. Society, relationships, and even the natural environment are internalized within individuals and their self-concept. Because social relations appear to be internalized within the individual from the beginning in the construction of selfhood, sociality can be experienced by an individual independent of external social interactions. The self is a social self even when it is alone; alternatively, one could say individuals are never truly alone, because our minds and brains always work socially in the construction of experience and meaning, even if we are physically isolated.

Sociality is therefore inextricable from habitus. All social phenomena, including loneliness, must be understood in conjunction with an understanding of self and self-concept, not as independent and nonsocial units but as units that have risen from social interaction that contain internalized social dynamics within themselves. This is why an internalized fear of social rejection can be dangerous even without any actual interpersonal social rejection taking place or even in the face of actual social support.

This dynamic process and the plasticity of subjectivity leave room for the cultivation of resilience to loneliness. My research on the Japanese introspective practice of Naikan demonstrated that individuals who were able to recall or maintain awareness of experiences of receiving affection and bonds with others in the past felt more connected with others and less alone.[34] Naikan is a practice that was secularized from a Buddhist meditation approach; it involves a full week of sustained introspection structured around three questions: What I have received from others? What have I given back? What trouble have I caused them?[35] By emphasizing memories of social support, Naikan establishes in those who undergo it a strong sense of having been cared for, supported, and accepted. This recognition of how one has been accepted despite one's failings directly undermines fear of social rejection and results in a strong sense of security and belonging. The emerging sense of secure attachment serves as a very powerful resilience factor when experiencing loneliness. The fact that someone is found meaningful by others who cared for them also establishes a sense of self-worth and self-acceptance that appears to strongly buffer against meaninglessness in life.

Diagrammatically, we could say that the sense and recognition of care from others leads to seeing oneself as an object of value and worth in the eyes of others. This leads to a sense of self-worth and value in one's own estimation, because meaning is socially constructed. As a result, this means one's life is meaningful, which is accompanied by secure attachment and secure relationships or bonds with others. This, in turn, is an experience of not being lonely. Alternatively, perceiving a lack of care or support from others leads to feeling that others do not see one as worthy, valuable, or meaningful. This may cause a crisis or questioning of one's value and meaning in life or a tension between one's striving for meaning and one's fear that others do not find one meaningful and valuable. This may be accompanied by insecure attachment, a weak sense of relational bonds with others, fear of social rejection, and perceived social isolation—namely, loneliness.

SHOPLIFTERS

In 2018 Kore-eda released the film *Shoplifters* (*Manbiki Kazoku*). It won the Palme d'Or prize at the Cannes film festival and has many similarities to the more well-known 2019 film *Parasite*, by Korean director Bong Joon-ho, which won multiple Academy Awards. *Shoplifters* follows the life of a three-generational family, the Shibatas, all living together in one house: apparently a grandmother (Hatsue), a couple in their thirties or forties (Osamu and Nobuyo), a younger woman in her twenties (Aki), and a boy of about twelve (Shota). The first scene in the film depicts Osamu (the father figure) and Shota engaging in coordinated shoplifting in a grocery store and then buying croquettes from a stall on the street. In the next scene, they pass by the living quarters of Yuri, a young girl of four or five. They hear her parents fighting, and Osamu decides to offer her a croquette and then take her home with them to their family of five. Nobuyo, his female partner, objects and insists they take Yuri home, but Osamu says it is too cold outside. The next day Osamu and Nobuyo are taking Yuri back to her home when they overhear Yuri's parents fighting violently again, and Yuri's mother saying, "I didn't want her either!" Nobuyo sinks to the ground, hugging Yuri tight and refusing to let her go, and we later learn that Nobuyo, too, was unwanted and discarded by her parents, as was Shota. They decide to keep Yuri and raise her as their own daughter.

As the film progresses, we learn that this is not an ordinary family at all, as none of these individuals is actually connected by blood ties; rather, they are all individuals who were "thrown away" (*suterareta*) like garbage (*gomi*). The grandmother figure, Hatsue, was abandoned by her husband in favor of another woman. Aki, who is like a daughter to her and who sleeps with Hatsue every night, is actually the natural granddaughter of Hatsue's ex-husband. Aki has run away from her parent's home and works in an establishment where young women partially strip and allow clients to rest on their laps in private rooms as a provision of commodified intimacy. Osamu and Nobuyo, who act like a married couple, are not in fact married, but are connected by the fact that Osamu helped Nobuyo bury the body of her abusive ex-husband, whom either she or they together killed in self-defense. And Shota is not Osamu's son, despite the fact that Osamu encourages Shota repeatedly to call him "father" and to call Yuri his "younger sister," but was found by Osamu and Nobuyo left in a car by himself as a small child.

Nearly every scene in the film contrasts the instrumental ties or bonds (*kizuna*) of society with bonds of real human connection. The film again and again makes the point that blood ties of family—which are foundational in traditional Japanese society—are not as strong or as genuine as one might think. By showing the kindness and mutual care of this family of poor misfits at the margins of Japanese society and contrasting that to the cruelty and indifference of families that are related by blood, Kore-eda subverts the traditional Japanese hierarchy of values. Through the vehicle of empathy, he provides an alternative narrative to the dominant singular national and nationalist narrative about family, blood ties, society, the homeless, shoplifters, sex workers, police, and so on. Claudia Strauss points to the importance of recognizing such diversity when she cautions against representing Japan (or any society) as a singular "abstract cultural subject," and when she notes, "Public culture does not simply reflect mass consciousness."[36]

In an interview, Kore-eda makes explicit his intentions to push against the traditional Japanese representations of what society and family should be: "One of my major life realizations . . . is that having a child is not enough to make you a parent. . . . I think my films reflect my own sense of crisis about that, and this film—in which the binding agent is ultimately neither the blood relationship nor the time the Shibatas spend together—brings that crisis to a head."[37] He notes, "After the 2011 earthquake, I didn't feel comfortable with people saying repeatedly that a family bond is important."[38] And he goes on to say, "The traditional concept of family was already being dismantled or destroyed in Japan, and 3/11 just made it obvious that was happening. I believe you can no longer interpret the true value or purpose of family based on the antiquated traditional tropes of Japanese society. In 'Shoplifters,' I was looking at three generations living together, because that's typically what you'd find in a Japanese household. But I wanted to play with that, and show that even within those terms the nuclear family is undergoing a permanent change."[39]

The contrast between the human bonds formed by the Shibata family and the conservative values of traditional Japanese society becomes most clear in the film's climax, when the entire family is arrested after Shota intentionally lets himself get caught shoplifting to protect Yuri. As the police question the members of the Shibata family one by one, they insist that they were connected only by crime, greed, and convenience. Within the frame of values of traditional Japan, it is not possible that they could be connected any other way; after all, they are not a "real family." But the members of the family reject these interpretations, and after they are released from police custody (or put in jail, as happens with Nobuyo, who elects to take the fall for Osamu), there is clear evidence that their bonds of love with each other remain, and their family built on bonds of choice is as strong as, if not stronger than, a family built on the bonds of blood. In the final scene between Shota and Osamu, Shota finally mouths the word *father*, despite the fact that they are being separated and may never see each other again.

SOCIETY AND COMPASSION

The film *Shoplifters* portrays in fictional form a deeper truth that I believe lies at the heart of this book and at the heart of the question of loneliness in Japan: a society creates loneliness when it instrumentalizes the value of its members and when it treats people as disposable. In such a society, every member is dehumanized, not just those who are marginalized, discarded, or at obvious risk of being forgotten. This is because when members, even those perceived to be "productive" or "successful," see others being discarded, they realize that they themselves could eventually lose their productive value and then be discarded: "If that person is thrown away, then I too could be thrown away." *Shoplifters* invites its viewers to rethink traditional notions of human connection and society dependent on conventional norms like blood ties and socioeconomic hierarchy and to imagine types of human connection that are built on inherent value, compassion, and choice.

When people are reduced to merely their productive value—when they have only instrumental or utilitarian value to others—then it means they have no intrinsic value. They are then merely objects, not human beings. And like any object that has lost its instrumental value, they can be thrown away like "trash" (*gomi*) when their value has ended, including through aging and disability. In some cases, those who were born with a disability may even be seen as useless from the beginning. But individuals without obvious productive value to a society still have value in the eyes of those who love and care for them.

Fear of social rejection comes about when there is a perceived lack of safety and trust among people. When people feel a high level of safety and security, they feel that even if they make a mistake or even if something negative about them is revealed, they will still be accepted, valued, and loved. Being able to have this level of trust implies a very close connection between people. Genuine human relationships do not depend on instrumental value, but are based on a sense of intrinsic value. Intrinsic value here does not mean value independent of the perceptions of others; it is rather that value that is seen by caring others to be intrinsic to the person in their eyes. When a person genuinely cares for or values another person, they see that person as valuable just for existing, not because of the productive or instrumental value they have or may have in the future.[40]

This is the relational theory of meaning, which posits that a person's sense of value and sense of purpose and meaning in life is constructed socially and depends largely on feeling that their life is meaningful in the eyes of others. If a person feels intrinsically valued by others, independent of performance or productivity, they may start to see their own life as valuable as well, because an individual's perspective tends to be highly shaped by those of others. This is a characteristic of being a social being: although we are capable of holding views that are diametrically opposed to those of others, it is harder to do so than to agree with a larger consensus, especially when one is personally connected with the individuals who make up that consensus.

Studies like Vij's and Bourdieu's, that investigate the interdependent relationship between political economy and subjectivity—especially subjective well-being—suggest that when a society treats its members as having only instrumental value, as merely producers and consumers, then its members come to see their worth only through the lens of their productivity or success.[41] This has an outsized impact on the sections of society that have least access to being "fully productive" members of society according to the norms set out by its political, economic, and social structures: the elderly because they have passed their time of economic "productivity," and the young because they do not yet have access to it and may in fact have uncertain access. By the same logic, those who do not fit into the societal mold of productivity for other reasons, even if they are neither young nor elderly, will experience similar problems.

This suggests that as societies change, they can change in ways that make their members feel more or less meaningful. As modes of relating, social relationships, and relationship structures and expectations change, people can feel more or less meaningful to one another; they can treat one another as more or less meaningful. This is something that must be studied in any approach to social, political, and economic structure. To allow neoliberal market forces to reshape society and corporate structures without considering that they are made up of—and fundamentally should be made to serve the interests of—human beings who have feelings, bodies, and minds, is to allow a society to move toward "the lonely society" without even putting up a fight.

EMPATHY AND METHODOLOGY

In this book I have argued that feeling (sentience and affect) is more universal and deep-seated, both evolutionarily and developmentally, than higher cognition and the various manifestations of higher cognition (language, reason, institutions, and so on). Much work, not just in anthropology but also in philosophy, psychology, and other disciplines, has neglected the domain of feeling, sensation, and affect. Once we start attending to feeling, we begin to see that it is a foundational dimension of subjectivity.

Loneliness itself is a feeling, an affective and subjective state of being. Lacking meaning in life too, I have argued, is about feeling and not just cognition: a feeling that one's life is not valuable, that one doesn't have a place to belong, that one is drifting, lost. Such feelings—such afflictions of subjectivity—cannot be addressed solely through the intellect. When it comes to interventions, people who experience such feelings cannot simply be given an intellectual answer to their problems; they have to be brought into a different state of feeling. In North Ibaragi the mental care workers were rejected not because nobody wanted their help, but because the help they were offering was a technical, material type of help, when what the people there needed was to be seen, respected, heard, and treated as equals: actions that would help them feel better. On the suicide websites, visitors were looking for community, a place where they could be seen, heard, and understood—where their mental pain would not be dismissed but taken seriously by others who could empathize with their situation and even their wish to die.

Some of the most important feelings—such as a sense of belonging, meaning, and connection—happen not just individually but between people, as manifestations of intersubjectivity. Approaching subjectivity therefore requires empathy, because reason or what we call higher cognition alone is insufficient and ill-suited to understanding the affective states of others. Fortunately, as mammals and social animals, we are equipped with an ability to not just reason about others, but also empathize with them: a process that involves both reason and feeling. It is my growing belief that the affective states of those who suffer from afflictions of subjectivity, like severe and chronic loneliness, often cannot be comprehended in a purely intellectual way even by those undergoing such afflictions. But they can be approached empathetically.

Precisely because affect is embodied in systems of the brain that predate many of our higher cognitive functions, it is harder to put into words and analyze conceptually than thought and language. Our analytical vocabulary may fall short, indicating that we need to pay more attention to this area and develop it more. Furthermore, there are aspects of scholarship itself that may hinder processes of empathy. Science, statistics, and scholarly research are objectifying by nature and easily result in generalized, experience-far representations of human experience and human suffering that bypass or impede empathy and that efface the subjectivity of those they claim to represent.

In this book I have sought to balance this tendency of scholarship by including extensive first- and second-person accounts and by consciously separating these at times from the third-person accounts. As I worked on the book and developed its methodological focus on empathy, I reworked the presentation of the first-person accounts extensively. While doing so, I realized there is a time dimension to empathy that can impact scholarship and scholarly writing, by which I mean that empathy can take time to develop and grow and has to be given space if it is to be attended to. In successive drafts, I tried to allow the voices of those who were sharing their thoughts and experiences to speak directly to the reader with minimal interference. Since empathy depends on both recognizing and acknowledging real difference while also maintaining identification and a sense of shared humanity, I considered at length how best to translate passages to preserve the distinctiveness and difference while still allowing for emotional resonance. I also sought to create space (*ma*) around the narratives. Sometimes this meant creating a pause between the presentation of a narrative or set of quotes and the later analysis. Sometimes it meant deleting my commentary about what I thought a narrative meant or how I felt it should be read. I came to the conviction that while thinking can proceed at a frenetic pace, we do need to slow down to listen and feel. Then we can learn. While I view this work as a preliminary attempt by myself to take empathy seriously on a methodological level, I found it encouraging, and I will pursue this further in subsequent work.

Naturally, if anthropologists are to employ critical empathy as a methodological approach, this cannot mean abandoning reason to feeling, nor can it mean mistaking empathic distress for compassion. Critical empathy means recognizing both the promise and perils of empathy. Studying afflictions of subjectivity and engaging with interlocutors who are suffering can easily result in feelings of empathic distress. In other cases, empathy may fail when a scholar claims to represent an experience that is not the other's but in reality their own. These failures of empathy should be avoided. If empathy is to be taken seriously as something that can contribute methodologically to anthropological research, anthropologists may benefit from intentionally engaging in training related to empathy, compassion, perspective taking, and so on. This is something scholars in the field of contemplative science have been encouraging for some time, but as yet very little has been done in this regard.

WHAT CAN WE LEARN FROM LONELINESS?

In his Tanner lectures, which have proved very influential on my views about subjectivity, Kleinman succinctly explains why it is productive for us to look at experience as inherently interpersonal and moral. Experience is inherently interpersonal because "it is a medium in which collective and subjective processes interfuse. We are born into the flow of palpable experience. Within its symbolic meanings and social interactions our senses form into a patterned sensibility, our movements meet resistance and find directions, and our subjectivity emerges, takes shape, and reflexively shapes our local world."[42] Experience is moral, he goes on to say, "because it is the medium of engagement in everyday life in which things are at stake and in which ordinary people are deeply engaged stake-holders who have important things to lose, to gain, and to preserve."[43]

Moreover, as I have argued elsewhere, experience is plastic—fluid and open to being transformed by historical and cultural conditions. These are "transformations of subjectivity . . . whereby construals of suffering changed across historical and cultural settings in ways that changed the experience of suffering for those societies."[44] Unlike in early Christianity times, when suffering had a salvific meaning, in contemporary times, "No one is expected anymore to merely endure pain and suffering. The methods for socializing children and the societal institutions that support moral meanings and practices do not reward endurance of misery or acceptance of the limits of repair and rescue. The salvific potential of suffering is at an all-time low."[45]

This is relevant for the study of loneliness in two ways. First, it supports the idea that transformations in society are resulting in transformations of subjectivity, resulting in more intense and more widespread experiences of loneliness. Second, it implies that construals of suffering, including afflictions of subjectivity like loneliness, could shift to increase resilience. If loneliness is understood in society as merely meaningless pain, if it is pathologized as some kind of disorder, or if it is characterized as a sign of a personality flaw, this can compromise the resilience and well-being of the individuals who experience it. On the other hand, if loneliness is understood as an inevitable condition of human existence, indeed as a result of the structures of subjectivity itself, then it may be easier to bear. This is not to say that minimizing chronic and severe loneliness has no value; it is merely to say that eliminating loneliness in its entirety may not be a realistic approach for either individuals or societies. As seen in the preceding chapters, both human and natural disasters can create experiences of loss that are not easily rectified: destroyed cities cannot be rebuilt in a day, lost loved ones cannot be brought back, and not all expectations in life can be fulfilled.

Indeed, I believe loneliness has something to teach us. While loneliness is certainly a subjective experience, it is not just an epiphenomenal one;

it is not merely a fleeting experience of unhappiness or distress. Rather, it is founded upon the very structure of subjectivity itself, including the fact that subjectivity is inherently intersubjective and relational, and yet aspects of our subjectivity are private and "closed off" from the minds and experiences of others. The interdependence of self and other in fact presupposes, rather than precludes, the differentiation of self and other.

Loneliness is a good example of our "dual inheritance," as it involves the complex interaction of structures that are evolutionary, developmental, and cultural. Evolutionarily, human beings are mammals who need others to survive, at all stages of life. Separation from others is a survival threat, and one source of our ability to feel loneliness. Developmentally, human beings develop theory of mind and the ability to differentiate one's own emotional and mental states from those of others; this simultaneously gives us the capacity to empathize with one another and engage in perspective taking and introduces the possibility that we might not be understood or empathized with. Here we find another source of loneliness.

Loneliness also has sources in our societies and our cultural norms and expectations. Societies express explicit and implicit expectations about social relationships, and failure to meet those expectations in one's life can result in loneliness. On a broader scale, not just individuals but entire groups and categories of people can experience marginalization, isolation, rejection, lack of respect, lack of acceptance, aggression, and oppression. Even if such threats to the value and self-worth of individuals and groups do not amount to threats to physical survival, they still constitute another source of loneliness.

The fact that loneliness stems from perceived and felt social isolation, not just actual physical isolation, means that it can be addressed through a shift in that perception and affect rather than by a change in the objective situations of a person's or community's life. This can happen on an individual level, a community level, or the level of an entire society. Herein lies its plasticity. My research on contemplative practices such as Naikan and Cognitively Based Compassion Training (CBCT) showed me that affect can be transformed when perceptions are changed. In Naikan, for example, clients recall their past from birth to present, remembering all the things they have been given by significant others in their lives. As clients start to recall the countless small acts of kindness they have received, they typically also start to let go of any sense of being unsupported, unloved, uncared for, disconnected, and alone. This practice of recollecting the past does not change the past, but it does change clients' perceptions of the past, resulting in a corresponding change in their affect. This is not merely an intellectual process, but a contemplative one that takes time and practice. Similarly, CBCT and other compassion training programs like Compassion Cultivation Training (CCT) and Compassionate Integrity Training (CIT) guide participants toward recognizing that their own perceptions and attitudes are shaping their current affect, and seek to empower participants to take responsibility for shifting those perceptions and attitudes toward ones that are more conducive to happiness. All of this suggests that while loneliness may be resulting from social and cultural conditions, the solutions to loneliness should not rely solely on changing external factors and structures, but should combine this societal change with recognition of the role of subjectivity and the potential for transformations of subjectivity through the shifting of perceptions.

On this basis, I conclude this book by offering five suggestions that I believe can help in addressing loneliness on individual and societal levels.

ACCEPT LONELINESS

Understanding the epidemic of loneliness should not lead to a pathologization of loneliness; it has to be accompanied by an understanding of loneliness's universality. This is all the more important because accepting temporary experiences of loneliness may be key to resilience. Not only loneliness, but related situations of rejection and isolation, are occasional states that happen with regularity in human life. Such experiences can be seen as part of our common humanity, rather than an individual tribulation to be faced alone. Not being able to accept or tolerate such experiences of suffering, and not being able to wait for them to pass, can lead to an intensification of psychological suffering and even suicidal ideation. On the other hand, accepting them and seeing them as natural parts of human life that everyone goes through at various times can enable one to have patience until they pass.

Accepting one's own loneliness as a natural part of one's humanity and seeing experiences of loneliness (both by oneself and others) as normal aspects of human life does not, of course, mean that one does not strive to address issues of loneliness. On the contrary, since unmet expectations for social relations are a key factor, the practice of accepting loneliness may be an important step toward decreasing one's loneliness and a key factor in developing resilience to loneliness.

ACCEPT OTHERS

Recognizing the universality of loneliness and its evolutionary, developmental, and cultural origins, and seeing it as a part of our common humanity, can help us reach out to others as well. While cultivating empathy toward others may be even more ideal, accepting others can be a first step. As shown in this book, individuals and even entire communities—especially those at risk of marginalization—need to feel accepted, need to be "seen" and recognized as worthwhile, and need to be cared for. Without this, it is only natural and only human to feel lonely, abandoned, and isolated. Rather than looking down on such people and such communities, as happened to young people who committed suicide in Japan, we can support such individuals and communities by recognizing and accepting their subjective experiences as legitimate.

Both the case of North Ibaragi and the situation of the suicide websites studied here suggest that it is important that such support not be offered paternalistically as a "cure," "treatment," or "service," but rather through the formation of genuine ties, respect, and community. A focus on an individual or a community's resilience can foster a sense of agency. It is important that lonely individuals feel this agency and recognize their own ability to form connections and reach out to others, since simply waiting for satisfying relationships to happen on their own is less likely to be successful.

For lonely individuals, a willingness to engage with others might be hampered by a fear of rejection. This fear can be lessened by recognizing it as a part of our common humanity, as noted in the preceding section, and also by recognizing that although one's need to affiliate has evolutionary and developmental roots that tie it to survival, which explains our natural fear of rejection, in actual human life, most instances of social rejection do not carry with them any actual threat to our physical survival. Reflecting on the origins of this fear of social rejection can help us to fear it less.

ACCEPT ONESELF

It is common for one's sense of self-worth and self-esteem to be highly dependent on one's relations with other people.[46] We have seen in this book how, for many young Japanese, meaning in life is tied to the "need to be needed." If one's perception of one's social relationships does not meet one's expectations, one may not only feel lonely, but may actually feel that one's life is not valuable. For this reason, it is crucial to cultivate a sense of self-worth that is at least in part independent of other people's approval. While recognition from others can bolster one's sense of self-worth, lacking other sources of self-worth places one in the risky situation of feeling that one's life is worthless when that recognition is not there anymore. It is important for each person to become convinced of their own intrinsic value and of the fact that no failure, lack of performance, or lack of productivity can invalidate that value.

FIND YOUR *IBASHO*

The many cases examined here suggest that finding a niche or place to belong, *ibasho*, can be very helpful for people experiencing loneliness, because loneliness is not just about a lack of relationships, but also about the lack of a context or environment in which one can feel at home and oneself. Caring relationships can provide that context, but the context can also be established through finding a community where others share similar interests or experiences. We have also seen the value of having *ikigai*, but it does not seem helpful to me to suggest that people experiencing loneliness find *ikigai*. If such people can, that is of course wonderful. But we have seen that *ikigai* is not just arbitrarily choosing a goal in life; it is above all a feeling that one's life is worthwhile and has purpose. While experiencing loneliness, many people do not feel they have a clear sense of *ikigai*. It therefore seems that finding *ibasho* first may be simpler, and through that *ibasho*, or else perhaps later in life, *ikigai* may become available.

On suicide websites, newcomers are often greeted with comments from site regulars, who say things like "Everything is okay now. Please feel that this place is your *ibasho*." Both the suicide websites and the 3.11 experiences examined here show that even when people feel alone, they are typically not alone in their suffering. Rather, their suffering is shared by others. If such people can find others who also have similar feelings and experiences, this can help them to experience being empathized with and can start to create a feeling of *ibasho*.

BUILD SYSTEMS OF ACCEPTANCE

Attention to subjectivity suggests that our cultural and social systems need to be consciously transformed so that they can enhance rather than limit agency. The four abovementioned steps can all be taken by individuals and communities, but they will work best when supported, rather than hindered, by the social and cultural systems such individuals and communities inhabit and co-constitute. Specifically, systems should be critically evaluated to see to what extent they (1) normalize and address loneliness as a public health issue and a common human issue, rather than a pathology or disorder; (2) facilitate niches and places of *ibasho*, especially for those at risk of marginalization, instead of stigmatizing subcultures and those who suffer from mental illness and other afflictions; (3) frame "citizenship" not just as one's relation to the state, but as one's relationship to one's fellow members of society; and (4) emphasize the worth of individuals as something irreducible to that person's productivity and recognize that the state plays a role not just in supporting economic well-being and national security, but also in affecting the subjective lives and experiences of all members of society.

As has been mentioned several times in this book, society and subjectivity are highly interrelated. Therefore, the transformation of society into systems of acceptance is not something that can happen independent of the understanding, perceptions, feelings, and actions of the members who constitute it. For this reason, the five suggestions made here may be most effective if integrated into the educational system. Schoolchildren can be taught about the universality of loneliness and how to deal with it, the importance of accepting and not stigmatizing others based on difference, the importance of forming bonds and cultivating empathy, and the intrinsic value of each child. Indeed, more and more social and emotional learning programs are seeking to do just this. In the long term, I believe these can play a very meaningful role in addressing the epidemic of loneliness in Japan.

MENTIONABLE AND MANAGEABLE

In 1993 Fred Rogers, of *Mister Rogers' Neighborhood* fame, appeared on the *Arsenio Hall Show*. Hall told Rogers the concern he felt about the hopelessness troubling children and young people in the world. Rogers replied, "There's no simple answer of course. But if we could through television programs as well as every other imaginable program let people know that each one of us is precious. Let everybody know that we have value in this life." Rogers felt that society had to employ all of its resources, and deploy its media, to transmit this vital message to each child. Almost twenty-five years earlier, testifying before the US Congress in 1969 to save public television, Rogers described his television show in the following way: "This is what I give. I give an expression of care every day to each child to help him realize that he is unique. I end the program by saying, 'You've made this day a special day by just your being you. There's no person in the whole world like you. And I like you just the way you are.' And I feel that if we in public television can only make it clear that feelings are mentionable and manageable, we will have done a great service for mental health."[47]

This message seems as relevant and topical today—if not more so—as it was when it was uttered more than half a century ago. Unlike then, it is now a statement backed up by several decades of research from a wide variety of fields.[48] The message that needs to be shared today is the same: loneliness is mentionable and manageable.

Ten years have passed since the 3.11 disasters and over twenty years since the spike in suicide rates in 1998, yet once again the year 2020 saw a rise in suicide rates, especially among women. Again loneliness and suicide are in the news, now prompted by the worldwide coronavirus pandemic, which has prompted more women to kill themselves—often not because they are physically sick or because of the economy, but because of shame, stigma, stress, and domestic violence. Once again, a natural disaster is being compounded by a social one, with more individual lives as the cost that is paid. Again, instead of treating victims of the pandemic with empathy, individuals are too often shamed and blamed for having contracted the illness through irresponsibility. In a *New York Times* article, suicide researcher Michiko Ueda is quoted as lamenting, "Unfortunately the current tendency is to blame the victim. . . .We don't basically support you if you are not 'one of us.' [. . .] And if you have mental health issues you are not one of us."[49] Cluster suicides have not gone away either. After the actress Yuko Takeuchi committed suicide in September 2020, suicides by women increased almost 90 percent the following month over the previous year, as if they had heard the message of permission: "It's okay to die."[50]

Societies do not have to be lonely. People do not have to languish alone. Suffering does not have to be pathologized and stigmatized. But it will take a serious look at both the internal and external structures of society and subjectivity to alter the course we are now on. It will take actions that change our behaviors and institutions, not just in Japan but in other societies as well. And it will take imagination to envision new ways of being and new ways of living together, ways that promote the well-being of all and that leave no one behind.

Notes

INTRODUCTION

Parts of this chapter are drawn from a reworking of Ozawa-de Silva and Parsons (2020).

Houghton quoted in Cook (2018).

1. Prime Minister's Office et al. (2018).

2. John (2018).

3. Quoted in John (2018).

4. Holt-Lunstad et al. (2015).

5. See, for example, the work of Barbara Fredrickson and Steve Cole (Fredrickson et al. 2015).

6. Beutel et al. (2017); Cacioppo and Patrick (2008); de Jong Gierveld, van Tilburg, and Dykstra (2018); Peplau and Perlman (1982).

7. Cacioppo and Patrick (2008); Hammond (2018); Harris (2015); Hafner (2016); Perry (2014).

8. Joiner (2005); Kral (1994); Lester (1987).

9. Keyes (2002, 2005); Keyes, Shmotkin, and Ryff (2002).

10. Ryff, Keyes, and Hughes (2003); Seligman (2002); Seligman and Csikszentmihalyi (2000); Steger et al. (2006); Steger, Oishi, and Kashdan (2009); Steger and Samman (2012); Zika and Chamberlain (1992).

11. Allison (2013); Amamiya and Toshihito (2008).

12. Ozawa-de Silva (2008, 2009, 2010).

13. Dalai Lama and Brooks (2016).

14. This concept of the "lonely society" is elucidated in detail in chapters 5 and 6. The idea is not to think of societies as individuals writ large, or to assume a homogeneous society that experiences a single collective form of well-being or suffering, but rather to shift our attention to the social and structural conditions that promote and express well-being and suffering at scale. An individual need not be lonely all the time to be a lonely individual; not every member of a community needs to be impacted for us to say that the community was affected. Similarly, it is not necessary to say that every member of a society is lonely for us to meaningfully say that it is a "lonely society."

15. Ozawa-de Silva (2006).

16. Cacioppo and Patrick (2008); Rochat (2009b).

17. Moustakas (1961); Rochat (2009b).

18. Weeks et al. (1980).

19. Cacioppo and Patrick (2008); Weeks et al. (1980).

20. Peplau and Perlman (1982).

21. American Psychiatric Association (2013).

22. Cacioppo and Patrick (2008); Cacioppo, Fowler, and Christakis (2009); de Jong Gierveld, van Tilburg, and Dykstra (2018).

23. Cacioppo and Patrick (2008).

24. Cacioppo and Patrick (2008).

25. Cacioppo and Patrick (2008); Rochat (2009b).

26. de Jong Gierveld, van Tilburg, and Dykstra (2018); Holt-Lunstad et al (2015); Victor (2011); Andrew Steptoe et al. (2013).

27. Klinenberg (2018).

28. Cacioppo, Fowler, and Christakis (2009); de Jong Gierveld, van Tilburg, and Dykstra (2018).

29. Cattan et al. (2005); Golden et al. (2009); Routasalo et al. (2006); Tomaka, Thompson, and Palacios (2006); Victor et al. (2000); Cornwell and Waite (2009).

30. De Jong Gierveld, van Tilburg, and Dykstra (2018).

31. Hawkley and Cacioppo (2010); Luhrmann and Marrow (2016).

32. De Jong Gierveld, van Tilburg, and Dykstra (2018, 394).

33. Cook (2018); Victor (2011).

34. Beutel et al. (2017, 6).

35. De Jong Gierveld, van Tilburg, and Dykstra (2018); Cacioppo, Fowler, and Christakis (2009).

36. De Jong Gierveld, van Tilburg, and Dykstra (2018); Perlman and Peplau (1981, 31).

37. Rubin (2017, 1853).

38. Moustakas (1961).

39. Moustakas (1961, 530).

40. Moustakas (1961, 542).

41. Moustakas (1961, 530).
42. Weiss (1974).
43. De Jong Gierveld, van Tilburg, and Dykstra (2018).
44. De Jong Gierveld, van Tilburg, and Dykstra (2018).
45. Ozawa-de Silva (2008).
46. Perlman and Peplau (1981).
47. Robbins (2013).

CHAPTER 1. SUBJECTIVITY AND EMPATHY

1. Bourdieu (1990, 53).
2. Another symbol that comes to mind is the Chinese yin-yang symbol, which has the added advantage of showing how each side contains a bit of the other in its constitution. What is nice about the figure of Janus, however, is that it is faces that are looking, pointing to the sensory and perspectival nature of subjectivity as a looking out and looking in. The image therefore evokes the dual natures of engagement with the world alongside introspection, sharing a world alongside privacy and isolation, interdependence alongside independence.
3. Rochat (2009b, 303).
4. In religious, spiritual, and mystical contexts—and even recently in scholarship on mindfulness—there does arise discussion of "non-dual" experience—that is, experience that does not involve a subject or object or in which the subject/object divide dissolves. Whether such experiences are possible or not lies beyond the scope of this book. Nevertheless, the model of subjectivity presented here, which stresses that the membrane between self and other is dynamic and porous, and that the differentiation itself is fundamentally a constructed one, does not preclude the possibility of non-dual experiences. See for example Dunne (2011).
5. Damasio (1999).
6. Singer et al. (2004).
7. In death, a person departs alone, and those left behind cannot follow them. Yet those who are left behind may feel that the person lives on in their minds and hearts. Again, this speaks to the two aspects of subjectivity: shared experience and aloneness. A person's existence, particularly the existence of someone whom one cares about, is not something purely external; their existence is represented within one's own subjectivity. Just as that representation does not cease when the person is far away, so does it not necessarily cease when the person dies. As Jose Mourinho said of the passing of Bobby Robson, "A person only dies when the last person who loved him dies." Jones and Clarke (2018).
8. Damasio (1999) calls these higher order levels of selfhood the "extended self" and differentiates it from the "proto-self," that is, the organism's basic differentiation of itself from its environment.

9. Markus and Kitayama (1991). See also Kondo (1990).

10. Kitayama articulates how culture functions as affordances: "[P]eople in any given cultural context gradually develop through socialization a set of cognitive, emotional, and motivational processes that enable them to function well—naturally, flexibility, and adaptively—in the types of situations that are fairly common and recurrent in the cultural context" (1245). Self and subjectivity are malleable. He writes: "Becoming a self (i.e., a meaningful cultural participant) will require a turning and coordinating of one's responses with the prevalent pattern of public meanings and situations—or cultural practices" (1247); "given this culturally shared and sanctioned view, the major cultural task is to create and affirm a social relationship in which the self is seen as participating by fitting into and adjusting to such a relationship" (1260). Kitayama et al. (1997).

11. Good (2012).

12. Biehl (2005); Biehl et al. (2007)

13. Ekman (2003).

14. Kirmayer (2008, 462).

15. See for example Waal (2009).

16. A great deal of data supports the idea that individuals and groups who are at higher risk of exclusion and marginalization as a result of difference are at higher risk for suicide and mental health disorders. See for example Haas et al. (2010).

17. Gordon et al. (2013).

18. Blakemore and Choudhury, (2006).

19. Jenkins (1996, 72).

20. Ortner (2005); Luhrmann (2006); Biehl, Good, and Kleinman (2007).

21. Ortner (2005, 31).

22. Ortner (2005, 33).

23. Biehl (2005).

24. I believe this is the argument made by Ortner (2005), but her use of terminology is slightly confusing. She first defines "subjectivity" as both the internal states of subjects and the cultural formations that shape those states, but later speaks of the latter (cultural formations) as shaping *subjectivities*. If "subjectivity" includes cultural formations, then it cannot itself be shaped by those same cultural formations, as that would be circular. The relevant passages read: "By subjectivity I will mean the ensemble of modes of perception, affect, thought, desire, fear, and so forth that animate acting subjects. But I always mean as well the cultural and social formations that shape, organize, and provoke those modes of affect, thought and so on. Indeed, this article will move back and forth between the examination of such cultural formations and the inner states of acting subjects." And later she writes of "the ways in which particular cultural formations shape and provoke subjectivities." I believe it is much clearer, and more standard, to refer to only the inner states as subjectivity, while recognizing that

such states exist interdependently with cultural formations. Moreover, as I argue in this book, that interdependence is a two-way street: cultural formations and social structures are also "shaped, organized and provoked" by the intersubjectivity of subjects. They are indeed a manifestation of such. This is a way of reconstructing a theory of collective agency.

25. *Oxford English Dictionary*, 11th ed., s.v. "emotion." This is not to say that the idea of affective states is new or only emerged in the nineteenth century. In the Western tradition, Aristotle delineated various "passions" that were later elaborated upon by Descartes and others, such as "wonder, love, hatred, desire, joy and sadness" Crivelli and Fridlund (2019). In Asian traditions, it is interesting that Buddhism, despite concentrating heavily on the regulation of mental and affective states, has no term that closely correlates to "emotion" in Tibetan or Sanskrit, the closest perhaps being the terms that are typically translated as "afflictive emotions" (but that includes afflictive mental states that would not be considered emotions in the West). See for example Dalai Lama and Goleman (2003).

26. Damasio (2006); Lutz (2017, 186).

27. Lutz (2017, 188).

28. Luhrmann (2006, 356).

29. Luhrmann (2006, 359).

30. Annas (1993).

31. I see the Dalai Lama's conception of "secular ethics" as a sounder basis for the development of an approach to ethics that can be universal, cross-cultural, and open to negotiation across diverse traditions. Unlike Aristotle, the fundamental human value in the Dalai Lama's approach is compassion, in part because biologically based compassion, as manifested in practices such as maternal care, is fundamental to the survival of the human species, as well as of all mammalian and bird species, while extended forms of compassion are fundamental to social cohesion, cooperation, and other ethical pursuits, and also support the intrinsic and noninstrumental value that I discuss in this book. See Dalai Lama (2012).

32. Decety and Ickles (2009, vii).

33. Bateson (2009, 3).

34. Eisenberg and Fabes (1990, 132).

35. Singer et al. (2004).

36. Eisenberg and Fabes (1990, 132).

37. Strauss et al. (2016, 19).

38. Throop and Hollan (2008).

39. Kirmayer (2008).

40. Hollan (2008).

41. Geertz (1975).

42. While this may have been less objectionable in Geertz's day, a great deal of recent research has focused on overcoming the false divide between emotions

and reason. This has been a recent topic of a significant amount of neuroscientific research. For a popular and readable work, see Damasio (2006). See also Lane and Nadel (2002).

43. Allison (2013).

44. Friedman (1951).

45. Friedman (1951).

46. Friedman (1951).

47. Friedman (1951).

48. Maruyama (1969).

49. Vij (2007, 199).

50. Vij (2007). Vij explains this phrase in the following way: "The main point about political economy being the 'external structure of subjectivity' is to recognize that the institutionalization of modern capitalist economy, and the way in which the boundary between state and market is set (a historical-political process) matters in that it creates the structure within which both social meaning and subjects are fashioned. Japan's productivist ethos structured not only the economy, but also the state and subjects. Work therefore is enormously valued for its contribution to the social (not just individual) good." Vij (2021).

51. Vij (2021, 198).

52. Allison (2013).

CHAPTER 2. TOO LONELY TO DIE ALONE

Parts of this chapter are drawn from an extensive updating and reworking of Ozawa-de Silva (2010) and Ozawa-de Silva (2008).

1. Za Keijiban (2003).

2. Cho (2006); Ozawa-de Silva (2008); Pinguet (1993).

3. Di Marco (2016); Pinguet (1993); Ozawa-de Silva (2008).

4. Di Marco (2016, 29).

5. In contrast to Di Marco, Inamura (1977, 21) gives the start date for suicide data collection as a year later, in 1900.

6. Takahashi (1997, 2006, 1998); Ozawa-de Silva (2008, 2010); Di Marco (2016); Inamura (1977).

7. Di Marco(2016, 34).

8. Di Marco (2016, 34–35).

9. It is commonly observed that suicide rates tend to drop during wars, as French sociologist Emile Durkheim noted in his research on suicide in 1897. See Durkheim (1951).

10. Di Marco (2016, 113).

11. Takahashi (1998, 26; 1997a, 26; 1997b, 19).

12. Di Marco (2016, 112).

13. Mita (1971, 2006); Di Marco (2016, 113).
14. Di Marco (2016, 154); Takahashi (1997b, 19–22).
15. Takahashi (1997b, 16).
16. Takahashi (1998); Di Marco (2016, 154).
17. Takahashi (1997b, 16–19; 1998, 59–64).
18. Di Marco (2016, 35). See also Takahashi (1998, iii).
19. Di Marco (2016, 71–73); Takahashi (1998, 126–29).
20. Takahashi (1998); Di Marco (2016, 71–73).
21. Di Marco (2016, 35).
22. Keisatsu Chou Seikatsu Anzen Kyokyu Chiiki ka (2006); Takahashi (2001).
23. Takahashi (1999).
24. Keisatsu Chou Seikatsu Anzen Kyokyu Chiiki ka (2006); McIntosh (2004).
25. Jisatsutaikougaiyou (2006).
26. Cho (2006); Motohashi (2006).
27. Motohashi (2006).
28. Allison (2013); Vogel (1980, 1993).
29. Nakane (1972).
30. Desapriya and Iwase (2003).
31. "Heisei 29nen Ban Jisatsu Taisaku Hakusho" (2017).
32. "Heisei 27nen Ban Jisatsu Taisaku Hakusho" (2015).
33. "Heisei 27nen Ban Jisatsu Taisaku Hakusho" (2015).
34. Takahashi (2001).
35. Takahashi (1997a, 2001).
36. "Heisei 27nen Ban Jisatsu Taisaku Hakusho" (2015); Takahashi (2001).
37. "Jisatsushasū No Sūji" (2014); "Wakamono-Sō No Jisatsu Wo Meguru Jyōkyō" (2014).
38. "Heisei 27nen Ban Jisatsu Taisaku Hakusho" (2015).
39. "Jisatsu Taisaku Ni SNS Sōdan" (2018).
40. Maita (2016).
41. Amamiya and Toshihito (2008); Maita (2016).
42. Tsurumi (1993). Interestingly, just two years earlier in 1991, a somewhat similar book was published in the United States: *Final Exit: The Practicalities of Self-Deliverance and Assisted Suicide for the Dying* by Derek Humphry. Although more focused on euthanasia and physician-assisted suicide, the book became a best seller in the United States and attracted controversy and criticism for serving as a "how-to" manual for suicide.
43. Maccha no jo (2018).
44. Kasutama (2018).
45. Ten Ten (2016).
46. Con (2006); Shibui (2007).
47. Horiguchi and Akamatsu (2005, 19–26).
48. Con (2006); Horiguchi and Akamatsu (2005); Shibui (2007).

49. Hi-ho Kai-in Support (2007).
50. Horiguchi and Akamatsu (2005); Horiguchi and Emoto (2005, 31–49).
51. Horiguchi and Akamatsu (2005); Takahashi (2009).
52. Ueno (2005).
53. "Takuhai Dokubutsu de Jisatsuhoujoyōgikeishichōsōsanettotūji Chūmonka" (1998).
54. "Twitter 'Hangers' 'I Want to Die' Identify the Identity of Eight Housewives" (2017).
55. "Suichiro Takashi Shiraishi's Suicidal 'Hanging Neck' Is a Hot Topic!" (2018).
56. "Twitter 'Hangers' 'I Want to Die' Identify the Identity of Eight Housewives" (2017).
57. "I Escaped from the 'Hanger' in This Way" (2017).
58. "Netto Ga Tsunagu Shūdan Jisatsu Ato Tatazu" (2018).
59. Cho (2006); Takahashi (1997a).
60. Kitanaka (2011).
61. Kitanaka (2011).
62. See for example Takahashi (1997b, 1999, 2001).
63. Yukio (n.d.).
64. Desjarlais et al. (1995).
65. Pinguet (1993); Takahashi (1997a, 1999, 2001); Traphagan (2004).
66. Pinguet (1993, 3).
67. Pinguet (1993, 11).
68. Pinguet (1993, 13).
69. Ueno (2005).
70. See for example Uneo (2005).
71. Lock (1986, 1988).
72. Long (2005).
73. Woman (2006).
74. Akira Tsutsumi (2004).
75. Shi Ni Itaru Wake (2003).
76. Shi Ni Itaru Wake (2003, 10).
77. Shi Ni Itaru Wake (2003, 10).
78. Ohsawa (1996).
79. Ohsawa (1996); Saito (2003); Usui (2002); Machizawa (2003).
80. Asahi (2003).
81. Kagawa and Mori (2004); Okonogi (2005); Muta (2007).
82. Asakura (2005).
83. Borovoy (2008); Machizawa (2003); Saito (1998).
84. Machizawa (2003).
85. Machizawa (2003).
86. Takeshima (2009); Ueda (2005).

87. Horiguchi et al. (2005, 19–26).
88. Horiguchi et al. (2005, 19–26).

CHAPTER 3. CONNECTING THE DISCONNECTED

Parts of this chapter are drawn from an extensive updating and reworking of Ozawa-de Silva (2010) and Ozawa-de Silva (2008).

1. Ghetto (n.d.).
2. Jisatsu Saito Jisatsu Shigansha No Ikoi No Ba (n.d.).
3. The bulletin board service (BBS) was a precursor to the World Wide Web and provided sites where individuals could share files and join online discussion forums and chat rooms using dial-up connections via modem. BBSs were popular in the 1980s and early 1990s before people commonly had internet access from their homes.
4. Jisatsu Saito No Tōhyō Rankingu (2005).
5. It is worth noting that numerous such support sites and forums now exist online for a wide variety of life experiences and conditions, ranging from anorexia to autism to spousal infidelity. A single platform like reddit contains hundreds of such support groups alone. It is interesting that in Japan, it was specifically suicide sites that attracted a great deal of interest in the late 1990s and early 2000s.
6. Hi-ho Kai-in Support (2007).
7. Ozawa-de Silva (2008).
8. Boiled Egg (2006).
9. Boiled Egg (2006).
10. Boiled Egg (2006).
11. Boiled Egg (2018)
12. Shadow (2016).
13. Saya (2006).
14. Kiki (2006).
15. Den Den (2006).
16. Melancholy (2017).
17. Shu Shu (2006).
18. Friends (2017).
19. Boa (2006).
20. Kurosuke (2006).
21. Jingi (2006).
22. Totoro (2006).
23. Aya (2006).
24. Poison (2018).
25. Love Heart (2016).
26. Cocoa (2015).

27. Puffy (2016).
28. Nameless (2016).
29. No Name (2006).
30. Chun Chun (2016).
31. Frog (2018).
32. Trash (2017).
33. Zoo (2006).
34. Ballet Girl (2010).
35. Kanata (2010).
36. Ballet Girl (2010).
37. Kanata (2010).
38. Suicidal Student (2013).
39. Alex (2015).
40. Oh No (2015).
41. Oh No (2015)
42. Wing (2015).
43. Defect (2017).
44. Yoshie (2018).
45. Reiko (2017).
46. Demon God (2017).
47. Zaza (2018).
48. Girl A (2017).
49. Demon God (2017).
50. Kuru (2006).
51. Alice (2006).
52. Nantonaku (2006).
53. Ozawa-de Silva (2008, 2010)
54. Ozawa-de Silva (2010).
55. Bum (2006).
56. Chibi (2018).
57. Ken (2019).
58. Issho (2006).
59. Cookie (2006).
60. Ellie (2006).
61. Together (2005).
62. Maru (2006).
63. Nightmare (2006).
64. Gunma (2006).
65. Misery (2006).
66. Run Run (2006).
67. Sasaki (2007).
68. Long (2001, 273).

69. Mimi (2006).
70. Knight (2006).
71. Kore-eda (1998).
72. LeTendre (2000); Mead (2000); Pike and Borovoy (2004); White (1994).
73. LeTendre (2000).
74. Pike and Borovoy (2004, 508).
75. White (1994).
76. Ozawa-de Silva (2008).
77. Kinsella (1994, 170–96); Sugiyama-Lebra (1984); Pike and Borovoy (2004, 502).
78. McVeigh (1997).
79. Buckley (2009, xxx–xxxvi).
80. Sono (2001); Shimizu (1998); Fukutani (2003); Kurosawa (2008).
81. Kon (2004).
82. Ozawa-de Silva (2008).
83. Buckley (2009, xxxv).
84. Translation courtesy of http://www.anime-kraze.com.
85. Ozawa-de Silva (2010, 402).
86. Samuels (2007).
87. Long (2001).
88. Kleinman (2002, x).
89. Cho (2006); Pinguet (1993); Sadakane (2008); Shimizu (2005, 77–86).
90. Durkheim (1951).
91. Durkheim (1951).
92. Durkheim (1951, 282).
93. Durkheim (1951, 282).
94. Durkheim (1951, 282).
95. Durkheim (1951, 282).
96. Kirmayer (2002).
97. Kirmayer (2002, 295).

CHAPTER 4. MEANING IN LIFE

Parts of this chapter are drawn, with major modification, from Ozawa-de Silva (2020).

1. Sadakane (2008).
2. Mathews (1996a).
3. Rosenberger (2007, 92).
4. The concepts of a "good death" and "how to die well" are highly debated in Japan, and the problem of dying alone without family members around (*kodokushi*) is a matter of national concern, as numerous anthropologists have

examined. See Long (2000, 2005, 2012, 2020); Lock (1993, 2001); Traphagan (2000, 2003, 2004, 2010); Danely (2010, 2014); Lynch and Danely (2013).

5. Mathews (1996a); Rosenberger (2007); Allison(2013); Biehl (2005); Chua (2014); Stevenson (2014).

6. García and Miralles (2017); Tamashiro (2019).

7. Mathews (1996a); Taguchi (2014); Yamamoto-Mitani and Wallhagen (2002).

8. Mathews (1996a, 718).

9. Mathews (1996a, 718).

10. Kavedžija (2019, 2).

11. Wada (2000); Kavedžija (2019, 2).

12. Yamamoto-Mitani and Wallhagen (2002, 404).

13. Kamiya (2004); Yamamoto-Mitani and Wallhagen (2002, 404).

14. Kamiya (2004); Taguchi (2014).

15. Kamiya (2004).

16. Yamamoto-Mitani and Wallhagen (2002).

17. Kamiya (2004).

18. Taguchi (2014).

19. Yamamoto-Mitani and Wallhagen (2002, 407–9).

20. Yamamoto-Mitani and Wallhagen (2002, 403).

21. Mathews (1996a, 734).

22. Mathews (1996a, 735).

23. Mathews (1996a, 735).

24. Mathews (1996b, 1996a, 2017); Holthus and Manzenreiter (2017c); Kavedžija (2019); Ozawa-de Silva (2020).

25. Mathews (1996a).

26. Mathews (1996a, 733).

27. Allison (2013). Prior to this work, Marilyn Ivy (1995) also investigated similar themes in *Discourses of the Vanishing: Modernity, Phantasm, Japan*. See also Strauss's (2006) comment on Ivy's work which points to the tension between a singular national narrative (commonly promoted in Japan, including on topics of suicide, *ikigai*, and *ikizurasa*) and the multiple alternative narratives that exist under its surface. The section in this book on *Shoplifters* shows how director Kore-eda raises an alternative narrative to question the standard national one.

28. Allison (2013, 63).

29. Amamiya and Toshihito (2008); Allison (2013).

30. Sugiyama-Lebra (1976).

31. Translating phrases like *jibun ga nai* literally as "having no self" can have the unintended consequence of exoticizing and orientalizing Japanese. Some have even gone so far as to interpret the use of phrases like *jibun ga nai* as implying that Japanese people have no sense of individual self at all; they just go along with others and have no individual preferences or opinions separate from that of

the group. This is clearly untrue, however. Individual preferences exist strongly even in nonhuman animals and infants, who prefer one type of food over another or one type of treatment over another. To imply that Japanese people do not have individual preferences is therefore absurd. Our translation of such phrases from one language and one culture to another must steer clear of such exoticization. One way of accomplishing this is not losing sight of common humanity. This does not mean that we reject cultural and linguistic differences, or that we need to find an equivalent colloquial phrase in English. As Doi (2001) pointed out in his classic work on the Japanese word *amae* and the concept of dependency, such a word or phrase can specify a certain type of experience that is either more common in Japan or more specific to Japan than elsewhere. Thus, my own appeal to scholars engaged in such work would be to seek a middle ground that acknowledges both common humanity and the way experience can be, and always is, particularized in context. Those particularities should never, however, transgress the limits of common sense and common humanity. I explore the thorny issue of "Japanese selfhood" in far greater detail in Ozawa-de Silva (2007).

32. Manzenreiter and Holthus (2017b); Holthus and Manzenreiter (2017c); Kavedžija (2019).

33. Manzenreiter and Holthus (2017b); Holthus and Manzenreiter (2017c).

34. Holthus and Manzenreiter (2017b, 1); Manzenreiter and Holthus (2017b, 1–21).

35. Jiménez (2008); Mathews and Izquierdo (2008); Miles-Watson (2010); Jackson (2011, Jackson (2013); Johnston and Colson (2012); Thin (2008); Robbins (2013).

36. Mathews and Izquierdo (2008, 1). In *Pursuits of Happiness*, Mathews and Izquierdo propose four experiential dimensions of happiness: (1) the physical (e.g., health, physical abilities), (2) the interpersonal (e.g., family relations, social networks), (3) the existential (e.g., ideas, value systems that give people a sense of meanings of their life), and (4) the structural (an overarching dimension of cultural institutions). Conceptions of happiness vary cross-culturally, and Mathews writes that happiness in Euro-American contexts is associated more with personal achievement than it is in East Asia, where happiness is understood in terms of interpersonal connectedness. Holthus and Manzenreiter argue that happiness can even be perceived as potentially negative, since individual happiness can endanger social harmony among East Asians, leading to a "fear of happiness." See Mathews (2017) and Manzenreiter and Holthus (2017b, 7–8).

37. Keyes (2002, 2005, 2014); Keyes, Shmotkin, and Ryff (2002); Ryff, Keyes, and Hughes (2003); Keyes and Simoes (2012).

38. Russell (1996); Austin (1983); McWhirter (1990); Shevlin, Murphy, and Murphy (2015).

39. Manzenreiter and Holthus (2017c, 260).

40. Bondy (2017).

41. Holthus and Manzenreiter (2017a).
42. Walker and Kavedžija (2016, 2).
43. Tiefenbach and Kohlbacher (2017, 250).

CHAPTER 5. SURVIVING 3.11

1. A number of anthropologists such as João Biehl and Jason Danely depict vividly what it feels like to be abandoned, uncared for, and forgotten at individual and community levels. Biehl uses the phrase "zones of social abandonment" to refer to communities that are abandoned due to drug use, mental illness, or age. See Biehl (2005). Danely, in his study of a group of older Japanese in Kyoto, describes how his aging interlocutors were turning their feelings of being abandoned into a means to establish bonds (*kizuna*) among fellow pensioners, a process very similar to what is described in this book for North Ibaragi. Danely describes how his interlocutors experienced "feelings of being discarded and abandoned (by one's family, by society, by the younger generation)" and how these experiences stem from Japanese collective cultural attitudes and the "political structuring of care" (2014, 33).
2. Miyazaki (1984); Otomo (1988); Anno and Tsurumaki (1995–1996).
3. Lindee (2016).
4. Tabuchi (2014).
5. Tabuchi (2014).
6. National Police Agency of Japan (2019).
7. Watabe (2014).
8. "7 and a Half Years after the Great East Japan Earthquake the Number of Evacuees Is Still 58,000" (2018).
9. Allison (2013).
10. Mora (2014, 25).
11. Of interest here is Paul Brodwin's assessment of the ethical dilemma faced by frontline mental health clinicians regarding their medical power and being ethical and compassionate caregivers when engaging in forced medical treatment against the will of those they treat. See Brodwin (2014).
12. Biehl (2005).
13. Fujiwara-san and the other names in this chapter, except for Dr. Ito and Dr. Kawano, are pseudonyms.
14. "Fukushima Genpatsujiko No Shinjitu To Hōshanō Kenkō Higai" (2019).
15. "Ishinomaki-Shi No Higai Gaikyō, Fukkō No Jyōkyō" (2012).
16. Quoting the tension Clifford described as "living here and remembering/desiring another place," Brodwin investigates how displaced people construct a diasporic group identity and group affiliation based on their lost homeland. Clifford (1997, 255), quoted in Brodwin (2003).

CHAPTER 6. THE ANATOMY OF RESILIENCE

1. Myers (2015); Nakamura (2013).
2. Shay (2014).
3. Farnsworth et al. (2014).
4. "Kokoro No Kea Tiimu" (n.d.).
5. Kitanaka (2011); Kleinman (1988).
6. Kitanaka (2011, 109).
7. Kitanaka (2011, 17).
8. Nakamura (2013, 154).
9. Ozawa-de Silva (2010).
10. Gibson (1979).
11. Gibson (1979, 127).
12. Gibson (1979, 127).
13. Gibson (1979, 130).
14. Gibson (1979, 128).
15. Gibson (1979, 129).
16. Gibson (1979, 128).
17. Gibson (1979, 130).
18. Kukihara et al. (2014, 524).
19. Lewis (2020, 46–47).
20. The model and definition I use was developed with Brendan Ozawa-de Silva and is elucidated in the materials of Emory University's SEE Learning program, an educational program for the cultivation of resilience across multiple domains and dimensions. Information on the program and its approach is available at seelearning.emory.edu.
21. Mattingly (2014).
22. Myers (2016).
23. Ozawa-de Silva (2006).
24. Buder (2018).
25. As mentioned earlier, both of these are features of mammalian life and are not unique to human beings. One may ask what the difference is between reciprocity and paid-for services. In the case of reciprocity, one person may provide a service to another person with the hope or expectation that a similar favor or service will be repaid at a future date. The open-ended nature of reciprocity, however, means that it is the choice of the other actor when and how they will repay the favor. There are typically no legal consequences for failing to repay such a favor, although there may be social ones. In the case of a monetary exchange, payment and services are both mandated, and the failure of either party to correctly engage in the exchange bears significant legal and social consequences. This means there is an element of force implicit in such exchanges (backed up by the state), and less of an element of choice. See for example Alexy (2020) and Alexy and Cook (2019)

26. Saya (2006).
27. Lester (2013, 754).
28. Lester (2013, 758).
29. Lester (2013, 759).
30. Lester (2013, 759).
31. Grabbe and Miller-Karas (2018); Miller-Karas (2015).
32. Gagné (2020).
33. Gagné (2020, 719).
34. Wada (2011).
35. Gibson (1979, 129).
36. Gibson (1979, 127–28).

CHAPTER 7. WHAT LONELINESS CAN TEACH US

1. Soble (2015).
2. Kondo (1990); Sugiyama-Lebra (1976); Markus and Kitayama (1991); Shimizu and LeVine (2001).
3. Suizzo (2004).
4. Shimizu (2001b, 206).
5. Rochat (2009a, 314).
6. Rochat (2009a, 306).
7. Rochat (2009a, 308).
8. Rochat (2009a, 306).
9. Cooley (1983); Mead (1934); Heidegger (1962).
10. Taylor (1989).
11. Doi (2001).
12. Doi (2001).
13. Nakane (1967).
14. Kimura (1972); Hamaguchi (1982).
15. Mead (1934, 5); Rochat, (2009a, 8).
16. There is a cultural difference in terms of what Bourdieu might call the doxic position, namely that position that is culturally taken for granted and therefore remains typically beyond the domain of conscious analysis. See Bourdieu (1977).
17. Rochat (2009b).
18. Shimizu (2001b, 219).
19. Shimizu (2001a, 12).
20. Takahashi (1998).
21. Takahashi (1997a, 1999, 2001).
22. Joiner (2005).
23. Niezen (2009, 179).

24. Rochat (2009a).
25. Rochat (2009a, 314).
26. Ozawa-de Silva (2008); Ozawa-de Silva and Ozawa-de Silva (2010).
27. Cacioppo and Patrick (2008).
28. Keyes (2014); Keyes and Simoes (2012); Steger et al. (2006).
29. Ozawa-de Silva (2015).
30. Ozawa-de Silva (2015).
31. Ozawa-de Silva (2015, 267).
32. Ozawa-de Silva (2015, 268–69).
33. Cacioppo and Patrick (2008).
34. Ozawa-de Silva (2006).
35. Chilson (2018).
36. Strauss (2006, 336). As noted earlier, this comes in a response to Ivy (1995).
37. Ehrlich (2018).
38. Ehrlich (2018).
39. Ehrlich (2018).
40. As mentioned throughout this book, the fact that this type of care is required for the survival of all human and mammalian infants provides a developmental and evolutionary argument for why it is so important to human psychological, physical, and social well-being.
41. Vij (2007).
42. Kleinman (1998, 359).
43. Kleinman (1998, 362).
44. Ozawa-de Silva (2015, 199).
45. Ozawa-de Silva (2015, 383). This section builds off a reading of Kleinman's work presented in Ozawa-de Silva (2015).
46. Neff and Vonk (2009).
47. Danieldeibler (2015).
48. Much of this research is cited throughout this book, but I am thinking in particular of research on trauma, adverse childhood experiences, emotion regulation, social and emotional learning, and so on.
49. Rich and Hida (2021).
50. Rich and Hida (2021).

References

Akira Tsutsumi. 2004. Comment posted on "Why Are Suicide Pacts on the Rise in Japan?" *BBC News*, October 15. http://news.bbc.co.uk/2/hi/talking_point/3737072.stm.

Alex. 2015. Issho Ni Ikiyō. August 25. https://wailing.org/.

Alexy, Allison. 2020. *Intimate Disconnections: Divorce and the Romance of Independence in Contemporary Japan*. Chicago: University of Chicago Press.

Alexy, Allison, and Emma Cook, eds. 2019. *Intimate Japan: Ethnographies of Closeness and Conflict*. Honolulu: University of Hawai'i Press.

Alice. 2006. Ikizurasa Kei No Fōramu. November 1. http://8238.teacup.com/hampen/bbs.

Allison, Anne. 2013. *Precarious Japan*. Durham, NC: Duke University Press.

Amamiya, Karin, and Kayano Toshihito. 2008. *"Ikizurasa" Nitsuite: Hinkon, Aidentiti, Nashonarizumu* [Concerning "hardship of life": Poverty, identity, nationalism]. Tokyo: Kobunsha Shinsho.

American Psychiatric Association. 2013. *Diagnostic and Statistical Manual of Mental Disorders (DSM-5)*. 5th ed. Washington, DC: American Psychiatric Association.

Annas, Julia. 1993. *The Morality of Happiness*. Oxford: Oxford University Press.

Anno, Hideaki, and Kazuya Tsurumaki. 1995–1996. *Evangelion*. Tokyo: TV Tokyo.

Asahi. 2003. "Netto Shinjyū To Dyurukemu no Jisaturon" [Internet group suicide and the theory of suicide by Durkheim]. Happy Campus. www.happycampus.co.jp/docs/963400369997@hc08/18202/.

Asakura, K. 2005. *Jisatsu No Shisou* [Ideology of suicide]. Tokyo: Ota Shuppan.

Austin, Bruce A. 1983. "Factorial Structure of the UCLA Loneliness Scale." *Psychological Reports* 53 (3): 883–89.

Aya. 2006. Ikizurasa Kei No Fōramu. November 22. http://8238.teacup.com/hampen/bbs.

Ballet Girl. 2010. Onigami Keijiban [Demon God Bulletin Board]. www3.ezbbs.net/cgi/bbs?id=onigami&dd=05&p=11.

Bateson, Daniel. 2009. "These Things Called Empathy: Eight Related but Distinct Phenomena." In *Social Neuroscience of Empathy*, edited by Jean Decety and William Ickles, 3–16. Cambridge, MA: MIT Press.

Baumeister, Roy F., and Mark R. Leary. 1995. "The Need to Belong: Desire for Interpersonal Attachments as a Fundamental Human Motivation." *Psychological Bulletin* 117 (3): 497–529.

Beutel, Manfred E., Eva M. Klein, Elmar Brähler, Iris Reiner, Claus Jünger, Matthias Michal, Jörg Wiltink, Philipp S. Wild, Thomas Münzel, Karl J. Lackner, and Ana N. Tibubos. 2017. "Loneliness in the General Population: Prevalence, Determinants and Relations to Mental Health." *BMC Psychiatry* 17 (97): 1–7.

Biehl, João. 2005. *Vita: Life in a Zone of Social Abandonment*. Berkeley: University of California Press.

Biehl, João, Byron Good, and Arthur Kleinman, eds. 2007. *Subjectivity: Ethnographic Investigations*. Berkeley: University of California Press.

Bishop, Claire. 2012. *Artificial Hells: Participatory Art and the Politics of Spectatorship*. New York: Verso Books.

Black Jack. 2018. Onigami Keijiban [Demon God Bulletin Board]. www3.ezbbs.net/cgi/bbs?id=onigami&dd=05&p=11.

Blakemore, Sarah-Jayne, and Suparna Choudhury. 2006. "Development of the Adolescent Brain: Implications for Executive Function and Social Cognition." *Journal of Child Psychology & Psychiatry* 47 (3/4): 296–312.

Boa. 2006. Ikizurasa Kei No Fōramu. October 28. http://8238.teacup.com/hampen/bbs.

Boiled Egg. 2006. "Site Guide." Ghetto. http://ghetto.hatenablog.com/entry/2019/10/31/siteguide.

———. 2018. *Tamagon No Burogu* [Boiled Egg's blog] (blog). July 7. https://ydet.hatenablog.com/entry/2018/07/07/123000.

Bondy, Christopher. 2017. "'A Really Warm Place': Well-Being, Place and the Experiences of Buraku Youth." In *Happiness and the Good Life in Japan*, edited by Wolfram Manzenreiter and Barbara Holthus, 181–94. New York: Routledge.

Borovoy, Amy. 2008. "Japan's Hidden Youths: Mainstreaming the Emotionally Distressed in Japan." *Culture, Medicine, and Psychiatry* 32 (4): 552–76.

Bourdieu, Pierre. 1977. *Outline of a Theory of Practice*. Cambridge: Cambridge University Press.

———. 1990. *The Logic of Practice*. Stanford, CA: Stanford University Press.

Brodwin, Paul. 2003. "Marginality and Subjectivity in the Haitian Diaspora." *Anthropological Quarterly* 76 (3): 383–410.

———. 2014. "The Ethics of Ambivalence and the Practice of Constraint in U.S. Psychiatry." *Culture, Medicine, and Psychiatry* 38 (4): 527–49.

Buckley, Sandra. 2009. Preface to *Encyclopedia of Contemporary Japanese Culture*, edited by Sandra Buckley, xxx–xxxvi. New York: Routledge.

Buder, Emily. 2018. "With Japanese Cry Therapy Company Ikemeso Danshi, You Can Pay to Shed Tears." *Atlantic*, December 10. www.theatlantic.com /video/index/577729/crying-man-japan/.

Bum. 2006. Ikizurasa Kei No Fōramu. October 15. http://8238.teacup.com /hampen/bbs.

Cacioppo, John T., James H. Fowler, and Nicholas A. Christakis. 2009. "Alone in the Crowd: The Structure and Spread of Loneliness in a Large Social Network." *Journal of Personality and Social Psychology* 97 (6): 977–91.

Cacioppo, John T., Louise C. Hawkley, John M. Ernst, Mary Burleson, Gary G. Berntson, Bita Nouriani, and David Spiegel. 2006. "Loneliness within a Nomological Net: An Evolutionary Perspective." *Journal of Research in Personality* 40 (6): 1054–85.

Cacioppo, John T., and William Patrick. 2008. *Loneliness: Human Nature and the Need for Social Connection*. New York: W.W. Norton.

Cattan, Mima, Martin White, John Bond, and Alison Learmouth. 2005. "Preventing Social Isolation and Loneliness among Older People: A Systematic Review of Health Promotion Interventions." *Ageing and Society* 25 (1): 41–67.

Chibi. 2018. Shinitai Hito No Kōryū Saito. September 2. http://blued.sakura.ne .jp/bbs/35/yybbs.cgi?pg=45.

Chibnik, Michael. 2015. "Goodbye to Print." *American Anthropologist* 117 (4): 637–39.

Chilson, Clark. 2018. "Naikan: A Meditation Method and Psychotherapy." *Oxford Research Encyclopedia of Religion*. https://doi.org/10.1093/acrefore /9780199340378.013.570.

Cho, Yoshinori. 2006. *Hito Ha Naze Jisatsu Suru Noka* [Why do people commit suicide?]. Tokyo: Bensei Shuppan.

Chua, Jocelyn Lim. 2014. *In Pursuit of the Good Life: Aspiration and Suicide in Globalizing South India*. Berkeley: University of California Press.

Chun Chun. 2016. Gensō Tōya. February 29. www2.ezbbs.net/cgi/bbs?id=ruruto &dd=05&p=3.

Clifford, James. 1997. *Routes: Travel and Translation in the Late Twentieth Century*. Cambridge, MA: Harvard University Press.

Cocoa. 2015. Gensō Tōya. June 9. www2.ezbbs.net/cgi/bbs?id=ruruto&dd=05&p=3.

Con, I. 2006. *Shinu Jiyū To Iu Na No Sukui* [Salvation in the name of "freedom or death"]. Tokyo: Kawade Shobo.

Cook, Michael. 2018. "Are We in the Middle of a Loneliness Epidemic?" Foundation for Economic Education. January 11. https://fee.org/articles/are-we-in-the-middle-of-a-loneliness-epidemic/.

Cookie. 2006. Ikizurasa Kei No Fōramu. September 14. http://8238.teacup.com/hampen/bbs.

Cooley, Charles Horton. 1983. "Looking-Glass Self." In *Human Nature and the Social Order*, edited by Charles Horton Cooley, 183–85. New Brunswick, NJ: Transaction Publishers.

Cornwell, Erin York, and Linda J. Waite. 2009. "Social Disconnectedness, Perceived Isolation, and Health among Older Adults." *Journal of Health and Social Behavior* 50 (1): 31–48.

Crivelli, Carlos, and Alan J. Fridlund. 2019. "Inside-Out: From Basic Emotions Theory to the Behavioral Ecology View." *Journal of Nonverbal Behavior* 43 (2): 161–94.

Dalai Lama [Bstan-'dzin-rgya-mtsho]. 2012. *Beyond Religion: Ethics for a Whole World*. New York: Random House.

Dalai Lama [Bstan-'dzin-rgya-mtsho], and Arthur C. Brooks. 2016. "Behind Our Anxiety, the Fear of Being Unneeded." *New York Times*, November 4. www.nytimes.com/2016/11/04/opinion/dalai-lama-behind-our-anxiety-the-fear-of-being-unneeded.html.

Dalai Lama [Bstan-'dzin-rgya-mtsho], and Daniel Goleman. 2003. *Destructive Emotions: How Can We Overcome Them? A Scientific Dialogue with the Dalai Lama*. New York: Bantam Books.

Damasio, Antonio R. 1999. *The Feeling of What Happens: Body and Emotion in the Making of Consciousness*. New York: Harcourt College Publishers.

———. 2006. *Descartes' Error: Emotion, Reason, and the Human Brain*. New York: Random House.

Danely, Jason. 2010. "Art, Aging, and Abandonment in Japan." *Journal of Aging Humanities and the Arts* 4 (1): 4–17.

———. 2014. *Aging and Loss: Mourning and Maturity in Contemporary Japan*. New Brunswick, NJ: Rutgers University Press.

Danieldeibler. 2015. "May 1, 1969: Fred Rogers Testifies Before the Senate Subcommittee on Communications." www.youtube.com/watch?v=fKy7ljRroAA.

de Jong Gierveld, Jenny, Theo G. van Tilburg, and Pearl A. Dykstra. 2018. "Loneliness and Social Isolation." In *The Cambridge Handbook of Personal Relationships*, edited by Anita L. Vangelisti and Daniel Perlman, 485–99. Cambridge: Cambridge University Press.

Decety, Jean, and William Ickles. 2009. *Social Neuroscience of Empathy.* Cambridge, MA: MIT Press.

Defect. 2017. "Shinitai Hito No Kōryū Saito" [Site for suicidal people to communicate with each other]. September 2. http://blued.sakura.ne.jp/bbs/35/yybbs.cgi?pg=45.

Demon God. 2017. Onigami Keijiban [Demon God Bulletin Board]. www3.ezbbs.net/cgi/bbs?id=onigami&dd=05&p=11.

Den Den. 2006. Kokoro No Hanazono. November 16. http://bbs1.nazca.co.jp/12/.

Desapriya, Ediriweera B. R., and Nobutada Iwase. 2003. "New Trends in Suicide in Japan." *Injury Prevention* 9 (3): 284.

Desjarlais, Robert R., Leon Eisenberg, Byron Good, and Arthur Kleinman. 1995. *World Mental Health: Problems and Priorities in Low-Income Countries.* Oxford: Oxford University Press.

Di Marco, Francesca. 2016. *Suicide in Twentieth-Century Japan.* New York: Routledge.

Doi, Takeo. 2001. *Amae No Kozo* [Anatomy of dependency]. Tokyo: Kobundo.

Dunne, John. 2011. "Toward an Understanding of Non-Dual Mindfulness." *Contemporary Buddhism* 12 (1): 71–88.

Durkheim, Emile. 1951. *Suicide: A Study in Sociology.* New York: Free Press.

Ehrlich, David. 2018. "Kore-eda Hirokazu's Masterpiece 'Shoplifters' Is the Culmination of His Career." *IndieWire.* November 20. www.indiewire.com/2018/11/shoplifters-hirokazu-kore-eda-interview-palme-d-or-ethan-hawke-1202022396/.

Eisenberg, Nancy, and Richard A. Fabes. 1990. "Empathy: Conceptualization, Measurement, and Relation to Prosocial Behavior." *Motivation and Emotion* 14 (2): 131–49.

Ekman, Paul. 2003. *Emotions Revealed: Recognizing Faces and Feelings to Improve Communication and Emotional Life.* New York: Times Books.

Eliot, George. 1956. *Middlemarch.* Boston: Houghton Mifflin.

Ellie. 2006. Ikizurasa Kei No Fōramu. August 14. http://8238.teacup.com/hampen/bbs.

Far Away. 2018. Onigami Keijiban [Demon God Bulletin Board]. www3.ezbbs.net/cgi/bbs?id=onigami&dd=05&p=11.

Farnsworth, Jacob K., Kent D. Drescher, Jason A. Nieuwsma, Robyn B. Walser, and Joseph M. Currier. 2014. "The Role of Moral Emotions in Military Trauma: Implications for the Study and Treatment of Moral Injury." *Review of General Psychology* 18 (4): 249–62.

Fredrickson, Barbara L., Karen M. Grewen, Sara B. Algoe, Ann M. Firestine, Jesusa M. G. Arevalo, Jeffrey Ma, and Steve W. Cole. 2015. "Psychological Well-Being and the Human Conserved Transcriptional Response to Adversity." *PLOS One* 10 (3): 1–17.

Friedman, Milton. 1951. "Neoliberalism and Its Prospects." *Farmand*. February 17.

Friends. 2017. Ikikurushindeiru Hitotachi No Tame No Keijiban. March 30. www2.ezbbs.net/cgi/bbs?id=ruruto&dd=05&p=2.

Frog. 2018. Shinitai Hito No Kōryū Saito. April 28. http://blued.sakura.ne.jp/bbs/35/yybbs.cgi?pg=45.

"Fukushima Genpatsujiko No Shinjitu To Hōshanō Kenkō Higai" [The truth about Fukushima nuclear accident and the damage of radiation on health]. 2019. April 17. www.sting-wl.com/category/.

Fukutani, Osamu. 2003. *Jisatsu Manual* [Suicide manual]. DVD. Amumo K.K.

Gagné, Isaac. 2020. "Dislocation, Social Isolation, and the Politics of Recovery in Post-Disaster Japan." *Transcultural Psychiatry* 57 (5): 710–23.

García, Héctor, and Francesc Miralles. 2017. *Ikigai: The Japanese Secret to a Long and Happy Life*. New York: Penguin Life.

Geertz, Clifford. 1975. "On the Nature of Anthropological Understanding: Not Extraordinary Empathy but Readily Observable Symbolic Forms Enable the Anthropologist to Grasp the Unarticulated Concepts That Inform the Lives and Cultures of Other Peoples." *American Scientist* 63 (1): 47–53.

Ghetto. n.d. *Hatena Blog*. http://ghetto.hatenablog.com/.

Gibson, James J. 1979. "The Theory of Affordances." In *The Ecological Approach to Visual Perception*, 127–37. Boston: Houghton Mifflin.

Gilbert, Gustave. 1950. *The Psychology of Dictatorship: Based on an Examination of the Leaders of Nazi Germany*. New York: Ronald Press.

Girl A. 2017. Onigami Keijiban [Demon God Bulletin Board]. February 5. www3.ezbbs.net/cgi/bbs?id=onigami&dd=05&p=1.

Golden, Jeannette, Ronán M. Conroy, Irene Bruce, Aisling Denihan, Elaine Greene, Michael Kirby, and Brian A. Lawlor. 2009. "Loneliness, Social Support Networks, Mood and Wellbeing in Community-Dwelling Elderly." *International Journal of Geriatric Psychiatry* 24 (7): 694–700.

Good, Byron J. 2012. "Phenomenology, Psychoanalysis, and Subjectivity in Java." *Ethos* 40 (1): 24–36.

Gordon, Ilanit, Avery C. Voos, Randi H. Bennett, Danielle Z. Bolling, Kevin A. Pelphrey, and Martha D. Kaiser. 2013. "Brain Mechanisms for Processing Affective Touch." *Human Brain Mapping* 34 (4): 914–22.

Grabbe, Linda, and Elaine Miller-Karas. 2018. "The Trauma Resiliency Model: A 'Bottom-Up' Intervention for Trauma Psychotherapy." *Journal of the American Psychiatric Nurses Association* 24 (1): 76–84.

Gunma. 2006. Ikizurasa Kei No Fōramu. November 4. http://8238.teacup.com/hampen/bbs.

Haas, Ann P., Mickey Eliason, Vickie M. Mays, Robin M. Mathy, Susan D. Cochran, Anthony R. D'Augelli, Morton M. Silverman, et al. 2011. "Suicide and Suicide Risk in Lesbian, Gay, Bisexual, and Transgender Populations: Review and Recommendations." *Journal of Homosexuality* 58 (1): 10–51.

Hafner, Katie. 2016. “Researchers Confront an Epidemic of Loneliness.” *New York Times*, September 5. www.nytimes.com/2016/09/06/health/lonliness-aging-health-effects.html.

Hamaguchi, Eshun. 1982. *Kanjin Shugi No Shakai Nihon* [Japan, society of contextualism]. Tokyo: ToyoKeizai Shinpou Sha.

Hammond, Claudia. 2018. “Five Myths about Loneliness.” *BBC Future*. February 13. www.bbc.com/future/article/20180213-five-myths-about-loneliness.

Harris, Rebecca. 2015. “The Loneliness Epidemic: We're More Connected Than Ever—But Are We Feeling More Alone?” *Independent*, March 30. www.independent.co.uk/life-style/health-and-families/features/the-loneliness-epidemic-more-connected-than-ever-but-feeling-more-alone-10143206.html.

Hawkley, Louise C., and John T. Cacioppo. 2010. “Loneliness Matters: A Theoretical and Empirical Review of Consequences and Mechanisms.” *Annals of Behavioral Medicine* 40 (2): 218–27.

Heidegger, Martin. 1962. *Being and Time*. New York: Harper & Row.

“Heisei 27nen Ban Jisatsu Taisaku Hakusho” [The white paper of suicide prevention in 2015]. 2015. Kōseirōdōshō [Ministry of Health, Labour and Welfare]. www.city.kumamoto.jp/common/UploadFileDsp.aspx?c_id=5&id=12213&sub_id=1&flid=80342.

“Heisei 29nen Ban Jisatsu Taisaku Hakusho” [The white paper of suicide prevention in 2017]. 2017. Kōseirōdōshō [Ministry of Health, Labour and Welfare]. www.npa.go.jp/safetylife/seianki/jisatsu/H29/H29_jisatsunojoukyou_01.pdf.

Hi-ho Kai-in Support. 2007. “Hikite Yaku Ni Hikizurarete Shudan Jisatsu: Jisatsu Saito No Kyofu” [Lured into group suicide by recruiters: The danger of suicide websites]. http://home.hi-ho.ne.jp/support/info/security/colum/column05.html.

Hollan, Douglas. 2008. “Being There: On the Imaginative Aspects of Understanding Others and Being Understood.” *Ethos* 36 (4): 475–89.

Holthus, Barbara, and Wolfram Manzenreiter. 2017a. “Conclusion: Happiness as a Balancing Act Between Agency and Social Structure.” In *Happiness and the Good Life in Japan*, edited by Wolfram Manzenreiter and Barbara Holthus, 243–55. New York: Routledge.

———. 2017b. “Introduction: Making Sense of Happiness in ‘Unhappy Japan.’” In *Life Course, Happiness and Well-Being in Japan*, edited by Barbara Holthus and Wolfram Manzenreiter, 1–30. New York: Routledge.

———, eds. 2017c. *Life Course, Happiness and Well-Being in Japan*. New York: Routledge.

Holt-Lunstad, Julianne, Timothy B. Smith, and J. Bradley Layton. 2010. “Social Relationships and Mortality Risk: A Meta-Analytic Review.” *PLOS Medicine* 7 (7): 1–20.

Holt-Lunstad, Julianne, Timothy B. Smith, Mark Baker, Tyler Harris, and David Stephenson. 2015. “Loneliness and Social Isolation as Risk Factors for

Mortality: A Meta-Analytic Review." *Perspectives on Psychological Science* 10 (2): 227–37.

Horiguchi, Itsuko, and Rie Akamatsu. 2005. "Shakai Ni Okeru Jittai Ni Kansuru Kenkyū: Shimbun Ni Okeru Houdo No Jittai" [Research on actual conditions in society: Actual conditions of news reports]. In *Web Saito Wo Kaishiteno Fukusuu Douji Jisatsu No Jittai To Yobō Ni Kansuru Kenkyu Hōkokusho* [Research report on the actual condition and prevention for the multiple-simultaneous suicide via internet websites], edited by Shigeru Ueda, 19–26. Tokyo: National Institution of Mental Health, NCNP.

Horiguchi, Itsuko, K. Cho, Rie Akamatsu, and Masaru Emoto. 2005. "Shakai Ni Okeru Jittai Ni Kansuru Kenkyū: Daigakusei Wo Taisho Toshita Focus Group Interview Chosa" [Research on actual conditions in society: Survey of focus group interviews targeting the college students]. In *Web Saito Wo Kaishiteno Fukusuu Douji Jisatsu No Jittai To Yobō Ni Kansuru Kenkyu Hōkokusho* [Research report on the actual condition and prevention for the multiple-simultaneous suicide via internet websites], edited by Shigeru Ueda, 19–26. Tokyo: National Institution of Mental Health, NCNP.

Horiguchi, Itsuko, and Masaru Emoto. 2005. "Shakai Ni Okeru Jittai Ni Kansuru Kenkyū: Terebi Ni Okeru Houdo No Jittai" [Research on actual conditions in society: Actual conditions of TV reports]. In *Web Saito Wo Kaishiteno Fukusuu Douji Jisatsu No Jittai To Yobō Ni Kansuru Kenkyu Hōkokusho* [Research report on the actual condition and prevention for the multiple-simultaneous suicide via internet websites], edited by Shigeru Ueda, 31–49. Tokyo: National Institution of Mental Health, NCNP.

Humphry, Derek. 1991. *Final Exit: The Practicalities of Self-Deliverance and Assisted Suicide for the Dying*. New York: Random House.

"I Escaped from the 'Hanger' in This Way: A Confession of a 21-Year-Old Woman Who Earned a Lifetime in Nine Deaths While Promising Cohabitation." 2017. *Daily Shincho*, December.

Inamura, Hiroshi. 1977. *Jisatugaku* [Suicidology]. Tokyo: Tokyo Daigaku Shuppansha.

Ip, Ka, Alison Miller, Mayumi Karasawa, Hidemi Hirabayashi, Midori Kazama, Li Wang, Sheryl Olson, Daniel Kessler, and Twila Tardif. 2020. "Emotion Expression and Regulation in Three Cultures: Chinese, Japanese, and American Preschoolers' Reactions to Disappointment." *Journal of Experimental Child Psychology* 20: 1–19.

"Ishinomaki-Shi No Higai Gaikyō, Fukkō No Jyōkyō" [The general situation of the Ishinomaki-City's damage and its recovery]. 2012. www.city.ishinomaki.lg.jp/cont/10181000/8320/siryo1.pdf.

Issho. 2006. Ikizurasa Kei No Fōramu. September 15. http://8238.teacup.com/hampen/bbs.

Ivy, Marilyn. 1995. *Discourses of the Vanishing: Modernity, Phantasm, Japan*. Chicago: University of Chicago Press.

Jackson, Michael. 2011. *Life within Limits: Well-Being in a World of Want.* Durham, NC: Duke University Press.

——. 2013. *The Wherewithal of Life: Ethics, Migration, and the Question of Well-Being.* Berkeley: University of California Press.

Jenkins, Janis H. 1996. "Culture, Emotion and Psychiatric Disorder." In *Handbook of Medical Anthropology: Contemporary Theory and Method,* edited by Carolyn Sargent and Thomas Johnson, 71–87. Westport, CT: Greenwood Press.

Jiménez, Alberto Corsín. 2008. *Culture and Well-Being: Anthropological Approaches to Freedom and Political Ethics.* London: Pluto Press.

Jingi. 2006. Jisatsusha No Sōgen. December 16. www.cotodama.org/cgi-bin/.

Jisatsu Saito Jisatsu Shigansha No Ikoi No Ba [Suicide site: A relaxing place for suicidal people]. n.d. http://izayoi2.ddo.jp/top/.

Jisatsu Saito No Tōhyō Rankingu [Ranking of suicide sites]. 2005. Site Rank. http://cat.jp.siterank. org/jp/cat/1100102562/.

"Jisatsu Taisaku Ni SNS Sōdan: Wakamono Shien No Kōka Ha? Kadai Ha?" [SNS Consultingfor Suicide Prevention: What Is the Effectiveness of Support for the Young? What Are the Tasks?]. 2018. *Asahi Shimbun,* June 20.

"Jisatsushasū No Sūji" [Shift in a Number of Suicides]. 2014. Kōseirōdōshō [Ministry of Health, Labour and Welfare]. www.mhlw.go.jp/wp/hakusyo /jisatsu/16/dl/1-01.pdf.

Jisatsutaikougaiyou. 2006. "Ikiyasui Shakai No Genjitsu Wo Mezashite" [Aiming for the society for comfortable living]. www8.cao.go.jp /jisatsutaisaku/sougou/taisaku/kaigi_2/data/s1.pdf.

John, Tara. 2018. "How the World's First Loneliness Minister Will Tackle 'the Sad Reality of Modern Life.'" *Time,* April 25. https://time.com/5248016 /tracey-crouch-uk-loneliness-minister/.

Johnston, Barbara R., and Elizabeth Colson. 2012. "Vital Topics Forum: On Happiness." *American Anthropologist* 114 (1): 6–18.

Joiner, Thomas E. 2005. *Why People Die by Suicide.* Cambridge, MA: Harvard University Press.

Jones, Torquil, and Gabriel Clarke. 2018. *Bobby Robson: More Than a Manager.* DVD. Noah Media Group.

Kagawa, R., and K. Mori. 2004. *Netto Ohji To Keitai Hime: Higeki Wo Fusagutame No Chie* [Internet king and mobile phone princess: Wisdom for preventing tragedy]. Tokyo: Chuo Koron-sha.

Kamiya, Meiko. 2004. *Ikigai Ni Tsuite* [On the meaning of Ikigai]. Tokyo: Misuzu-Shobo.

Kanata. 2010. Onigami Keijiban [Demon God Bulletin Board]. www3.ezbbs.net /cgi/bbs?id=onigami&dd=05&p=11.

Kaori. 2006. Jisatsusha No Sōgen. December 22. www.cotodama.org/cgi-bin/.

Kasutama. 2018. "Review of 'The Complete Manual of Suicide' by Wataru Tsurumi." Amazon Japan. October 18. www.amazon.co.jp/-/en/%E9%B6%B4

%E8%A6%8B%E6%B8%88/dp/4872331265/ref=sr_1_3?dchild=1&keywords=%E8%87%AA%E6%AE%BA&qid=1623001044&s=books&sr=1-3.

Kavedžija, Iza. 2019. *Making Meaningful Lives: Tales from an Aging Japan.* Philadelphia: University of Pennsylvania Press.

Keisatsu Chou Seikatsu Anzen Kyokyu Chiiki ka. 2006. "Heisei 16 Nen Ni Okeru Jisatsu No Gaiyou Shiryō" [Abstract resources on suicide in 2004]. www.npa.go.jp/safetylife/seianki/jisatsu/H16/H16_jisatunogaiyou.pdf.

Ken. 2019. Shinitai Hito No Kōryū Saito. January 12. http://blued.sakura.ne.jp/bbs/35/yybbs.cgi?pg=45.

Keyes, Corey L. M. 2002. "The Mental Health Continuum: From Languishing to Flourishing in Life." *Journal of Health and Social Behavior* 43 (2): 207–22.

———. 2005. "Mental Illness and/or Mental Health? Investigating Axioms of the Complete State Model of Health." *Journal of Consulting and Clinical Psychology* 73 (3): 539–48.

———. 2014. "Mental Health as a Complete State: How the Salutogenic Perspective Completes the Picture." In *Bridging Occupational, Organizational and Public Health: A Transdisciplinary Approach*, edited by Georg F. Bauer and Oliver Hammig, 179–92. New York: Springer.

Keyes, Corey L. M., Dov Shmotkin, and Carol D. Ryff. 2002. "Optimizing Well-Being: The Empirical Encounter of Two Traditions." *Journal of Personality and Social Psychology* 82 (6): 1007–22.

Keyes, Corey L. M., and Eduardo J. Simoes. 2012. "To Flourish or Not: Positive Mental Health and All-Cause Mortality." *American Journal of Public Health* 102 (11): 2164–72.

Kiki. 2006. Nageki Keijiban. October 13. http://wailing.org/freebsd/jisatu/index.html.

Kimura, Bin. 1972. *Hito To Hito No Aida: Seishin Byōriteki Nihonron* [The space between people]. Tokyo: Kobundo.

Kinsella, Sharon. 1994. "Cuties in Japan." In *Women, Media, and Consumption in Japan*, edited by Brian Moeran and Lisa Skov, 170–96. Honolulu: University of Hawaii Press.

Kirmayer, Laurence J. 2002. "Psychopharmacology in a Globalizing World: The Use of Antidepressants in Japan." *Transcultural Psychiatry* 39 (3): 295–322.

———. 2008. "Empathy and Alterity in Cultural Psychiatry." *Ethos* 36 (4): 457–74.

Kitanaka, Junko. 2011. *Depression in Japan: Psychiatric Cures for a Society in Distress.* Princeton, NJ: Princeton University Press.

Kitayama, Shinobu, Hazel Markus, Hisaya Matsumoto, and Vinai Norasakkunkit. 1997. "Individual and Collective Processes in the Construction of the Self: Self-Enhancement in the United States and Self-Criticism in Japan." *Journal of Personality and Social Psychology* 72 (6): 1245–67.

Kleinman, Arthur. 1988. *The Illness Narratives: Suffering, Healing, and the Human Condition.* New York: Basic Books.

——. 1998. "Experience and Its Moral Modes: Culture, Human Conditions, and Disorder." Lecture presented at the Tanner Lectures on Human Values, Stanford University, April 13–15.

——. 2002. Preface to *Reducing Suicide: A National Imperative*, edited by Institute of Medicine, 4–7. Washington, DC: National Academies Press.

Klinenberg, Eric. 2018. "Is Loneliness a Health Epidemic?" *New York Times*, February 9. www.nytimes.com/2018/02/09/opinion/sunday/loneliness-health.html.

Knight. 2006. Nageki Keijiban. December 20. http://wailing.org/freebsd/jisatu/index.html.

"Kokoro No Kea Tiimu" [Mental health care teams]. n.d. Kōseirōdōshō [Ministry of Health, Labour and Welfare]. https://saigai-kokoro.ncnp.go.jp/activity/pdf/activity04_02.pdf.

Kon, Satoshi. 2004. *Paranoia Agent*. Tokyo: WOWOW.

Kondo, Dorinne. 1990. *Crafting Selves: Power, Gender, and Discourses of Identity in a Japanese Workplace*. Chicago: University of Chicago Press.

Kore-eda, Hirokazu. 1998. *Afterlife (Wandafuru Raifu* [Wonderful life]*)*. DVD. Engine Film.

Kral, Michael J. 1994. "Suicide as Social Logic." *Suicide & Life Threatening Behavior* 24 (3): 245–55.

Kukihara, Hiroko, Niwako Yamawaki, Kumi Uchiyama, Shoichi Arai, and Etsuo Horikawa. 2014. "Trauma, Depression, and Resilience of Earthquake/Tsunami/Nuclear Disaster Survivors of Hirono, Fukushima, Japan." *Psychiatry and Clinical Neurosciences* 68 (7): 524–33.

Kurosawa, Kiyoshi. 2008. *Tokyo Sonata*. DVD. Django Film.

Kurosuke. 2006. Kokoro No Hanazono. November 19. http://bbs1.nazca.co.jp/12/.

Kuru. 2006. Ikizurasa Kei No Fōramu. October 17. http://8238.teacup.com/hampen/bbs.

Lane, Richard D., and Lynn Nadel, eds. 2002. *Cognitive Neuroscience of Emotion*. Oxford: Oxford University Press.

Lester, David. 1987. *Suicide as a Learned Behavior*. Springfield, IL: Charles C. Thomas.

Lester, Rebecca. 2013. "Back from the Edge of Existence: A Critical Anthropology of Trauma." *Transcultural Psychiatry* 50 (5): 753–62.

LeTendre, Gerald K. 2000. *Learning to Be Adolescent: Growing up in U.S. and Japanese Middle Schools*. New Haven, CT: Yale University Press.

Lewis, Sara E. 2020. *Spacious Minds*. Ithaca, NY: Cornell University Press.

Lindee, Susan. 2016. "Survivors and Scientists: Hiroshima, Fukushima, and the Radiation Effects Research Foundation, 1975–2014." *Social Studies of Science* 46 (2): 184–209.

Lock, Margaret. 1986. "Plea for Acceptance: School Refusal Syndrome in Japan." *Social Science & Medicine* 23 (2): 99–112.

———. 1988. "A Nation at Risk: Interpretations of School Refusal in Japan." In *Biomedicine Examined*, edited by Margaret Lock and Deborah R. Gordon, 377–414. Boston: Kluwer Academic.

———. 1993. *Encounters with Aging: Mythologies of Menopause in Japan and North America*. Berkeley: University of California Press.

———. 2001. *Twice Dead: Organ Transplants and the Reinvention of Death*. Berkeley: University of California Press.

Long, Susan, ed. 2000. *Caring for the Elderly in Japan and the U.S.: Practices and Policies*. New York: Routledge.

———. 2001. "Negotiating the 'Good Death': Japanese Ambivalence about New Ways to Die." *Ethnology* 40 (4): 271–89.

———. 2005. *Final Days: Japanese Culture and Choice at the End of Life*. Honolulu: University of Hawaii Press.

———. 2012. "Ruminations on Studying Late Life in Japan." *Anthropology & Aging* 33 (2): 31–37.

———. 2020. "Family, Time, and Meaning Toward the End of Life in Japan." *Anthropology & Aging* 41: 24–45.

Love Heart. 2016. Gensō Tōya. October 24. www2.ezbbs.net/cgi/bbs?id=ruruto&dd=05&p=3.

Luhrmann, Tanya M. 2006. "Subjectivity." *Anthropological Theory* 6 (3): 345–61.

Luhrmann, Tanya M., and Jocelyn Marrow, eds. 2016. *Our Most Troubling Madness: Case Studies in Schizophrenia across Cultures*. Berkeley: University of California Press.

Lutz, Catherine. 2017. "What Matters." *Cultural Anthropology* 32 (2): 181–91.

Lynch, Caitrin, and Jason Danely, eds. 2013. *Transitions and Transformations: Cultural Perspectives on Aging and the Life Course*. New York: Berghahn Books.

Maccha no jo. 2018. "Review of 'The Complete Manual of Suicide' by Wataru Tsurumi." Amazon Japan. August 19. www.amazon.co.jp/-/en/%E9%B6%B4%E8%A6%8B-%E6%B8%88/dp/4872331265/ref=sr_1_3?dchild=1&keywords=%E8%87%AA%E6%AE%BA&qid=1623001044&s=books&sr=1-3.

Machizawa, Shizuo. 2003. *Hikikomoru Wakamonotachi* [Withdrawn youths]. Tokyo: Daiwa Shobo.

Maita, Toshihiko. 2016. "Zetsubō No Kuni Nihon Ha Sekai Ichi 'Wakamono Jisatsusha' Wo Ryōsan Shiteiru" [Desperate country Japan has been producing "Suicide Among Young People"]. *President Online*, January 12. https://president.jp/articles/-/17058.

Manzenreiter, Wolfram, and Barbara Holthus, eds. 2017a. *Happiness and the Good Life in Japan*. New York: Routledge.

———. 2017b. "Introduction: Happiness in Japan Through the Anthropological Lens." In *Happiness and the Good Life in Japan*, edited by Wolfram Manzenreiter and Barbara Holthus, 1–22. New York: Routledge.

———. 2017c. “Reconsidering the Four Dimensions of Happiness across the Life Course in Japan.” In *Life Course, Happiness and Well-Being in Japan*, edited by Barbara Holthus and Wolfram Manzenreiter, 256–72. New York: Routledge.

Markus, Hazel R., and Shinobu Kitayama. 1991. “Culture and the Self: Implications for Cognition, Emotion, and Motivation.” *Psychological Review* 98 (2): 224–53.

Maru. 2006. Ikizurasa Kei No Fōramu. November 7. http://8238.teacup.com/hampen/bbs.

Maruyama, Masao. 1969. *Thought and Behavior in Modern Japanese Politics*. London: Oxford University Press.

Mathews, Gordon. 1996a. “The Stuff of Dreams, Fading: Ikigai and ‘The Japanese Self.’” *Ethos* 24 (4): 718–47.

———. 1996b. *What Makes Life Worth Living? How Japanese and Americans Make Sense of Their Worlds*. Berkeley: University of California Press.

———. 2017. “Happiness in Neoliberal Japan.” In *Happiness and the Good Life in Japan*, edited by Wolfram Manzenreiter and Barbara Holthus, 227–43. New York: Routledge.

Mathews, Gordon, and Carolina Izquierdo. 2008. *Pursuits of Happiness: Well-Being in Anthropological Perspective*. New York: Berghahn Books.

Mattingly, Cheryl. 2014. *Moral Laboratories: Family Peril and the Struggle for a Good Life*. Berkeley: University of California Press.

McIntosh, John L. 2004. “Year 2004 Official Final Data on Suicide in the United States.” American Association of Suicidology. www.suicidology.org.

McVeigh, Brian J. 1997. *Life in a Japanese Women’s College: Learning to Be Ladylike*. New York: Routledge.

McWhirter, Benedict T. 1990. “Factor Analysis of the Revised UCLA Loneliness Scale.” *Current Psychology* 9 (1): 56–68.

Mead, George Herbert. 1934. *Mind, Self, and Society*. Chicago: University of Chicago Press.

Mead, Margaret. 2000. *Coming of Age in Samoa*. New York: Harper Perennial Modern Classics.

Melancholy. 2017. Shinitai Hito No Kōryū Saito. August 29. http://blued.sakura.ne.jp/bbs/35/yybbs.cgi?pg=45.

Miles-Watson, Jonathan. 2010. “Political Economy, Religion and Wellbeing: The Practices of Happiness.” In *Ethnographic Insights into Happiness*, 125–33. New York: Routledge.

Miller-Karas, Elaine. 2015. *Building Resilience to Trauma: The Trauma and Community Resiliency Models*. New York: Routledge.

Mimi. 2006. Nageki Keijiban. December 11. http://wailing.org/freebsd/jisatu/index.html.

Misery. 2006. Ikizurasa Kei No Fōramu. September 15. http://8238.teacup.com/hampen/bbs.

Mita, Munesuke. 1971. *Gendai Nihon No Shinjō To Ronri* [Sentiment and logic in contemporary Japan]. Tokyo: Kōbundō.

———. 2006. *Shakaigaku Nyūmon* [Introduction to sociology]. Tokyo: Iwaba Shoten.

Miyazaki, Hayao. 1984. *Nausicaa of the Valley of the Wind*. VHS. Toei Company.

Mora, Ralph B. 2014. "Lessons Learned about PTSD from the Disaster in Fukushima." *Journal of Healthcare, Science and the Humanities* 4 (2): 23–39.

Motohashi, Yutaka. 2006. *Stop: Jisatsu* [Stop: Suicide]. Tokyo: Kaimeisha.

Moustakas, Clark E. 1961. *Loneliness*. New York: Prentice Hall.

Muta, T. 2007. *Netto Izon No Kyofu* [Fear of the internet addiction]. Tokyo: Kyuiku Shuppan.

Myers, Neely Laurenzo. 2015. *Recovery's Edge: An Ethnography of Mental Health Care and Moral Agency*. Nashville, TN: Vanderbilt University Press.

———. 2016. "Recovery Stories: An Anthropological Exploration of Moral Agency in Stories of Mental Health Recovery." *Transcultural Psychiatry* 53 (4): 427–44.

Nakamura, Karen. 2013. *A Disability of the Soul: An Ethnography of Schizophrenia and Mental Illness in Contemporary Japan*. Ithaca, NY: Cornell University Press.

Nakane, Chie. 1967. *Tate Shakai No Ningen Kankei* [Human relationships in the vertical society]. Tokyo: Kodansha Shinsho.

———. 1972. *Japanese Society*. Berkeley: University of California Press.

Nameless. 2016. Onigami Keijiban [Demon God Bulletin Board]. October 31. www3.ezbbs.net/cgi/bbs?id=onigami&dd=05&p=11.

Nantonaku. 2006. Jisatsusha No Sōgen. December 24. www.cotodama.org/cgi-bin/.

National Police Agency of Japan. 2019. "Damage Situation and Police Countermeasures Associated with 2011 Tohoku District—Off the Pacific Ocean Earthquake." www.npa.go.jp/news/other/earthquake2011/pdf/higaijokyo_e.pdf.

Neff, Kristin D., and Roos Vonk. 2009. "Self-Compassion Versus Global Self-Esteem: Two Different Ways of Relating to Oneself." *Journal of Personality* 77 (1): 23–50.

"Netto Ga Tsunagu Shūdan Jisatsu Ato Tatazu: Jyūtaku Ni Danjo 5 Itai" [Never ceasing internetrelated group suicide: 5 dead bodies of men and women at a residence]. 2018. *Nihon Keizai Shimbun*, July 22.

Niezen, Ronald. 2009. "Suicide as a Way of Belonging: Causes and Consequences of Cluster Suicides in Aboriginal Communities." In *Healing Traditions: The Mental Health of Aboriginal Peoples in Canada*, edited by Laurence J. Kirmayer and Gail Valaskakis, 178–95. Vancouver: University of British Columbia Press.

Nightmare. 2006. Ikizurasa Kei No Fōramu. November 6. http://8238.teacup.com/hampen/bbs.

No Name. 2006. Jisatsusha No Sōgen. July 14. www.cotodama.org/cgi-bin/.

Oh No. 2015. Issho Ni Ikiyō. March 20. https://wailing.org/.

Ohsawa, Masaki. 1996. *Kyōko No Jidai No Hate: AUM To Sekai Saishu Sensou* [The end of the era of fiction]. Tokyo: Chikuma Shobo.

OK. n.d. Gensō Tōya. www2.ezbbs.net/cgi/bbs?id=ruruto&dd=05&p=3.

Okonogi, Keigo. 2005. *Keitai Netto Ningen No Seishin Bunseki* [Psychoanalysis of mobile phone and internet people]. Tokyo: Asahi Shimbun-sha.

Onigami. 2017. Onigami Keijiban [Demon God Bulletin Board]. October 5. www3.ezbbs.net/05/onigami/.

Ortner, Sherry B. 2005. "Subjectivity and Cultural Critique." *Anthropological Theory* 5 (1): 31–52.

Otomo, Katsuhiro. 1988. *Akira*. VHS. Toho.

Ozawa-de Silva, Brendan. 2015. "Becoming the Wish-Fulfilling Tree: Compassion and the Transformation of Ethical Subjectivity in the Lojong Tradition of Tibetan Buddhism." PhD diss., Emory University.

Ozawa-de Silva, Chikako. 2006. *Psychotherapy and Religion in Japan: The Japanese Introspection Practice of Naikan*. New York: Routledge.

———. 2007. "Demystifying Japanese Therapy: An Analysis of Naikan and the Ajase Complex through Buddhist Thought." *Ethos: Journal of the Society for Psychological Anthropology* 35 (4): 411–46.

———. 2008. "Too Lonely to Die Alone: Internet Suicide Pacts and Existential Suffering in Japan." *Culture, Medicine and Psychiatry* 32 (4): 516–51.

———. 2009. "Seeking to Escape the Suffering of Existence: Internet Suicide in Japan." In *Understanding and Applying Medical Anthropology*, edited by Peter J. Brown and Ronald L. Barrett, 246–58. Mountain View, CA: Mayfield.

———. 2010. "Shared Death: Self, Sociality and Internet Group Suicide in Japan." *Transcultural Psychiatry* 47 (3): 392–418.

———. 2017. "Wakamono No Jisatsu Kara Mieru Seizonteki Kunō" [Existential suffering and suicide among youth.] *Clinical Psychology* 17 (4): 568–69.

———. 2020. "In the Eyes of Others: Loneliness and Relational Meaning in Life Among Japanese College Students." *Transcultural Psychiatry* 57 (5): 623–34.

Ozawa-de Silva, Chikako, and Brendan Ozawa-de Silva. 2010. "Secularizing Religious Practices: A Study of Subjectivity and Existential Transformation in Naikan Therapy." *Journal for the Scientific Study of Religion* 49 (1): 147–61.

Ozawa-de Silva, Chikako, and Michelle Parsons. 2020. "Toward an Anthropology of Loneliness." *Transcultural Psychiatry* 57 (5): 613–22.

Peplau, Letitia Anne, and Daniel Perlman. 1982. *Loneliness: A Sourcebook of Current Theory, Research, and Therapy*. New York: Wiley.

Perlman, Daniel, and Letitia A. Peplau. 1981. "Toward a Social Psychology of Loneliness." In *Personal Relationships 3: Personal Relationships in Disorder*, edited by Robin Gilmour and Steve Duck, 31–43. London: Academic Press.

Perry, Philippa. 2014. "Loneliness Is Killing Us—We Must Start Treating This Disease." *Guardian*, February 17. www.theguardian.com/commentisfree/2014/feb/17/loneliness-report-bigger-killer-obesity-lonely-people.

Pike, Kathleen M., and Amy Borovoy. 2004. "The Rise of Eating Disorders in Japan: Issues of Culture and Limitations of the Model of 'Westernization.'" *Culture, Medicine and Psychiatry* 28 (4): 493–531.

Pinguet, Maurice. 1993. *Voluntary Death in Japan*. Hoboken, NJ: Wiley.

Poison. 2018. Issho Ni Ikiyō. October 25. https://wailing.org/.

Prime Minister's Office, Department for Digital, Culture, Media & Sport, Office for Civil Society, and The Right Honourable Theresa May. 2018. "PM Launches Government's First Loneliness Strategy." GOV.UK. October 15. www.gov.uk/government/news/pm-launches-governments-first-loneliness-strategy.

Puffy. 2016. Gensō Tōya. March 4. www2.ezbbs.net/cgi/bbs?id=ruruto&dd=05&p=3.

Qualter, Pamela, Janne Vanhalst, Rebecca Harris, Eeske Van Roekel, Gerine Lodder, Munirah Bangee, Marlies Maes, and Maaike Verhagen. 2015. "Loneliness across the Life Span." *Perspectives on Psychological Science* 10 (2): 250–64.

Reiko. 2017. Onigami Keijiban [Demon God Bulletin Board]. October 14. www3.ezbbs.net/05/onigami/.

Rich, Motoko, and Hikari Hida. 2021. "As Pandemic Took Hold, Suicide Rose among Japanese Women." *New York Times*, February 23. www.nytimes.com/2021/02/22/world/asia/japan-women-suicide-coronavirus.html.

Robbins, Joel. 2013. "Beyond the Suffering Subject: Toward an Anthropology of the Good." *Journal of the Royal Anthropological Institute* 19 (3): 447–62.

Rochat, Philippe. 2009a. "Commentary: Mutual Recognition as a Foundation of Sociality and Social Comfort." In *Social Cognition: Development, Neuroscience, and Autism*, edited by Tricia Striano and Vincent Reid, 303–17. Malden, MA: Blackwell.

———. 2009b. *Others in Mind: Social Origins of Self-Consciousness*. Cambridge: Cambridge University Press.

Rosenberger, Nancy. 2001. *Gambling with Virtue*. Honolulu: University of Hawaii Press.

———. 2007. "Rethinking Emerging Adulthood in Japan: Perspectives from Long-Term Single Women." *Child Development Perspectives* 1 (2): 92–95.

Routasalo, Pirkko E., Niina Savikko, Reijo S. Tilvis, Timo E. Strandberg, and Kaisu H. Pitkälä. 2006. "Social Contacts and Their Relationship to Loneliness Among Aged People—A Population-Based Study." *Gerontology* 52 (3): 181–87.

Rubin, Rita. 2017. "Loneliness Might Be a Killer, but What's the Best Way to Protect against It?" *Journal of the American Medical Association* 318 (19): 1853–55.

Run Run. 2006. Ikizurasa Kei No Fōramu. September 14. http://8238.teacup.com/hampen/bbs.

Russell, Daniel W. 1996. "UCLA Loneliness Scale (Version 3): Reliability, Validity, and Factor Structure." *Journal of Personality Assessment* 66 (1): 20–40.

Russell, Daniel W., Carolyn E. Cutrona, Cynthia McRae, and Mary Gomez. 2012. "Is Loneliness the Same as Being Alone?" *Journal of Psychology* 146 (1–2): 7–22.

Ryff, Carol D., Corey L. M. Keyes, and Diane L. Hughes. 2003. "Status Inequalities, Perceived Discrimination, and Eudaimonic Well-Being: Do the Challenges of Minority Life Hone Purpose and Growth?" *Journal of Health and Social Behavior* 44 (3): 275–91.

Sadakane, Hideyuki. 2008. "A Sociological Investigation on 'Group Suicides through the Internet' in Japan." *Japanese Sociological Review* 58 (4): 593–607.

Saito, Kan. 2003. "Iki Kihaku Sa, Kontei Ni" [On the fundamental thinness of life]. *Asahi Shimbun*.

Saito, Tamaki. 1998. *Shakai Teki Hikikomori* [Social withdrawal]. Tokyo: PHP Shinsho.

Sato, Keisuke. 2018. "Jisatsu Taisaku Ni SNS Sōdan: Wakamono Shien No Kōka Ha? Kadai Ha?" [SNS consulting for suicide prevention: What is the effectiveness of support for the young? What are the tasks?]. *Asahi Shimbun*, June 20. https://digital.asahi.com/articles/ASL6N23PVL6NUBQU002.html.

Samuels, David. 2007. "Let's Die Together." *Atlantic*, May. www.theatlantic.com/magazine/archive/2007/05/let-s-die-together/305776/.

Sasaki, Tishinao. 2007. "Otte Masukomi Intānetto Shinjyū Hōdō No Otoshiana" [The catch of the major mass media reports on internet suicide pacts]. http://homepage3.nifty.com/sasakitoshinao/pcexplorer_5.html.

Saya. 2006. Nageki Keijiban. October 12. http://wailing.org/freebsd/jisatu/index.html.

Schinka, Katherine C., Manfred H. M. VanDulmen, Robert Bossarte, and Monica Swahn. 2012. "Association Between Loneliness and Suicidality during Middle Childhood and Adolescence: Longitudinal Effects and the Role of Demographic Characteristics." *Journal of Psychology* 146 (1–2): 105–18.

Seligman, Martin E. P. 2002. *Authentic Happiness: Using the New Positive Psychology to Realize Your Potential for Lasting Fulfillment*. New York: Free Press.

Seligman, Martin E. P., and Mihaly Csikszentmihalyi. 2000. "Positive Psychology: An Introduction." *American Psychologist* 55 (1): 5–14.

"7 and a Half Years after the Great East Japan Earthquake the Number of Evacuees Is Still 58,000." 2018. *Mainichi News*, September 10. https://mainichi.jp/articles/20180911/k00/00m/040/127000c.

Shadow. 2016. Issho Ni Ikiyō. June 22. https://wailing.org/.

Shay, Jonathan. 2014. "Moral Injury." *Psychoanalytic Psychology* 31 (2): 182–91.
Shevlin, Mark, Siobhan Murphy, and Jamie Murphy. 2015. "The Latent Structure of Loneliness: Testing Competing Factor Models of the UCLA Loneliness Scale in a Large Adolescent Sample." *Assessment* 22 (2): 208–15.
Shibui. 2012. "It Is Lonely to Die Alone." October. https://biz-journal.jp/2012/10/post_883_3.html.
Shibui, T. 2007. *Wakamono Tachi Ha Naze Jisatsu Surunoka* [Why do young people commit suicide?]. Tokyo: Nagasaki Shuppan.
Shimizu. 2018. Shirabee. August 17. https://sirabee.com/2018/08/17/20161754117/.
Shimizu, Hidetada. 2001a. "Introduction: Japanese Cultural Psychology and Empathic Understanding: Implications for Academic and Cultural Psychology." In *Japanese Frames of Mind: Cultural Perspectives on Human Development*, edited by Hidetada Shimizu and Robert A. LeVine, 1–26. Cambridge: Cambridge University Press.
———. 2001b. "Beyond Individualism and Sociocentrism: An Ontological Analysis of the Opposing Elements in Personal Experiences of Japanese Adolescents." In *Japanese Frames of Mind: Cultural Perspectives on Human Development*, edited by Hidetada Shimizu and Robert A. LeVine, 205–27. Cambridge: Cambridge University Press.
Shimizu, Hidetada, and Robert A. LeVine, eds. 2001. *Japanese Frames of Mind: Cultural Perspectives on Human Development*. Cambridge: Cambridge University Press.
Shimizu, Hiroshi. 1998. *Ikinai* [Not going to live]. DVD. Office Kitano.
Shimizu, Shinji. 2005. "Gendai Nihon No Ningen Pataan To Jyoho Kiki Komunikaishion" [Human relation patterns and information equipment communication for modern people]. In *Web Saito Wo Kaishiteno Fukusuu Douji Jisatu No Jittai to Yobō Ni Kansuru Kenkyū Hōkokusho* [Research report on the actual condition and prevention for the multiple-simultaneous suicide via internet websites], edited by Shigeru Ueda, 77–86. Tokyo: National Institution of Mental Health, NCNP.
"Shi Ni Itaru Wake" [Reasons to reach death]. 2003. *AERA*.
Shu Shu. 2006. Ikizurasa Kei No Fōramu. December 13. http://8238.teacup.com/hampen/bbs.
Singer, Tania, Ben Seymour, John O'Doherty, Holger Kaube, Raymond J. Dolan, and Chris D. Frith. 2004. "Empathy for Pain Involves the Affective but Not Sensory Components of Pain." *Science* 303 (5661): 1157–62.
Soble, Jonathan. 2015. "Japan to Pay Cancer Bills for Fukushima Worker." *New York Times*, October 20. www.nytimes.com/2015/10/21/world/asia/japan-cancer-fukushima-nuclear-plant-compensation.html.
Sono, Sion. 2001. *Suicide Circle* [Suicide club]. DVD. Earthrise.
"Sorry That I'm Alive." 2018. Onigami Keijiban [Demon God Bulletin Board]. www3.ezbbs.net/cgi/bbs?id=onigami&dd=05&p=11.

Steger, Michael F., Patricia Frazier, Shigehiro Oishi, and Matthew Kaler. 2006. "The Meaning in Life Questionnaire: Assessing the Presence of and Search for Meaning in Life." *Journal of Counseling Psychology* 53 (1): 80–93.

Steger, Michael F., Shigehiro Oishi, and Todd B. Kashdan. 2009. "Meaning in Life across the Life Span: Levels and Correlates of Meaning in Life from Emerging Adulthood to Older Adulthood." *Journal of Positive Psychology* 4 (1): 43–52.

Steger, Michael F., and Emma Samman. 2012. "Assessing Meaning in Life on an International Scale: Psychometric Evidence for the Meaning in Life Questionnaire-Short Form among Chilean Households." *International Journal of Wellbeing* 2 (3): 182–95.

Steptoe, Andrew, Aparna Shankar, Panayotes Demakakos, and Jane Wardle. 2013. "Social Isolation, Loneliness, and All-Cause Mortality in Older Men and Women." *Proceedings of the National Academy of Sciences* 110 (15): 5797–801.

Stevenson, Lisa. 2014. *Life Beside Itself: Imagining Care in the Canadian Arctic.* Berkeley: University of California Press.

Strauss, Clara, Billie Lever Taylor, Jenny Gu, Willem Kuyken, Ruth Baer, Fergal Jones, and Kate Cavanagh. 2016. "What Is Compassion and How Can We Measure It? A Review of Definitions and Measures." *Clinical Psychology Review* 47: 15–27.

Strauss, Claudia. 2006. "The Imaginary." *Anthropological Theory* 6 (3): 322–44.

Sugiyama-Lebra, Takie. 1976. *Japanese Patterns of Behaviour.* Honolulu: University of Hawaii Press.

———. 1984. *Japanese Women: Constraint and Fulfillment.* Honolulu: University of Hawaii Press.

"Suichiro Takashi Shiraishi's Suicidal 'Hanging Neck' Is a Hot Topic! Looking for SuicideApplicants with Multiple Accounts." 2018. *Yomiuri News*, September 10.

Suicidal Student. 2013. Issho Ni Ikiyō. May 16. https://wailing.org/.

Suizzo, Marie-Anne. 2004. "Mother-Child Relationships in France: Balancing Autonomy and Affiliation in Everyday Interactions." *Ethos* 32 (3): 293–323.

Tabuchi, Hiroko. 2014. "Unskilled and Destitute Are Hiring Targets for Fukushima Cleanup." *New York Times*, March 17. www.nytimes.com/2014/03/17/world/asia/unskilled-and-destitute-are-hiring-targets-for-fukushima-cleanup.html.

Taguchi, Kazunari. 2014. *Ikigai Toha Nanika: Ikigai Wo Meguru Isshiron* [What is ikigai? One theory on ikigai]. n.p. Kindle.

Takahashi, Yoshitomo. 1997a. "Culture and Suicide: From a Japanese Psychiatrist's Perspective." *Suicide and Life-Threatening Behavior* 27 (1): 137–46.

———. 1997b. *Jisatu No Shinrigaku* [Psychology of suicide]. Tokyo: Kōdansha Gendai Shinsho.

———. 1998. *Gunpatsu Jisatu* [Cluster suicide]. Tokyo: Chuo Shinsho.

———. 1999. *Seishounen No Tameno Jisatsu Yobō Manuaru* [A suicide manual for young people]. Tokyo: Kongo Shuppan.
———. 2001. *Jisatsu No Sain Wo Yomitoru* [Reading a signal of suicide]. Tokyo: Kodansha.
———. 2006. *Jisatsu Yobō*. Tokyo: Iwanami Shinsho.
———. 2009. Personal communication with the author, May.
Takeshima, Tadashi. 2009. *Netto Sedai No Jisatu Kanren Kōdo To Yobō No Arikata Ni Kansuru Kenkyū*. [Research on the suicide-related behaviors among internet generation and prevention]. Tokyo: National Institution of Mental Health, NCNP.
"Takuhai Dokubutsu de Jisatsuhoujoyōgikeishichōsōsanettotūji Chūmonka" [Assisting suicide via home delivery of poison through the internet? The police investigation]. 1998. *Asahi Shimbun*, December 25.
Tamashiro, Tim. 2019. *How to Ikigai: Lessons for Finding Happiness and Living Your Life's Purpose*. Coral Gables, FL: Mango Media.
Taylor, Charles. 1989. *Sources of the Self: The Making of Modern Identity*. Cambridge, MA: Harvard University Press.
Ten Ten. 2016. "Review of 'The Complete Manual of Suicide' by Wataru Tsurumi." September 15. Amazon Japan. www.amazon.co.jp/-/en/%E9%B6%B4%E8%A6%8B-%E6%B8%88/dp/4872331265/ref=sr_1_1?dchild=1&keywords=%E8%87%AA%E6%AE%BA%E3%83%9E%E3%83%8B%E3%83%A5%E3%82%A2%E3%83%AB&qid=1623004337&s=books&sr=1-1.
Thin, Neil. 2008. "'Realising the Substance of Their Happiness': How Anthropology Forgot About *Homo gauisus*." In *Culture and Well-Being: Anthropological Approaches to Freedom and Political Ethics*, edited by Alberto Corsín Jiménez, 134–55. London: Pluto Press.
Throop, Jason, and Douglas Hollan, eds. "Special Issue: Whatever Happened to Empathy?" *Ethos* 36, no. 4 (2008): 385–489.
"The Truth of the Fukushima Nuclear Accident and Radiation Health Damange." n.d. www.sting-wl.com/category/.
Tiefenbach, Tim, and Florian Kohlbacher. 2017. "Fear of Solitary Death in Japan's Aging Society." In *Life Course, Happiness and Well-Being in Japan*, edited by Barbara Holthus and Wolfram Manzenreiter, 238–55. New York: Routledge.
Together. 2005. Omae Ha Mou Shindeiru. December 24. http://jamu.cc/2ch/test/ read.cgi/xyz/#1.
Tom. 2018. Onigami Keijiban [Demon God Bulletin Board]. www3.ezbbs.net/cgi/bbs?id=onigami&dd=05&p=11.
Tomaka, Joe, Sharon Thompson, and Rebecca Palacios. 2006. "The Relation of Social Isolation, Loneliness, and Social Support to Disease Outcomes among the Elderly." *Journal of Aging and Health* 18 (3): 359–84.
Totoro. 2006. Kokoro No Hanazono. November 19. http://bbs1.nazca.co.jp/12/.

Traphagan, John. 2000. *Taming Oblivion: Aging Bodies and the Fear of Senility in Japan*. Albany, NY: State University of New York Press.

———. 2003. "Older Women as Caregivers and Ancestral Protection in Rural Japan." *Ethnology* 42 (2): 127–39.

———. 2004. "Interpretations of Elder Suicide, Stress, and Dependency among Rural Japanese." *Ethnology* 43 (4): 315–29.

———. 2010. "Intergenerational Ambivalence, Power, and Perceptions of Elder Suicide in Rural Japan." *Journal of Intergenerational Relationships* 8 (1): 21–37.

Trash. 2017. Shinitai Hito No Kōryū Saito. November 2. http://blued.sakura.ne.jp/bbs/35/yybbs.cgi?pg=45.

True Blue. 2018. Onigami Keijiban [Demon God Bulletin Board]. www3.ezbbs.net/cgi/bbs?id=onigami&dd=05&p=11.

Tsurumi, Wataru. 1993. *Kanzen Jisatsu Manyuaru* [The complete manual of suicide]. Tokyo: Ōta Shuppan.

"Twitter 'Hangers' 'I Want to Die' Identify the Identity of Eight Housewives." 2017. *Kozitech*, November 10.

Ueda, Shigeru, ed. 2005. *Web Saito Wo Kaishiteno Fukusuu Douji Jisatsu No Jittai To Yobō Ni Kansuru Kenkyū Hōkokusho* [Research report on the actual condition and prevention for the multiple-simultaneous suicide via internet websites]. Tokyo: National Institution of Mental Health, NCNP.

Ueno, Kayoko. 2005. "Suicide as Japan's Major Export: A Note on Japanese Suicide Culture." *Revista Espaco Academico*, no. 44 (January). https://web.archive.org/web/20141219085031/http://www.espacoacademico.com.br/044/44eueno_ing.htm.

Umi. 2006. Ikizurasa Kei No Fōramu. http://8238.teacup.com/hampen/bbs.

Usui, Mafumi. 2002. "Internet Shinrigaku" [Internet psychology]. www.n-seiryo.ac.jp/~usui/net/.

Victor, Christina, Sasha Scambler, John Bond, and Ann Bowling. 2000. "Being Alone in Later Life: Loneliness, Social Isolation and Living Alone." *Reviews in Clinical Gerontology* 10 (4): 407–17.

Victor, Christina R. 2011. "Loneliness in Old Age: The UK Perspective." In *Safeguarding the Convoy: A Call to Action from the Campaign to End Loneliness*. Abingdon: Age UK Oxfordshire. https://campaigntoendloneliness.org/wp-content/uploads/downloads/2011/07/safeguarding-the-convey_-_a-call-to-action-from-the-campaign-to-end-loneliness.pdf.

Vij, Ritu. 2007. *Japanese Modernity and Welfare: State, Civil Society and Self in Contemporary Japan*. London: Palgrave Macmillan.

———. 2012. Personal communication with author, February 2.

Vogel, Ezra F. 1980. *Japan as Number One: Lessons for America*. Cambridge, MA: Harvard University Press.

———. 1993. *The Four Little Dragons: The Spread of Industrialization in East Asia*. Cambridge, MA: Harvard University Press.

Waal, F. B. M. de. 2009. *The Age of Empathy: Nature's Lessons for a Kinder Society*. New York: Harmony Books.
Wada, Hideki. 2011. *Shinsai Torauma* [Natural disaster trauma]. Tokyo: Besuto Shinsho.
Wada, Shuichi. 2000. "Kōreishakai Ni Okeru 'Ikigai' No Ronri" [The logic of "ikigai" in aging society]. *Ikigai Kenkyū* [Study of ikigai] 12: 18–45.
"Wakamono-Sō No Jisatsu Wo Meguru Jyōkyō" [Circumstances surrounding suicide among the young generation]. 2014. Kōseirōdōshō [Ministry of Health, Labour and Welfare]. www.city.kumamoto.jp/common/UploadFileDsp.aspx?c_id=5&id=12213&sub_id=1&flid=80342.
Walker, Harry, and Iza Kavedžija. 2016. "Introduction: Values of Happiness." In *Values of Happiness: Toward an Anthropology of Purpose in Life*, edited by Harry Walker and Iza Kavedžija, 1–28. Chicago: Hau Books.
Watabe, Makoto. 2014. "Kantou Gen" [Forward?]. In *Shinsai Ikou: Owaranai 3.11* [After the natural disaster: Never ending 3.11], edited by T. Shibui, K. Murakami, Makoto Watabe, and N. Oota. Tokyo: 31 Shobo.
Weeks, David G., John L. Michela, Letitia A. Peplau, and Martin E. Bragg. 1980. "Relation between Loneliness and Depression: A Structural Equation Analysis." *Journal of Personality and Social Psychology* 39 (6): 1238–44.
Weiss, Robert Stuart. 1974. *Loneliness: The Experience of Emotional and Social Isolation*. Cambridge, MA: MIT Press.
White, Merry I. 1994. *The Material Child: Coming of Age in Japan and America*. Berkeley: University of California Press.
Wing. 2015. Issho Ni Ikiyō. https://wailing.org/.
Woman. 2006. "Nihon De Kyūzō Suru Netto Jisatsu: 2 Nen Kan de 3 Bai Ni" [Internet suicide on the rise in Japan: It has tripled in the last 2 years]. http://ameblo.jp/babanuki/entry-1001013 8363.html.
Yamamoto-Mitani, Noriko, and Margaret I. Wallhagen. 2002. "Pursuit of Psychological Well-Being (Ikigai) and the Evolution of Self-Understanding in the Context of Caregiving in Japan." *Culture, Medicine and Psychiatry* 26 (4): 399–417.
Yang, Ryan. 2013. "Mr. Rogers on Arsenio Hall." www.youtube.com/watch?v=1geWczVpUbE.
Yoshie. 2018. Onigami Keijiban [Demon God Bulletin Board]. August 28. www3.ezbbs.net/05/onigami/.
Yukio, Saito. n.d. Personal communication with the author.
Za Keijiban. 2003. "Jisatsu Shitai Hito Ha Oide Yo Bisshitto Shikatte Ageru Kara" [Come here, those of you who want to commit suicide, and I'll give you a stern scolding!]. http://psychology.dot.thebbs.jp/1050136588.html.
Zaza. 2018. Onigami Keijiban [Demon God Bulletin Board]. January 18. www3.ezbbs.net/05/onigami/.

Zielenziger, Michael. 2006. *Shutting Out the Sun: How Japan Created Its Own Lost Generation*. New York: Vintage.

Zika, Sheryl, and Kerry Chamberlain. 1992. "On the Relation Between Meaning in Life and Psychological Well-Being." *British Journal of Psychology* 83 (1): 133–45.

Zoo. 2006. Ikizurasa Kei No Fōramu. December 21. http://8238.teacup.com/hampen/bbs.0911/k00/00m/040/127000c.

Index

Founded in 1893,
UNIVERSITY OF CALIFORNIA PRESS
publishes bold, progressive books and journals on topics in the arts, humanities, social sciences, and natural sciences—with a focus on social justice issues—that inspire thought and action among readers worldwide.

The UC PRESS FOUNDATION
raises funds to uphold the press's vital role as an independent, nonprofit publisher, and receives philanthropic support from a wide range of individuals and institutions—and from committed readers like you. To learn more, visit ucpress.edu/supportus.

www.ingramcontent.com/pod-product-compliance
Lightning Source LLC
Chambersburg PA
CBHW030344270326
41926CB00009B/952

9780520383494